BEYOND *the* TEXT

Jewish Literature and Culture *Series Editor, Alvin Rosenfeld*

BEYOND *the* TEXT

A Holistic Approach To Liturgy

LAWRENCE A. HOFFMAN

INDIANA UNIVERSITY PRESS
Bloomington and Indianapolis

First Midland Book edition 1989

Manufactured in the United States of America

Library of Congress Cataloging-in-Publication Data

Hoffman, Lawrence A., 1942-
Beyond the text.

(Jewish literature and culture)
Includes index.
I. Judaism—liturgy. I. Title. II. Series.
BM660.H626 1987   296.4   85-45886
ISBN 0-253-31199-3 cl.
ISBN 0-253-20538-7 pbk.

2   3   4   5   6   93   92   91   90   89

CONTENTS

Acknowledgments   vii

1. Introduction: The Focus on Holism   I

2. *Havdalah:* A Case of Categories   20

3. Rites: A Case of Social Space   46

4. American Jewish Liturgies: A Study of Identity   60

5. Sacred Myths: I. Premodern Jewish Perspectives   75

6. Sacred Myths: II. After the Enlightenment   116

   Appendix to Chapter 6
   Inclusion in the Myth: The Case of Women   145

7. The Numinous: A Problem of Recognition   149

8. Conclusion: A Holistic View of Liturgy   172

Notes   183
Index   207

Acknowledgments

The first chapters of this book were typed over five years ago, on an early model of a word processor. A failure to depress "Save," coupled with I-know-not-what error on my part, resulted in a chapter's complete and sudden disappearance into what I presumed to be everlasting oblivion. A quick call for help to my son (who understands these mysteries) was met by good news. The chapter was recallable from the inner synapses of the computer's memory by a programming device known as a memory dump. It occurred to me at the time that whatever final title might be devised for the work when it was completed, I could do a lot worse than "Memory Dump," for in fact, that is largely what this book is: a dumping onto paper, albeit in an orderly fashion, of the contents of a decade's worth of memory. No matter what project, book, article, or lecture I had been working on, the final object of research turns out in retrospect to have been this book, which maps out a new liturgical landscape of which the other pieces are individual items in the foreground.

The point of the analogy is that a complete listing of people to whom I am beholden for this single volume ought properly to extend beyond the book to the formation of the specific memory file it reflects. I include a variety of academic and spiritual mentors, students, colleagues, and associates—all of whom led me at various times to see something I had never noticed before about the extension of the word "liturgy" to denote more than an inherited text of prayer. It all began when I attended my first meeting of the North American Academy of Liturgy and heard Gerald Lardner give two sterling lectures on communications and the social sciences as sources for liturgical awareness. I later met others who instructed me—some, like Mary Collins, who had lectured to the Academy before I discovered it, and others too numerous to mention who were to guide our deliberations thereafter and open the very possibility of going "Beyond the Text." I convey profound thanks to these, my colleagues in that most collegial of societies, the Academy.

I wish to dedicate my work to two of the world's grandest human beings, who died while the work was in progress: Rabbi Morris N. Kertzer and Dr. Allen A. Small. Both in their own way instructed me on the important things in life, and followed what I did with the truest of love. Their names go unmentioned in what follows, but not a page is without their influence. May their memory be eternally a blessing.

BEYOND *the* TEXT

ONE

Introduction

The Focus on Holism

This book is about a household activity, if not a household word; an activity that engages us all with that very degree of regularity which breeds indifference: liturgy, or, to be more precise, worship, or, to be more precise still, the variety of rituals in which religious people, particularly, engage. Liturgy ranges from the most elaborate Holy Day ceremonial to the simple sacred markings of otherwise pedestrian time: like grace before and after meals, or weddings, which bestow cosmic significance on the decisions of men and women to live together, or funerals, which cast equal grace on events no one chooses at all. An academic association that worries about such things, The North American Academy of Liturgy, recently honored one of its members, Father Robert Taft, who responded by speaking for all of those millions of others who celebrate religious ritual without giving it a moment of thought: "I had never heard the word liturgy," he said, "until I entered the Jesuits in August 1949. Of course I went to Church, but like Molière's Monsieur Jourdain, who did not know he was speaking prose, I did not know that what we did in church was liturgy."[1]

But what is it that one does in church that liturgy is? What exactly should a liturgist study? Since the middle of the nineteenth century, when both Christians and Jews generally date the genesis of liturgy as an independent academic discipline, the church (or synagogue) activity deemed worthy of investigation has been the prayers of the faithful, which are based on the sacred texts enshrined by tradition. To study liturgy was taken as the equivalent of exercising expertise in the reconstitution of the recension history of those prayers. By that definition, usually assumed as unquestioned and unquestionable, however, Taft's attitude preceding his personal Enlightenment when he entered the Jesuits turns out to be not so wrong. "I did not know that what we did in church was liturgy," he observes wryly; indeed, by that definition it wasn't. Religious services in synagogue and church may vary widely from place to place and time to time; they may have within them all manner of activities; they may feature singing, reading, bowing, preaching, and a variety of other communicative means. These ac-

1

tivities may or may not revolve about a sacred text, but even when they do, what
worshipers do with that text at the moment of praying is a far cry from what
nineteenth-century liturgists envisioned as they defined the proper object of their
study to be the text as independent literary tradition. Taft, who is a better student
of the text than most, knows this very well. To know liturgy, says he, "one must
study much more than liturgy. . . . We need to study not just the Roman Mass
through the ages as Jungmann did, but liturgical life in southern Gaul or Northern
Italy at some chosen period, and we must do it within the sociocultural context of
that time. We must plunge into what Jacques Le Goff has called the 'archeology
of the everyday.' "[2]

Taft's call for the expanding of the borders to go beyond the text of prayer
itself is more than an interesting critique of the liturgical establishment from
within. First, the field is so small, one wonders whether there is an establishment; second, if there is one, the audience to whom Taft spoke is it. What we see
is a discontent shared by many, who may not readily go so far as to admit that
"what we do in church is not liturgy," but at least feel that "what we have been
doing in the academic discipline of liturgy is not what people do in church" and
may even come to the thoroughly revisionist conclusion that it should be. For
Taft's uneasy stance before the tradition of his own craft is, if anything, mild,
compared to what others have been saying: that liturgical theology ought to be
conducted in the "borderlands between theology and some of its neighboring
human disciplines, such as the sociology of knowledge, the philosophy of language, the anthropology of ritual, the psychology of belief, and the theory of
action";[3] that "the formal object of . . . liturgical studies [ought to be] the
actual worship life of the living offering praying Church";[4] or, on the Jewish
side of things, that "Jewish liturgy certainly warrants more than a mention in
passing in such subjects as Hebrew language and literature, Jewish history,
Halakhah, Kabbalah, archeology and art, musicology, Jewish religious thought,
and phenomenology and social anthropology."[5] Perhaps a discipline as young
and as small as liturgy has no right to suffer from a mid-life crisis in its normal
operating procedure; but if that is not so, it seems to me indubitable that we are in
the process of a radical reevaluation of its paradigms and cannot easily go home
again untouched by the fruitful interaction of interdisciplinary attention, which,
in fact, has come to characterize the social sciences in general.[6]

But before us is the promise not merely of revamping a little-known discipline,
but of opening a new window on the life of religious people the world over, a
window that looks out on the very essence of religious celebration, the way in
which a holy calendar takes its shape, a committed life unfolds, a community of
faithful takes its stand. It is not the text, then, but the people who pray it, that
should concern us.

I have divided this book into chapters that elaborate some suggestive ways in which the text of the past becomes a window onto the worshipers then, a source of insight into the way religious consciousness is formed, nurtured, and lived. And not only in the past, but now too. People ritualize their lives now as much as they ever have, not always in accepted religious fashion, but in some way: in hymns like John Philip Sousa's marches at the annual fireworks display on the Fourth of July; sermons like those given every four years by the candidates of each major party about to rally the faithful for a march to the White House; responsive readings like the antiphonal cheering between cheerleaders and crowd at the annual homecoming game; or even obeisance to iconic symbols, as when a corporation spawns images to which its workers attach ultimate loyalty.[7] Not that I argue for these expressions as the true religion of our time—my point is by no means polemical, one way or the other (though, of course, I have my own opinion on things). I want only to shout as loudly as I may in favor of taking such things seriously as liturgies, that is, as acted-out rituals involving prescribed texts, actions, timing, persons, and things, all coming together in a shared statement of communal identity by those who live with, through, and by them. If we learn to see the liturgy as transcending words, even great words, we inherit a window on the past and present alike, in which the image on the other side of the glass may look remarkably like ourselves.

How that may be the case is the subject of this book. But before going further into it, a closer look at the topic of this chapter is in order. So let me turn to a more detailed account of how the dominant paradigms for liturgical research came into being, and the types of critique that might be leveled at them.

The modern study of Jewish liturgy (which is my case study here) is almost two centuries old now. Its roots have been traced back even earlier, of course— everything can always be traced back "even earlier"—but few current studies find the need to cite pioneering scholars who lived before the time of Leopold Zunz (1794–1886).[8]

Zunz embodied the spirit that was to guide the study of liturgy up to and including our time. Given his stature, it is no surprise to find that the details of his life and thought are well known now. His place in the history of liturgical research is both documented and assured. Little need be said here, then, beyond one all-important fact (for this study)—namely, that Zunz was at home in books, and, whether he knew it or not, what he was really studying in his classification of liturgical forms was not the liturgy as it is "lived" in that human activity we call "worship," but its literary remains. There is nothing innately wrong with such an approach, as long as one keeps it firmly in mind at all times. The problem has been that the people who talk about liturgy have not always kept it in mind.

Behind Zunz's all-embracing passion for Jewish literature as a topic for inves-

tigation was the ninteenth-century doctrine of philology, which Zunz learned
from his mentor, Friedrich August Wolff. The Age of Reason had given way to
the romantic era and the latter's implicit claim against the former to the effect
that pre-Napoleonic universalistic pretensions had only masked the real and
indelible cultural differences that separate one nation-folk from another. In Germany's case, the new romantic agenda now sent intellectual leaders scurrying
back to the cultural evidence of German uniqueness, which was thought to reveal
the essence of German genius. It was Wolff's contention that literary remnants
bore the all-important clues to the Germanic spiritual heritage. And what was
true about German literature for Wolff was true of Jewish literature for Zunz.
Though on the face of it, Zunz was studying Jewish literature, on a deeper level
he sought to reveal the history of the Jewish spirit as it had unfolded through the
centuries.

Not many people still maintain Wolff's romantic zeal. *Heilsgeschichte* of
every sort is distinctly unpopular in the circles of "objective" scholars these
days, as are teleological investigations in general; under the influence of con-
trolled, scientifically oriented investigations, all-encompassing statements about
the nature of entire cultures, based on a sampling of their literary remains, are
generally eschewed. So the theoretical moorings of Zunz's methodology have
been not only abandoned, but even forgotten. His method, however, remains.
Philology is alive and well in the study of Jewish liturgy,[9] and though there is
nothing wrong with that, one should at least recognize that, as with all theories,
philology has its distinct limitations in terms of what we can reasonably expect it
to achieve.

One such limitation has been the topic of a debate launched just over two
decades ago, by the publication of a landmark volume by the late Joseph Heinemann.[10] Until then, even though academicians had abandoned the romantic era's
claim that philology might reveal a nation-folk's entire spiritual legacy, they still
maintained that it could at least unearth the literary origin of a specific prayer
text. Scholars still went about the philological task of comparing alternative
manuscript readings of the prayer in question, "deducing" what "must be" its
"original wording" (its *Urtext*), and then positing a likely period or event in
antiquity in which to place the prayer's message. They presupposed such things
as a centralized rabbinic social structure in which authoritative texts might be
legislated, and from which they could be successfully disseminated; and the
absence of "authentic" diversity, in that non-normative but parallel early worship traditions must (by definition) be either heretical or unimportant when
compared with the centralized authoritative norm. All deviations from the so-
called original text (known because they were cited by early authors, or were still
extant in other manuscripts) were thus regarded as later accretions to or diminu-
tions of the pure paradigmatic wording of the *Urtext*, and were plotted on a time

line whereby the same historicist perspective sought to unearth the events that lay behind each of them. When all was said and done, a given prayer in use today stood revealed as a multiply stratified, or layered, literary document. The "original" prayer and subsequent additions to it were all explained as arising in response to various events and periods, as if prayer must always be a rational response to political persecution, a reaction to a foreign ideology, a blow against heresy, or an organism's response to the thousand and one other data that constitute a nation-folk's history. This being reconstituted by scholarship, the prayer was said to be explained.

But as much as literature may be the obvious way to think about most texts, Heinemann challenged that assumption in the case of prayers. He charged that Jewish prayer in classical times must be seen as originally oral, its wording unencumbered by the norms of single authoritative texts. His critique was not universally accepted, to be sure, but at least one had an alternative method, what Heinemann and, even before him, Arthur Spanier (1884–1944) preferred to call form-criticism, which could be used as a substitute for the Zunzian model. Much like form-critics in biblical studies,[11] liturgists of the Heinemann school were encouraged to give up the fruitless attempt to reconstruct a nonexistent original text, to exercise caution in matching up so-called later accretions with historical circumstances that sounded vaguely as if they might have produced political conditions appropriate to the prayer in question, and, instead, to separate prayers according to style. Then they could locate each such genre within a social milieu, preferably known, but sometimes only postulated, within Jewish society of ancient times. Like the philological position that it criticized, the form-critical analysis of liturgy proved itself able to accomplish a great deal; and, again, like the methodology it claimed to supersede, it has its shortcomings.

Here we require a complete critique of form-criticism no more than we do a thoroughgoing analysis of philology. More to the point is our recognition of a consistent similarity that underlies even these presumably rival systems of research. That is, Heinemann's form-criticism is just as much a text-centered phenomenon as is Zunz's philology, since his goal too is the attainment of a critical stance regarding texts, even if it means postulating a pretextual oral period of recension. This text-centeredness might seem obvious and even necessary in studies of antiquity, which must gather their evidence in literary remains, the only thing we have left, at times, of cultures long destroyed by the ravages of history. But there is no necessity involved. Of course research must begin with the literature in which the evidence is embedded; that indeed is necessary. But both philology and form-criticism end with that literature as well; and that is not necessary at all.

Both vantage points are essentially analyses of literary works, as if a complete comprehension of the words of prayers (and of the books that carry them) were equivalent to an understanding of the liturgical life of the people who pray. To this claim, the following remark by Saussure is in order. He used to begin his course on general linguistics by noting the curious fact that "philological criticism is still deficient [in that] it follows the written language too slavishly and neglects the living language."[12] To be sure, Saussure's context was not Zunz's; by philology, they meant different things; the contrast to which Saussure points, that of the grammatically formalized system of written speech as opposed to oral utterance, is not identical with the distinction between written prayer records and the ritualized act of rehearsing those records. Still, Saussure's insight is not beside the point for us. We may well paraphrase him with regard to both philology and form-criticism, inasmuch as they claim to be studying liturgy. Slavishly addicted to the study of liturgical texts, these methods neglect the living liturgy itself. In other words, the methods entailed in unraveling textual conundrums are excellently suited to the task of literary analysis, but liturgy—like linguistics—is not a literary matter in the first place. Like it or not, liturgists must eventually confront the disturbing recognition that though their evidence from the past is essentially literary, the human activity of worship is not. People who pray already know this. Though hardly gifted with complete comprehension of what they are about when they worship, those who do so certainly know better than to confuse the text of a prayer with the act of praying. Every liturgist has thus been in the uncomfortable position of lecturing on the origin of this or that prayer, only to be asked by a layperson why we pray it in the first place. Referring the question to the local theologian will not do. If we are to take our métier seriously, we liturgists must develop some context for handling prayer qua prayer, not just prayer qua literature. We will have to acknowledge the common-sense recognition that prayers are not readings, and prayer books are not literary specimens.

The question of what exactly liturgy is has been debated from many perspectives; the claim has even been made recently that Jewish worship is not liturgy at all.[13] But we need not establish a universally accepted definition of liturgy to agree that, whatever it is, it goes beyond literature, or at least that we do no intellectual damage to the concept of liturgy by extending our purview to include not only the books of prayer but the people who pray as well, the worshiping community for whom the prayers exist as something to be prayed, not read.

Prayers are unique human cultural extensions of those who pray them, indistinguishable as prayers, in fact, as long as they are separated from the act of praying. By analogy, consider what we call a recitation, the word we use to describe both the act of reciting something (a poem or dramatic monologue, perhaps) and the thing recited as well. Without the reciter doing the reciting (either actually or in our imagination), we have no recitation, but only a reading; and in the act of declaiming the literary piece in question, the whole nature of the piece is itself changed. So too, to study prayers as if they were inert literary specimens separable from the praying actors is not to comprehend their very nature as prayers. But even the act of declaiming differs from prayer, in that reading someone else's prayer aloud does not in and of itself make it a prayer, unless by reading it, the reader intends to appropriate it as his or her own. Prayer thus has its own subcategory of private prayer, that is, a spontaneous, or at least individualistic, prayer that, by definition, belongs to oneself and oneself alone; whereas there is no such similar category of private poem or reading. Even a prayer by someone else is not really a prayer until I, the worshiper, usurp it as if it were my own; and that is why prayer books usually find it superfluous, even misleading, to ascribe their contents to particular authors; whereas books of poetry must necessarily say who the poet was. When we say that a prayer is "a Psalm of David" (as the superscriptions to the psalms often attest), or a prayer of St. Francis, we mean to gloss the words involved with a commentary that says something about the spirituality implicit in the content and transferable to us, the praying community who appropriate the contents as our own. But without such an appropriation, we have mere literary records that may be called poetry or readings, perhaps, but not yet prayers. The study of written records of prayers, then, without an equivalent investigation into a given worshiper's act of making that record his or her own extension of self, falls short of being an adequate investigation of prayer.

Clearly, scholars have the right to study anything they want, and, equally clearly, those who continue bringing to our attention more accurate recensions of ancient prayer material will also continue to receive the proper adulation of those who recognize that without these data we could say nothing at all of the communities who once composed them. But equally clearly, it is the obligation of others in the scholarly community to take the next step and postulate pictures of those communities.

It may be objected at this point that Heinemann surely cannot be charged with ignoring the spiritual institutions of the Jewish people; and that even Zunz, who clearly held literature to be central to his concerns, had much to say about the worshipers of the past. And to a point, this objection is valid. For example, Zunz, assuming that a people is essentially a political reality, used his considerable knowledge of Jewish history in antiquity to explain the addition of blessings in the prayer known as the *Tefillah*.[14] The problem he faced was that this amalgam of benedictions apparently reached its final form after many years, perhaps centuries, in which newer blessings were added to older ones, until eventually, it contained nineteen such blessings. Yet it is known not only as the *Tefillah*, but as the *Shemoneh Esrei* (The *Eighteen* Benedictions). By applying his political model for liturgical creativity, and following the lead of the Babylonian Talmud (Berakhot 28b), he was able (he thought) to identify the "extra," "nineteenth" benediction as the blessing that now comes twelfth in order, it being, in fact, not a benediction at all, but a malediction against heretics, whom Zunz identified as sectarians such as Jewish Christians.[15]

With the benefit of almost two hundred years of more advanced study of Jewish history, Heinemann exchanged this one-sided, political view of Jewish nationhood with a more sophisticated conceptualization of a set of interlocking institutions, each with its own function and creative style. So for him the question was whether a given prayer displayed a style congruent with that which emerged from one institution rather than from another: from the house of study, say, or from the Temple and its attendant cult, or from the nascent synagogue, or from the law court, and so on. Thus I certainly do not mean to charge that all consideration of the actual people is absent in the accounts of these scholars, to whom we are all indebted in no small measure, but only that the worshiping community as a worshiping community is not central. That is, both philologists and form-critics begin with already-established notions of the nature of the community and use those preconceptions to help them form theories about the nature of the prayer texts. From the people, they argue to the texts.

There are at least two potential objections here. First, we might dispute the blithe assumptions about the nature of the people. Zunz and his followers may be wrong to put such emphasis on its political essence, for example, so that—to cite the situation at its most extreme—they may be entirely incorrect in understanding liturgical creativity as arising out of the felt need to excoriate enemies and appease friends.[16] Heinemann may at times have insufficient evidence to postulate details about the functioning of a given social institution, the workings of which he takes for granted in his etiology of a given prayer. I will argue here, for example, that prayer rarely emerges from cold calculated political decisions on the part of leaders, that worship is a category of human experience with rules of its own, and that these rules function in their own way to result in the formation of a liturgy.

But second, and far more fundamental, is the recognition that we might reverse the process itself: rather than arguing from the people to the texts, we should be going the other way around. The essential unknown, that which cries out for clarification, after all, is not the texts; what little we know of them, they are at least before us and are amenable to restoration in more or less accurate facsimile by virtue of manuscript evidence. It is the people about whom we know virtually nothing, at least insofar as they constituted worshiping communities in various ages of Jewish history. We ought not to argue from the people to the texts, then, but from the texts to the people.

An example might clarify what I have in mind. An exceptionally problematic text is the second chapter of Mishnah Taanit, which describes fast-day ritual said to have taken place some time in the century or so before the turn of the common era. I will cite it in translation, and then see how philologists and form-critics have handled it.

1. What was the order of fasting? They would bring the ark (*tevah*) into the town square and put wood ashes on it and on the heads of the *Nasi* and the *Av Bet Din*. Everyone took ashes and put them on his head. The *Zaken* among them said words of admonition: Brothers, it is not written of the Ninevites, "God saw their sackloth and their fasting," but, "God saw their deeds in that they turned from their evil way" (Jon. 3:10). And [Joel], in his protest says, "Rend your heart, not your garments" (Joel 2:13).

2. They stood up to pray the *Tefillah*. They send before the ark a *Zaken* well versed [in prayer (?)], one who had children but a house that was empty [of sustenance], so that he would be wholehearted in prayer. Before them, he recites twenty-four benedictions: the eighteen used daily to which he adds six more.

3. These are they: (1) *zikhronot* [biblical verses on the theme of remembrance], (2) *shofarot* [biblical verses about the ram's horn, or *shofar*], (3) "I called out to the Lord in my distress, and He answered me" (Ps. 120), (4) "I lift up my eyes to the hills" (Ps. 121), (5) "From the depths I cry out to You, Lord" (Ps. 130), (6) "A prayer of the afflicted when he is overwhelmed" (Ps. 102). Rabbi Judah says: One need not recite the *zikhronot* and the *shofarot*, if in their stead he recites, "If there be famine and pestilence in the land" (1 Kings 8:37), and, "The word of the Lord that came to Jeremiah concerning the drought" (Jer. 14:1).

3a. And he says their concluding eulogies.

4a. After the first, he says, "May He who answered our father Abraham at Mt. Moriah answer you and hearken to your voice which cries out this day. Blessed art Thou, Lord, redeemer of Israel."

4b. After the second, he says, "May He who answered our fathers at the Red Sea answer you and hearken to your voice which cries out this day. Blessed art Thou, Lord, who remember that which is forgotten."

4c. After the third, he says, "May He who answered Joshua at Gilgal answer you. . . . Blessed art Thou, Lord, who hear the sound of the *shofar* blast."

4d. After the fourth, he says, "May He who answered Samuel at Mizpah answer you. . . . Blessed art Thou, Lord, who hear those who cry out."

4e. After the fifth, he says, "May He who answered Elijah at Mt. Carmel answer you. . . . Blessed art Thou, Lord, who hear prayer."

4f. After the sixth, he says, "May He who answered Jonah in the belly of the whale answer you. . . . Blessed art Thou, Lord, who answer in times of trouble."

4g. After the seventh, he says, "May He who answered David and Solomon his son at Jerusalem answer you. . . . Blessed art Thou, Lord, who have compassion on all the earth." [17]

Now what have scholars done with this text? Since it deals with a complete description of a ritual that can easily be dated very early in the history of Jewish liturgy, it has received considerable attention. Especially is this the case, since the recension before us is clearly problematic.

To begin with, I have divided paragraph 3 into two parts (3 and 3a), to indicate the fact that 3 itself is a comment upon 2, probably coming some time after 2, and explaining what 2 meant. Paragraph 2 tells us the number of blessings, and 3 lists what they are. But 3a is probably part of 2, the connection between 2 and 3a being broken by the intrusion of 3, at that point in the narrative where the explanation that we now call 3 fits best. Thus, originally, we probably had:

> 2. . . . Before them, he recites twenty-four benedictions: the eighteen used daily, to which he adds six more [3a] and he says their concluding eulogies.

But this complete report was interrupted later in time with an explanation of what the "six more" were, and then the last clause about the eulogies was tacked back on. The addition (3) is purely academic, taking place far after the event described, and, in fact, it is itself a composite of two alternative interpretations, an anonymous opinion and a "minority" report of Rabbi Judah.

The most glaring textual problem, however, is the patent discrepancy between the number of extra benedictions claimed, and the number of eulogies (with their benedictions) listed. Paragraph 2 says there are six extra blessings, and paragraph 3, presumably, tells us what the six blessings are. But the several subsections that constitute paragraph 4—which I have divided, to facilitate clarity— cite seven, not six, eulogies. Should we conclude, then, that the list of eulogies (4a–g) is a late addition grafted onto the earlier text in the same way that a definition of the blessings (3) was? Just as later redactors felt the need to add a list of the requisite blessings (3) after the words "six more [blessings]," so too, perhaps, they felt obliged to specify the eulogies (4a–g), after the words "their eulogies," either by fabricating their own list, or by drawing on an earlier fragment that they possessed and that seemed to belong here.

Whatever the case, we are still left with the essential discrepancy. Were there six extra blessings added, or, following the number of eulogies listed, were there seven? And if seven, were there not eighteen standard benedictions to which they were added, but seventeen? Or should we revise the total to twenty-five? These are the sorts of questions to which scholars have addressed themselves.

But the problem did not have to await the eye of enlightened scholarship. The contradiction is so apparent that even the Talmud could not accept the Mishnah's account without explaining it. Taking a Tosefta report,[18] which explained that these benedictions were inserted not at the end of the daily *Tefillah* but after the seventh blessing there, the one asking for deliverance, and noting the fact that the first of our seven eulogies is almost identical to the normal eulogy for that seventh benediction, the Talmud concludes that the first so-called extra blessing is really just a variant of the usual seventh benediction, and that the list of seven eulogies includes within it both this one (which was said regularly) and the six extras that are specially appended.[19]

The talmudic debate has by now been augmented by a veritable library of articles by philological scholars for whom the textual conundrum was ideal. As far back as 1903,[20] Israel Lévi drew attention to another observation of the Talmud, notably, that the seventh eulogy—the one with David and Solomon— seems out of place, in that all the other people who are cited as models of being worthy recipients of God's response are listed according to the chronological order in which they lived—with the exception, that is, of David and Solomon, who lived before Jonah. So one would have expected to find the formula with David and Solomon before, not after, the one with Jonah.

Further, Lévi divided each eulogy into two stylistically distinct units: first, the phrase beginning, "May He who answered . . . ," and then the concluding "Blessed art Thou . . ." fragment. Here too, the David and Solomon formula differs from the others, at least in content, if not in style, in that its second half does not refer back to some event in the life of the people who constitute the subject of the first half. Instead, we find a reference to a universalistic divine quality, God's mercy over all the earth. So the seventh eulogy is not only out of place, but general rather than specific. From these two anomalous characteristics, Lévi concluded that it is not part of the original string of eulogies, but a late addition tacked on to the end.

Lévi was a keen scholar, and here, as elsewhere, his observations are insightful. Were this the place to solve the philological squabble over the original text, we could continue at length to cite not only Lévi's very complex and challenging solution in all its detail—how the seventh got added, its relationship to yet other eulogies contained in the talmudic account, and so on—but also alternative theories by Aptowitzer, Albeck, and others.[21] The point, however, is that no matter how superior these accounts may be judged, their focus always remains the text itself, as if reconstructing the text were a sufficient goal for the student of liturgy.

I have selected this textual difficulty partly because it illustrates not only philology at its best, but form-criticism too. Indeed, insofar as Lévi himself analyzed the form of the material, emphasizing, for example, the dual nature of the eulogy, he anticipated by many decades form-criticism as a liturgical method. Heinemann, who was able to take the method much further, is also at his best here. He provides a marvelous illustration of what the form-critical method can offer.

Heinemann begins with the assumption that there is no original text at all, and asks instead that we determine the formal characteristics that allow us to posit the social institution out of which this fast-day liturgy emerged. What surprises him is that the people here are addressed in the second person. This is never the case with normative synagogue-based prayers, he holds, since the synagogue prayers were always couched in such a way as to include the precentor (or prayer leader) along with the congregation. The normal form there would have been the first-person plural. Indeed, even the medieval authorities were surprised by this apparent exclusivity of the speaker, and went so far at times as to emend the object of God's remembering in the eulogy from "you" to "us." But the second-person address was common in the Temple, where the priests blessed the assembled throng in the course of the daily offering. Thus, concludes Heinemann, we have an instance of Temple-based prayer that was transferred to the synagogue upon the emergence of the latter as a significant institution in its own right.[22]

So far, so good. We have learned something about the people of Israel meeting in prayer. Going from the text, a question of words, Heinemann has deftly taken us to a consideration of institutions and the people who made them up. But even Heinemann is essentially doing textual study, so he abandons any attempt to take the social situation further and analyze it with any sort of criteria that might make manifest the nature of the liturgical experience to the worshiping community in Temple or synagogue. Instead, he now returns to the text. What we have, he concludes, is an ancient Temple liturgy in which

> . . . two elements came to be conjoined: the congregational prayer of the people (in the "we"-style), and, following it, a kind of confirmation by the priests in the appropriate "you"-style of the "benediction by which a man blesses his fellow." The form of this prayer . . . should then be considered an attempt to adapt the original ceremony of the Temple for use outside it. On the one hand, the response of the priests after each of the additional benedictions was no longer appropriate in the synagogue-style prayer, but on the other hand, there was a strong desire not to do away with these formulae, so characteristic of the fast-day liturgy; thus they came to be included in the body of the benediction itself.[23]

With this conclusion, Heinemann's task is ended. He now comprehends the text before him. He has moved from the problematic element in it to the institution that gave it birth, and from there back to a solution that restores the text to acceptability as a valid document bearing witness to its time. No less than the philologists whom he opposes, Heinemann too both begins and ends with the text.

I emphasize that there is no reason why Heinemann, or for that matter, Lévi, Aptowitzer, and Albeck, should have been expected to do otherwise. I do not question the value of philology and form-criticism in the same way that they question the validity of each other. Philology and form-criticism, after all, stand opposed in their presumptions regarding the nature of the material being studied, so that those who adopt one approach must generally occupy a critical stance vis-à-vis the other. What I am suggesting, on the other hand, need not be seen as a denial of either of these two standpoints that have dominated the study of

Jewish liturgy so far. I wish only to extend the perspective of both. What else, then, could have been asked regarding the liturgical example we have looked at?

For one thing, it is immediately evident that we have an entire ritual being described here, not just a textual recension. Rituals have been studied by anthropologists with field experience the world over. What would an anthropologist say about our description? Is this ritual classifiable by type or identifiable according to the social structure that gives rise to it? And would it then tell us something that these worshipers shared with other religionists in places and times that differ from what we have here, but whose situation and aspirations remain the same? Or, knowing a common typology that is applicable across religious lines, might we then see the reverse, that is, how Jewish ritual here differed from others, such that the uniqueness of Jewish experience in Palestine at the turn of the century becomes evident?

Or, if that is too much to expect, can we at least tell something about the social structure of the society that this ritual mirrors, simply by expanding our view beyond the text to include also the ritual as it was performed? Is it coincidental, for example, that the prayer leader is (1) a *Zaken*, a term denoting as the ideal type an old man, who (2) addresses those assembled in the masculine "Brothers . . ." (*acheinu*) and (3) cites only men as his biblical paradigms of people who merited hearing God's response to prayer? The Bible does not lack for examples of women whose prayers were answered: witness Hannah, Deborah, and Leah, for example. But in our instance, they are passed over as if they did not exist. Women may or may not have been physically present in these fast-day gatherings of first-century Judaism, but even if they were, from a sociological perspective, they were absent.

Suppose now we take the instance of covenantal initiation liturgy, the rituals that admit new generations into Israel's covenant with God. Even without going into any great detail, it becomes evident that the life cycle for males properly begins with such a ritual: the *brit milah* (covenant of circumcision). Here, the male carrier of the covenanted status (the father) is instructed to pass on the covenanted condition to his male heir.[24] Until that time, the boy does not even have a name, which he receives only upon successful conclusion of the covenantal operation.[25] Sociologically speaking, as a Jew, the boy is not even present until the moment of the *brit milah*. To some extent, he has the same status as an adult male non-Jew, in that both lack the social distinction of being gifted with covenanted standing (though both may attain it—the latter by his own initiative, if he decides to become a proselyte, and the former by his father's act on his behalf).

To the modern American mentality, with our accent on personal growth and uniqueness, the *brit milah* seems part of a single person's life cycle, the marking of birth. But to the classical Jewish perspective, birth has nothing to do with it, not birth physically speaking, at least. Girls too are born, but their birth goes completely unrecognized in rabbinic liturgical ritual, after all. The only reason the birth of boys seems to be a matter of cultural recognition is that boys, unlike girls, are admitted into convenantal status, and the ritual that accomplishes that rite of passage happens to take place at a moment sufficiently close to the moment of birth. To moderns, who care about birthdays anyway, it appears to correspond to the moment of birth, which is still fresh in our mind.

If, now, we consider together our two separate instances of liturgical ritual—fast-day worship and the *brit milah* ceremony for initiating boy-children into the covenant—we find that in both cases women are without independent sociologically meaningful existence; that is, they exist only by virtue of belonging within the orbit of men. No wonder the Mishnah must allot an entire order to determining what to do with these female creatures who are liable to change orbits, and hence status, vis-à-vis the men who chance to encounter them.[26] Unlike the moment of their births, the movement of these women to and from the orbits of different men will be marked by appropriate liturgical ceremonial, but even then, women will never actively betroth, marry, or divorce; they will *be* betrothed, married, and divorced, for not they but their husbands stand in covenantal relationship to God, and thus may initiate action with covenantal consequences. To be sure, all living beings are recipients of God's mercy, so that women too may remain personally involved with the Creator of all. But for rituals calling for representatives of the covenanted people to stand before God—as here, in the fast-day prayer—only those with covenanted status are counted. So a man addresses other men and recalls ancestors who were other men still. If there were women present, they go unaddressed and unrecognized. Not covenanted themselves, they are not considered paradigmatic as group petitioners, and they are excluded in a ritual that calls for a man to represent God's people.

To those schooled in liturgy as a textual discipline, it may seem that our example goes far afield. The whole point of this book is precisely that it does not. We managed to combine two discrete liturgical examples that seemed on the face of it to have little in common, and in so doing, to say something about the system of signification that dominated the way the rabbis carved up experience. I do not mean to suggest that my own expansion of the question before us is in any way definitive; some may even find it trivial (though I do not). At any rate, I have not taken pains here to analyze the matter in all its detail so as to prove this particular case. It was intended only as an example of where, tentatively, one might open up new avenues of exploration. Nor do I maintain (either here or in the chapters that follow, for that matter) that I have managed to manufacture the final set of correct questions for which solutions may even be available. At this point, I want only to take an instance of liturgy as it has been studied, and studied with some success, by prominent representatives of both liturgical schools of thought available in the literature, so as to demonstrate their competence at their craft, and their understandable hesitancy to violate the boundaries of that craft by including questions beyond its ability to offer solutions. They could and did tell us much about the liturgical texts that people used. They did not tell us much about the people using them. Even if it should turn out that the additional questions raised here with regard to fast-day liturgy are not fully answerable—even if, that is, the example of fast-day worship does not immediately lend itself to a successful demonstration of going from a prayer text to the community who prays it—my intention is that the studies in succeeding chapters will.

Perhaps an image is in order before I proceed further. Michael Polanyi speaks of a pregiven Gestalt governing perception, and Gregory Bateson describes what he calls predefined systems of meaning.[27] In both cases, we are warned against limiting our view to the particular concatenation of stimuli—or, in our case, data—that we prejudge as somehow existing independently of its constituent units, on the one hand, and of the larger field of reality in which it exists, on the other. We are in the situation of watching a television screen and being warned not to confuse the two-dimensional picture rendered by the camera crew for the totality of reality on the site of the program's shooting. What we wish to be able to do is to control the camera, allowing it to sweep back and forth, including and excluding this or that part of reality, regularly zeroing in and then stepping back, constantly changing the center of focus, until we have a good mastery of the whole, not just a single part that happens to fit conveniently on the screen. Polanyi calls this mastering not only the focus but the subsidiary, and concludes, "Scientific discovery reduces our focal awareness of observations into a subsidiary awareness of them, by shifting our attention from them to their theoretical coherence."[28] Studies have hitherto isolated one element in the act of worship—the text—until it emerged as the focus. But we are our own camera operator. We can, if we like, swing the camera around at the other aspects of worship, until the text becomes subsidiary, and we discover a new coherence to worship that does justice to the people performing it. Since this is an attempt to integrate the entire act of worship into the study of liturgy, I should like to call it holistic.[29]

Even a holistic integration of data requires some predetermined notion of the set of questions that will be raised, and it is this to which I alluded when I said above that our example of the fast-day liturgy combined with the ritual of *brit milah* led us to "the system of signification that dominated the way the rabbis carved up experience" I can think of no better general description of what I am about than that suggested by Clifford Geertz, whose self-conscious analysis of his own craft sounds remarkably like what is being suggested here.

> The thing to ask about a burlesqued wink or a mock sheep raid is not what their ontological status is. It is the same as rocks on one hand and dreams on the other—

they are things of this world. The thing to ask is what their import is: what it is, ridicule or challenge, irony or anger, snobbery or pride, that in their occurrence and through their agency, is getting said.[30]

What goes for "a burlesqued wink or a mock sheep raid" goes equally for a prayer. Unless we know the cultural significance of "what is getting said," we flatter ourselves by thinking we know anything at all of liturgical importance.

Geertz pictures the field anthropologist watching some people going about their daily rituals, and asking the shaman what is transpiring. The shaman has never been asked before. But now, so as to satisfy the anthropologist, our shaman concocts an explanation. This, Geertz labels a construction of reality, rather than reality itself. The verbal explanation is one step removed from the reality of the ritual being described. But the matter does not end there. The anthropologist returns to his or her study to fashion a scholarly account of the shaman's interpretation. The native language will have to be translated into terms familiar to modern Western culture. It will be in English, say, and fit into the straitjacket of current anthropological jargon. What emerges is removed yet a step further from the reality of ritual in action; it is now a construction of a construction. Geertz concludes, "What we call our data are really our own constructions of other people's constructions of what they and their compatriots are up to. . . . Analysis, then, is sorting out the structures of signification."[31]

What should interest us, therefore are the liturgical "structures of significa-tion." We too have reports by shamans, so to speak; that is to say, the writers of records regarding the ritual life of the Jewish people in times past. What is this documentary evidence that we have inherited from times past, if not con-structions of reality; and who are the authors, if not each generation's experts in the rules governing the propriety of Jewish ritual and in the interpretation of its religious signification? We must learn to utilize the discussions and reports in ancient and medieval sources as if they were answers to hypothetical anthropolo-gists, ourselves, whose task it is to go back in time and ask, "What are you doing, and why?".

To be sure, the reorientation I suggest is not easily arrived at. Since people take their rituals for granted, they rarely stop to suggest what they think they are doing by them. In Geertz's instance, it is only the actual presence of the an-thropologist that results in the shaman's remarks; in our own case, what we have is less an ordered interpretation arranged to suit our enquiries than it is a random recounting of signification contained within a literary corpus that was designed with wholly other rules of organization. Still, we have a lot: prayer books, of course; and legends and myths and stories about the world's composition; and theological assertions; and seemingly endless documentation of legal debate over details of ritual behavior. Even when, as in these instances, the medium of communication between generations past and present remains our texts, what is communicated need not be confined to textual information. A debate in the Talmud, for example, may tell us something about the status of the Haggadah text at that time, and it is this information that is, strictly speaking, textual, and that scholars have been interested in primarily; but it may also tell us something about the people who lived then, how they viewed Passover eve, and what they anticipated in their seder ceremony. This is the sort of information that should interest us here.

Furthermore, we have the nonliterary sources, the music and art of previous eras: the mosaic floor at the synagogue of Beth Alpha, or the biblical panorama at that of third-century Dura Europus; fifteenth-century Haggadah representations of Elijah and the messiah; the shape of synagogues in American suburbs; nineteenth-century art music in Germany, but guitars at youth camps in twentieth-century United States. None of this is irrelevant. Everything is potentially pregnant with meaning. What did people argue about? What did they envision? What did they act out? Who did the acting? What were—and what now are—the structures of signification?

At times, we shall discover that this sort of investigation is not amenable to the same sort of rigorous proofs that the science of textual analysis demands, because the rules of the textual game permit us to limit the scope of its enquiry in advance to that range of topics about which such certainty is *a priori* demonstrable. Unfortunately, items of cultural signification are not on that list; were we to insist on an equal degree of confirmation here, we should have to abandon our task at the outset. Naturally, we shall require considerable evidence for any claims we make, but in essence, the nature of a claim regarding a medieval Jew's notion of sacred history, or the role of synecdochal vocabulary in apprehending the numinous—to take as illustrative two items discussed in the pages that follow—differs from that of a claim regarding the presence or absence of any given word in a specific edition of this or that prayer book. The latter claim is textual and thus patently provable by formally agreed-upon conventions of defining certainty. The former questions are not.

But it is those questions that occupy us here, since this book is intended for those who, like myself, want to know exactly this: what liturgy is all about. This group is essentially a "newly evolved species" of liturgists, of whose "interdisciplinary character" Daniel Stevick writes:

The group that represents passionate commitment to liturgy is extremely diverse—historians, theologians, artists, architects, musicians, poets, dancers. Some teach; some write—at a range of levels; some are in close touch with parishes; some work with children; some serve with official worship commissions. Some are themselves creative people in liturgy. Some study the creativity of others. The list could go on and on. [The important thing is that] *all recognize the need of one another. . . . To be a liturgist is not to be one sort of thing.*[32]

With such a diverse group in mind, I am led to conclude very quickly that as much as my own expertise may be assured in one area, it is sorely lacking in others. But I have found it necessary to try to find insights available from many disciplines. This interdisciplinary mutual encroachment in an effort to avoid reductionism has been well under way elsewhere, so that my recourse to it here should surprise no one. As Geertz characterizes our condition, things have gone so far that "one waits only for quantum theory in verse, or biography in algebra." The inclusion of Jewish liturgy in the overall "blurring of genres" should have the beneficial result of unwrapping the hermetic seal that has hitherto kept it in its own discrete package, and opening it up to the fresh gaze of the academy-at-large, whose "woods are full of eager interpreters," each one bent on picturing human society from the vantage point of his or her own camera lens.[33]

To the extent that my own interdisciplinary encroaching on the boundaries of others has generated errors of a novice, I apologize. But I take it as an elementary truth that liturgists must take the risk of stretching the contours of tried and true textual study; and *mutatis mutandis*, artists and scientists who wish to apply their crafts to liturgy must learn to be at home in the arcane world that traffics in the coin of literary conceits, stratified pericopes, and manuscript comparisons.

I have tried to make my own specialized entry into the larger field of liturgy accessible to those who approach it in their own ways, by relegating (as far as possible) to the notes all abstruse textual analyses of Hebrew and Aramaic sources, or even foregoing heavy-handed textual analysis altogether, when such an exercise is not absolutely necessary for the argument at hand. But that has not always been possible. Initial readers of Freud will recall their grudging recognition of the necessity of wading through reports of subjects' dreams; anthropology has its convoluted kinship descriptions; and the raw data of Jewish liturgy, historically speaking, are the Mishnah, the two Talmuds, and the rest of what constitutes a Jewish library of voices from the past bearing witness on what was. Usually I have been able to bypass the need for overly long citations, but sometimes it was necessary to listen at some length to what these voices were saying, without prior editorial interruption. I have at least translated everything, including Hebrew prayers from the standard prayer book, and I have supplied equally standard background information and cross-references to available editions of prayer books in English, so that the reader can refer to the original prayer in its context. At the same time, wanting to widen the field of reference for liturgists of all perspectives, who, like myself, may have been raised on the limited fare of a textual diet drawn from a single tradition, I have supplemented the usual bibliographic references with introductory and summary works that I found helpful somewhere along the line; they ought not to be excluded here just because they were written nontechnically and well.

To be sure, the choice of terminology presented problems. At times, I used technical terms already available in the scientific literature, not because I wanted to clutter these pages with jargon, but because the ability to name something in a properly descriptive way simplifies comprehension and furthers the transferral of ideas from one situation to another. For this reason, when I found accepted terminology lacking, I did not hesitate to redefine old words or make up new ones to describe the process in question.

I generally draw my examples from the world of Jewish liturgy, the only body of evidence about which I have any pretensions of knowledge. I know enough about the depth of Christian liturgy to avoid the temptation of dabbling in it. I have no doubt that the same is true of other religious traditions as well. But those who are at home in Christian liturgy should be able to apply some of my notions to their situation, and the same may be true of worship for others. My examples, then, are particularistic, but the conceptual framework is not.

In what follows, the first problem I tackle (chapter 2) is the structuring of experience through cultural categories that are reenforced by ritual. In terms of empirical demonstration, this is the least provable of all my claims, and precisely because it is so tentative, I was tempted to bury it somewhere near the end of the book. But it is also the most obvious example of asking new questions that go beyond the text, so I decided to begin there anyway, risking the possibility that the reader might close the book without going on to the surer subjects that follow. Next (chapters 3 and 4), I redefine liturgical rites, so that they are seen as reflective of social rather than geographical space. This places the worshiping community and its perception of self properly at the center of our attention. That community's ritualized sacred history, its "sacred myth" as I call it, forms the substance of chapters 5 and 6, beginning with biblical and rabbinic Jewish liturgy, and concluding with the dominant myth presented by the new Jewish liturgies of today. Finally, I attempt the hardest, but probably the most satisfying, task: to arrive at a cross-cultural model by which the liturgical sense of the numinous can be charted and studied. For me, this chapter alone made the overall research worthwhile.

Thus, the chapters that follow draw consciously on many times and places; they also focus on different liturgical situations; and they use equally as evidence any cultural expression of the signification people find in their liturgy, from respected rabbinic texts to the scribbled drawings on throw-away pamphlets. What all my examples have in common is that they lend themselves to an attempt to ask new questions of our material, so as to go beyond that material: to proceed to the worshiping community that lives beyond the text.

TWO

Havdalah

A Case of Categories

Havdalah is the name for one of the oldest and, still today, one of the most colorful Jewish rituals. The word itself means "separation." Ironically, by exploring the ritual of separation from an interdisciplinary standpoint, we shall be flying in the face of the separation of academicians into separate disciplines. We will understand *havdalah* only by bringing together two sets of disciplines that have hitherto developed apart from each other. A consideration of this academic separation is instructive at the outset.

On the one hand, we have the various departments of Jewish studies. Most universities and seminaries in which serious Jewish study is pursued have such departments, and the people staffing them think of themselves as teaching and researching within the boundaries of certain standard "areas of expertise." The definitions of these areas, however, are rarely thought out; they partake almost of the mystical, in that it is as if they went back to some distant hazy *Urzeit* in which all great decisions were made. They are taken as given. One is in Jewish history or philosophy, for example. These subjects in turn may be broken down further into ancient, modern, or medieval, and so on.

Another way of making distinctions, however, a method particularly popular in seminaries, is to label people by the kind of literature they have mastered. For example, a relatively sharp dichotomy is made between Bible and postbiblical literature, the latter being known as Rabbinics. When asking for someone's specialty, it is common to receive the answer that one is in Bible or Rabbinics, as a first-order response; and then, if the questioner is him or herself within the club of Judaica specialists, one receives a more precise answer, particularly with regard to Rabbinics, which has within it such fields as Talmud, Midrash, and Commentaries.

So the field of Jewish studies employs two rival taxonomies. The second, or textually oriented one, is derived from the internal traditional Jewish world, and reminds one immediately of the bias in favor of selecting literature as the proper object of scholarly investigation, a bias going back (as we saw) to Leopold Zunz.

True, Zunz was encouraged in his pursuit by the philological ideas of mentors like Wolff; but he certainly brought with him an already established proclivity for that study, in that he had been trained as a boy in the traditional world of the yeshivah, the medieval institution whose entire curriculum was built on the study of the many and varied literary works of the rabbis. When the Enlightenment enabled people like Zunz to move into the modern world of letters, they simply transferred their expertise in books to the world of the secular university. Some items, like mysticism, they preferred to ignore. Others, like Talmud, were so central to any study of Judaism that they had to be maintained. Yet others, like Midrash, were newly accentuated, since they lent themselves easily to demonstrations of Jewish ethics and spirituality.

The first category of specialization that I mentioned differs from the second primarily in that it is not derived at all from traditional Judaism but, instead, is borrowed from general academia. Scholars fully assimilated into the university milieu entered departments that bore secular titles like History, Philosophy, or Near Eastern Studies. To this day, seminaries are overloaded with the traditional categories, both in their personnel and in their curricular organization, while general universities have managed to translate Jewish disciplines into their own recognizable fields. Two people expert in the same body of data, and using identical methodologies, may be classified as a medievalist at Harvard, and a Commentaries specialist at the Hebrew Union College. Both of these departments, however, share a common focus: they are both Jewish studies.

By contrast, there exists yet another branch of scholarship that until recently had little to do with the Judaica experts, even though both groups had much to say to each other. I mean the social scientists. To be sure, some of the masters, like Weber, explored biblical society, for example, but the literature on Judaica written by Jews who still thought of themselves as Bible or Talmud people rarely bothered with such analyses as these. There was sometimes good reason for this. Those "within" recognized gross errors in the facts cited by those "without." Those "without" were more interested in using biblical or rabbinic society to prove sweeping sociological generalizations in any case, and it was just those general rules which those "within" considered beside the point.

So over the course of time these two groups of researchers have gone about building two separate sets of data, and two mutually exclusive academic circles. Only recently, with the coming of age of the postwar baby-boom children, and the consequent burgeoning of doctoral candidates, have the hundreds of people anxious to publish discovered the fortuitous combination of traditional Judaica and social science. In the field of Jewish liturgy, it is still rare to find recognized experts even referring to anthropological studies of religious experience, say, or the sociology of space. Those who do cite such findings risk being treated with suspicion by their elders, who still classify secular studies of internal Jewish phenomena as uninformed incursions from without. I should like to argue that the mutual mistrust that one finds between, for example, the anthropologist who studies the structural implications of biblical food prohibitions, and the philologist who seeks to understand the Bible from within, has direct relevance to the ritualization of category-separation, or *havdalah*. The commonality between these two apparently unrelated phenomena is, first, that human beings institutionalize differences in terms of categories of experience, and then, that they expect themselves and others to honor these distinctions. One crosses the boundaries of separate categories only with great difficulty.

The departmentalizing systems of academia, then, are marvelously homologous to *havdalah*. To summarize in advance, my study of *havdalah* will argue that human epistemology proceeds through the process of categorization. Cultures categorize their worlds differently, presenting alternative social constructions of reality to their adherents. *Havdalah* is a ritual of categorization, in that it presents the Jewish categorization scheme. The ritual is celebrated precisely at that point in time when the categories threaten to break down, when the Sabbath is about to fade into weekday secularity, and light is becoming dark. It thus reinforces elementary categories of opposition, protecting the scheme from breaking down. As with all systems of separation—our example above was mixing rival academic taxonomies—the potential breakdown through mixing of opposites is perceived as dangerous, and to be avoided at all costs. Thus, we shall see that the *havdalah* ritual attracts mythology regarding the perils inherent in the very time frame in which the ritual is celebrated; further, recognition of these perils generates protective devices that are built into the ritual itself.

We will have to consider two somewhat separate questions in the course of this analysis. First, we will look at the ritual itself, along with traditional Jewish explanations, including, in the latter, scholarly opinions derived from the traditional "inside" worlds of the study of Jewish texts. I have already indicated that these tend to be translated into the agendas of philology and form-criticism. This will leave us with a specific case of the general dilemma posited in the last chapter: an instance in which liturgy as text is defined, probed, discussed, and stratified, while liturgy as human activity is ignored. We will then face the challenge of asking new questions, so the second task will entail choosing from among the many perspectives available in the competing models generated by social sciences. Finally, having selected the one best suited here, we can turn to our own analysis of *havdalah*, and demonstrate the thesis that I outlined in general terms in the paragraph above.

What, then, is *havdalah*? Let us proceed to describe it. The word refers to two separate but related entities. One is a liturgical insertion at the close of Sabbaths and festivals, which serves to note formally the fact that holy time (the Sabbath or festival) is over and mundane time is beginning. That, at least, is the content of the prayer when the next day is a weekday. On occasion, the next day is a holy day, and differentiation must be made between the degrees of holiness represented by the Sabbath and the festival following, rather than between the holy and the profane per se. Wording in the rites varies somewhat, but the "normative texts" in the Ashkenazic tradition, that is, the ones hailing from central and eastern Europe and representing the majority practice in America, are as follows.

On Sabbaths and holy days preceding weekdays, one says the prayer we will refer to as "A."

(A) You have favored us with knowledge of Your Torah, and taught us to perform the laws You want. Lord our God, You have separated holy from profane, light from darkness, Israel from [other] peoples, the seventh day from the six days of work. Our Father, our King, grant that the approaching days begin for us in peace; may we be withheld from all sin, cleansed from all iniquity and devoted to the veneration of You.[1]

On Saturday nights before a holy day, one says the following. Call it "B."

(B) Lord, our God, You have informed us of Your righteous statutes, and taught us to perform the laws You want. Lord, our God, You have given us righteous ordinances, true teachings and good laws and commandments. You have bequeathed to us times of joy, holy festivals, and feasts for free will offerings. You have granted us the holiness of the Sabbath, the glory of the festival, and the festive offering due on the pilgrimage festival. Lord, our God, You have divided holy from profane, light from darkness, Israel from [other] peoples, the seventh day from the six days of work. You have distinguished between the holiness of the Sabbath and the holiness of a holy day. You have sanctified the seventh day as opposed to the six days of work. You have separated Your people Israel in Your sanctity.[2]

There is, however, yet another *havdalah*, this one a fully discrete ritual that takes place in the home, as opposed to the above prayers, which are added to the service of the synagogue. It is further distinguished from the others by its own technical title, *havdalah al hakos,* or "*havdalah* over the cup [of wine]." The ritual features a blessing that parallels A and B above, but it also contains other items that should be described, if not quoted in full. The word *havdalah* is used for the core paragraph itself and for the ritual as a whole.

This *havdalah* begins with a series of biblical verses, the selection of which varies from rite to rite. The practice as we know it dates from eleventh-century France—it is part of the liturgical compendium known as *Machzor Vitry*—but the use of biblical verses in a somewhat similar manner is known to the Geonim, the intellectual leaders of Jewish society under the Abbasid caliphate, ca. 757–1038. There then follow three short benedictions, praising God for creating wine, spices, and fire, respectively. They are accompanied by some wine, sweet spices that are inhaled, and a candle made from several wicks twisted together.

During the benediction regarding fire, one observes the flame. Finally we come
to the core *havdalah* benediction itself, which we label "C":

> (C) Blessed art Thou Lord our God, Sovereign of the universe, who has separated
> holy from profane, light from darkness, Israel from [other] peoples, the seventh day
> from the six days of work. Blessed art Thou, Lord, who has separated holy from
> profane.[3]

The ritual concludes with several poems and songs. The themes vary, according to the selection particular to each rite, but the most common elements are a
petition for forgiveness of sin, coupled with a greeting of Elijah the prophet, who
is expected to arrive with the good news that the messiah has come. These two
elements are also medieval. The petition for forgiveness is of uncertain origin,
though our version is usually traced to the eleventh-century Spanish authority,
Isaac ibn Giyyat. The greeting of Elijah will occupy our attention later. Suffice it
to say at this point that medieval society after the turn of the millennium featured
Elijah's appearance at the Passover seder and at the ceremony of a child's
circumcision (*brit milah*), as well as at *havdalah* time.

In sum, by dividing C further, we have the following:

C1. Introduction: Bible verses
C2. Blessings over wine, spices, light
C. The actual *havdalah* blessing itself
C3. Conclusion: songs seeking forgiveness, and the coming of Elijah

What is it, now, that traditional liturgical investigation has had to say about
havdalah? Our goal is not to cite and to adjudicate among every known study,
deciding in favor of this or that theory, but to indicate the textual nature of the
question addressed and the range of answers provided. We shall then be able to
turn to those questions which are necessarily excluded by the text-centered focus
of philology and form-criticism.

In many ways, Isaac Seligman Baer (1825–97) was paradigmatic in the pioneering of the study of Jewish liturgy. Though he never held a university
position or boasted rabbinic education, he did study under the master bibliophile
Wolf Heidenheim, and inherited from his teacher a passion for preparing fault-
less texts of Jewish liturgical classics. In 1868 Baer published what he had
decided was an authoritative collection of Jewish prayers. To this, he appended
footnotes explaining his editorial decisions and providing supportive cross-references to the Jewish sources whence the prayers and relevant traditions regarding
them were derived.[4]

He has only a little to say about the scriptural verses (C1). Basically, he cites
authorities who tell us that they are not as critical as the blessings that they
introduce. The sixteenth-century legalist Moses Isserles thought they were in the
ritual just for good luck (*siman tov*). Baer notes the existence of different collec-

tions of verses that earlier rabbis had mentioned in their writings, and he himself records some variants in manuscripts of the Roman rite. After deciding which verses to include, Baer tells us where we can find them in the Bible.

For the blessings (C2), Baer has much more to add. Most striking is the etiology he imagines for them, a series of folk tales drawn from the tradition. A blessing over wine needs no explanation, but the benediction over the spices does. We are told that on the Sabbath we are visited by an extra soul, which, however, is saddened when it has to leave us on Saturday night. The sweet-smelling spices cheer it up. We bless fire because of Adam. Two versions of the story are given. According to the first, Adam was afraid of the dark, and God gave him two stones to rub together to make fire. In the second version, he feared the return of the snake who might lead him astray, so God sent a pillar of fire to protect him.

Baer passes over the *havdalah* blessing itself (C) with no comment other than providing the talmudic source whence it is derived, but he is a wealth of information on the songs (C3). In each case he traces the lyrics back to their biblical paradigms, explaining as well who the authors were, and what the allusions to the rest of rabbinic literature are. Particularly with regard to "Elijah the Prophet" does Baer give us detail. The prophet Malachi predicted that Elijah would herald the messiah, and tradition has determined that one likely time for the fulfillment of his prophecy is Saturday night. No one is quite clear why this is so, but Baer bravely surveys Jewish opinion on the subject. According to a twelfth/thirteenth-century source (*Hamanhig*) hailing from Provence, we expect Elijah as soon as the Sabbath is over because the Talmud tells us that Elijah would not travel on the Sabbath itself; it follows that he must be anxious to come as soon as he can on Saturday night. A fourteenth/fifteenth-century authority (Maharil) cites his teacher (Maharash) to the effect that earlier Jewish sources (second and fifth centuries respectively) remember how Elijah sits in the Garden of Eden under the tree of life, counting the merit of those who keep the Sabbath. And Israel is to be redeemed only because of the Sabbath that its members keep.

Baer has no discursive summary of his remarks. He is a conscientious publisher of books who has ferreted out the proper readings and justified his work in notes that provide a running study guide for Jewish readers. His book of prayer has become a book of study, running some 800 pages long and weighing far too much to be considered seriously as a widely used worship text. I cite him because he is paradigmatic of Jewish liturgical study.

It is Baer as scholarly paradigm that should concern us. In that regard, we should note, above all, that Baer has expanded a synchronic work into a diachronic one, allowing the reader of prayers to arrest the flow of liturgy and to pause momentarily to consider any single word or group of words with respect to its historical development. The reader may proceed page by page or stop to consult the history behind each unit. But the structure of the first dimension has determined the structure of the second. The synchronic structure of a prayer book is determinative in terms of what it allows Baer to do. That is to say, his commentary must follow the order of the service, proceeding prayer by prayer, page by page. Nowhere is he free, say, to excerpt all the Elijah passages in the liturgy and ask questions about the function of Elijah generally in Jewish prayer. Instead, he must handle Elijah here, and then wait patiently until Elijah turns up again, when he will discuss Elijah *de novo*. But questions about Elijah's overall liturgical role are not part of Baer's vocabulary. His interest is limited to the determination of the correct wording of prayers, and then to tracing down the origins thereof.

Baer's agenda remained the same for later philologists as well.[5] Over time, they may have increased their willingness to exercise critical judgment on the theories they proposed, an "advance" due primarily to the information gain brought about by increasing numbers of newly discovered manuscripts. But their questions were still limited by their literary orientation. It is as if they could not escape the image of a hypothetical book of prayer that was going to be printed above a line, for which they were preparing the commentary that would go below. Like Baer, they rarely went beyond a consideration of the one particular text that would have appeared above the imaginary line at that point. When their articles or books were published, one could easily imagine them being set as a running commentary to the order of prayer, both the prayer and the commentary hewing faithfully to the arbitrary strictures of a book. For them, liturgy was still literature.

The master liturgist, Ismar Elbogen (1874–1943), demonstrates this dependence on literary structure. In his comprehensive and classic 1913 study of the synagogue service[6]—in many ways, still the basic work today—Elbogen proceeded as if the prayer book were printed above the line; he discussed the prayers in their liturgical order, stopping at each one to give us its history, and to establish the proper reading of words that are in doubt. Unlike Baer, he had a wealth of modern secondary studies on which to draw, and many more original sources—including Genizah fragments (that is, the cache of documents unearthed in the synagogue of old Cairo, at the turn of this century)—to guide him; and his doctoral training at the University of Breslau had inculcated a heightened sense of sophistication regarding the theories worth advancing. Where Baer felt free to include both scientific grammatical comparisons and mythological folklore drawn from midrash, Elbogen stayed firmly within the bounds of the scientific, accenting his generation's notion of "historical development," with the phrase "in seiner geschichtlichen Entwicklung" even dominating the title of his work.

But a more sophisticated theory of a text's origin is still only a theory about a text's origin. As desirable, even necessary, as such theories may be, we wish to do what Baer and Elbogen and anyone else constrained by literary structure cannot do: extend our view beyond the text.

Still, let us look at Elbogen and gain what we can from him. He is at his best in his treatment of the *havdalah*. He sees it as developing naturally out of community meals eaten together by "tableship groups" known as *chavurot*. Since people regularly drank wine at the end of their meals then, no special explanation is necessary for the first of our blessings in C2, the one over wine. But why do we say benedictions over fire and spices? Elbogen hypothesizes that with the end of the Sabbath ban on starting fires, which occurred after dinner Saturday night, people deliberately brought in lamps to light, and also incense to burn on the coals. The latter was intended to remove the smell of the food from dinner. So blessings over fire and spices became the norm. As for *havdalah* itself (C), Elbogen assumes it developed from a logical insertion into the grace after meals for Saturday night. Beyond this, Elbogen has little to add. He cites new manuscript information regarding differences in the rites, and omits Baer's traditionalistic folk tales, which he dismisses as inappropriate for scholarly inclusion. Since the songs (C3) and biblical verses (C1) are either optional or of lesser stature than the blessings themselves, he barely mentions them.

The textual bias of the philological school is particularly evident in Elbogen's treatment of Elijah. He knows he is studying a book, not a lived liturgical ritual. What counts, then, is the material that would necessarily be printed in the book under discussion. The fact that the people praying from the book might project greater subjective significance to a folk custom associated with the book, though not necessarily appearing within it as a *bona fide* prayer text, is of no concern to Elbogen. So he dispenses with Elijah in one short sentence fragment: " . . . and in Spain, they have even added a section from the poem 'Elijah the Prophet.' "[7]

So the order of blessings (C2) is dealt with at length. Elijah (C3) is hardly considered at all. And the further question, the meaning of the *havdalah* ritual in the prayer life of the Jewish people, is not even asked. What we have in Elbogen is another diachronic expansion of the normative text accompanying a ritual. If Baer's version was rich in legend, Elbogen's is highly scientific. So, scientifically speaking, Elbogen's account is truer. If our purpose is to understand the ritual act of *havdalah*, however, it is not necessarily better.

I have hammered home the shortcomings of the philological methodology enough by now. It is time to balance the picture. What philologists have done exceptionally well is to provide raw data without which serious consideration of prayers would be impossible. Let us look, then, at some of these data that will be particularly useful for us later.

First, as Elbogen correctly noted, the *havdalah* ceremony is very old. The practice of making *havdalah* is attested in the earliest rabbinical literature, and

the Hillelites and the Shammaites, the parties to the debates there, can be dated to
the period preceding the fall of the Jerusalem Temple (70 C.E.).[8] They already
know of the practice of saying all of the blessings (C2 and then C), though not
the biblical verses (C1) or the songs (C3). Exact texts, however, are rarely
specified, and when they are, we should not assume that they were the only ones
in use.

Similarly, in the *havdalah* inserted in the synagogue prayer service (A and B
above), we find agreement neither on the wording of the texts, nor on the proper
time when that *havdalah* should be introduced. All agree that the *havdalah*
should be inserted in the prayer known as the *tefillah*, but three options are
advanced regarding the precise benediction of the *tefillah* that should be selected
as the locus for *havdalah*'s inclusion. As late as the geonic period (ca. 757–
1038),[9] disagreement continued, particularly in the Land of Israel, which continued to create new alternative texts and to insert them into the *tefillah* at
different places.[10]

Perhaps the most interesting report in the entire corpus of literature on *havdalah* is a statement attributed to Rabbi Jochanan, a third-century Palestinian
authority. "The men of the Great Synagogue," he says, "instituted blessings,
prayers, sanctifications, and separations for Israel."[11] What could this pithy
semihistorical recollection mean? Our translation prejudices the case, so let us
look at the original Hebrew words for the four items in question: *berakhot*,
tefillot, *kedushot*, and *havdalot*. Clearly, *havdalot* is the plural of *havdalah*, and,
therefore, of interest to us here. What exactly did the Great Assembly do regarding *havdalah*?

To answer that question, we should first determine the identity of the Great
Assembly. Unfortunately, there is no scholarly consensus here, but most people
think it was an official body of lay and religious leaders established by Ezra upon
his return from Babylonian exile in the middle of the fifth century B.C.E. It would
have lasted until the Pharisaic age, which, again, is not clearly established in our
sources, but which, at the latest, cannot be placed after the Hasmonean revolt of
167 B.C.E. The only actual name preserved from the Assembly is Simon the Just,
who is said to be one of its last members, and who is normally identified as one
of two people with that name, both of whom functioned as the High Priest, the
first around 280 B.C.E., and the second roughly one hundred years later.[12] On the
other hand, it has also been argued that the Assembly was not a governing body
that met regularly throughout the centuries after Ezra's demise, but a legislature
that met on only one occasion, that being the coronation of Simon the Hasmonean, who should be identified as our Simon the Just.[13] Finally, it has been
suggested that the Great Assembly never existed at all.[14] What we have is a
reification of a presumably existent entity, so as to explain the functioning of the
Jewish polity in an earlier period about which later generations knew nothing.

Seeking to preserve the chain of tradition that went back to biblical days, the rabbis invented the fiction of a leadership body that transmitted Torah diligently and faithfully to those who came after them.

However we decide the issue, it is clear at least how the rabbis use the concept of the Great Assembly. Plainly they have no precise idea of the nature of the group, which, if it existed at all, did so only in the distant past. But it is that very ancient status which makes the Great Assembly a useful construct in the first place. Unlike the Torah, which, the rabbis insist, goes back to Sinai, the liturgy is regularly linked to historical circumstance. So the Great Assembly provided the means of explaining those liturgical innovations for which no actual event in recent history existed as a reliable explanatory mechanism. Whenever the rabbis encountered a liturgical tradition that they assumed to be sound, but whose origins were shrouded in the dim past, they classified it as an innovation of the Men of the Great Assembly.[15] This was tantamount to saying that the prayer or practice or doctrine under discussion was authentic, but so old that it was impossible to know for sure the name of the sage who had created it.

So Rabbi Jochanan means to inform us that the four liturgical items in question are very old, and so central to Judaism that their authenticity is beyond question. Let us take them in turn. *Berakhot* means blessings, and *tefillot* means prayers. Yet we are told only that the Assembly ordained them, generally; no specific blessings or prayers are cited. We are surely not being told that the Great Assembly ordained all our blessings and prayers, since elsewhere in the same rabbinic literature specific ones are dated according to discrete events or persons clearly datable only after the Assembly ceased functioning, frequently within recent memory of the speaker. Of course, the sense of the communication could still be that the Great Assembly ordained *some* blessings and prayers but not *all* of them. But if that is the case, we are hardly being informed of anything useful, since we are not told which ones are which.

Thus, I suggest Rabbi Jochanan is telling us something altogether different: he is describing an elementary and very early categorization of Jewish prayer. There are four essential categories that go back as far as anyone can remember. Two of them are *berakhot* and *tefillot*, blessings and prayers.

Consider now the other two terms, *kedushot* and *havdalot*, sanctifications and separations. Several possible interpretations come to mind, not all of them liturgical. We might be discussing theological concepts, for example, the things that are holy rather than profane, or those that should be maintained in isolation from others. It is more likely, though, that Jochanan would have strung together four items that are members of the same class. So he was probably denoting *kedushot* and *havdalot* as liturgical entities. He is telling us that besides blessings and prayers, sanctifications and separations also constitute essential categories of Jewish prayer. By sanctifications, he means those technical sections in the liturgy which contain the trishagion of Isaiah 6:3, "Holy, holy, holy . . . "—the *kedushot hashem*, or "sanctifications of the name of God," as they are known technically.[16] By separations, he means the prayers in question here, the *havdalah* liturgies that we have labeled A, B, and C.

What we have is nothing less than an elementary ordering of the primary categories of Jewish liturgy, by none other than the most prominent Palestinian rabbi of the third century. There are other categories too, of course. We should not assume that Jochanan meant to include everything in his fourfold scheme. Psalms, for example, are older than the Great Assembly and precede the rabbinic imagination. Confessions (*viduyim*) and biblical or rabbinic descriptions of sacrifices once offered in the Temple (*korbanot*) would be other categories that Jochanan excluded, possibly because they were not so old or not so central to the inherent structure that he considered basic to Jewish worship. The point, then, is not that *everything* has to be subsumed under blessings, prayers, sanctifications, and separations; only that these categories are basic, primary, prior to any others that arise over the course of time, and that must either fit within the first four or be debated anew until the tradition establishes what to do with them. Each of our primary items exists independently in the sense that each inhabits its own field of meaning; each elaborates its own canons of style, its own rules of liturgical recitation. One stands for sanctifications, for example, but not for blessings. One necessarily includes the name and sovereignty of God in blessings but not in separations. And so on. Eventually, a defining complex of structural, theological, and attitudinal hallmarks for each category develops. Expectations of worshipers will be defined by which of the four essential items they see themselves as praying at any given moment.

On the other hand, it is indisputable that by Jochanan's day, these elementary categories had not only been augmented by other liturgical forms (such as *korbanot* or *viduyim*, mentioned above), but they also had merged with one another to the point where they no longer constituted wholly independent categories, at least insofar as we consider their literary style. But unless Jochanan was deliberately being redundant, there must have been a time in which the four categories did not overlap. I expect that he was either citing a fragment of an earlier communication that reflected the state of liturgical compartmentalization then actually in existence; or he was displaying remarkable insight into an earlier stage of liturgical evolution, linking the distant era of the Great Assembly to an elementary fourfold categorization scheme that once was in fact the case.

In any event, by Jochanan's generation, the blessing as liturgical form had encroached on the other categories, so that *havdalot*, *kedushot*, and *tefillot* were now styled according to canons of taste once typical only of *berakhot*. This growth of the blessing as the preferred prose form for the rabbis is in keeping with what we know elsewhere in our sources: the exchange of the ten commandments for a blessing affirming revelation, before the *Shema*, for example; or the gradual selection of one set of rules regarding the wording of blessings, such as Heinemann has documented. But we would be wrong to assume that the *eventual* stylistic mastery of the blessing *form* must presuppose a common set of worship expectations *whenever* that form is encountered in the worship experience. To this day, each worship system contains subsets of prayer material that carry with them differentiated feeling tones. So categories still exist today, even if they are no longer quickly distinguishable in terms of compositional style. Every worshiper knows that even though a *tefillah* is written in blessing form, it is not simply another blessing. The *kedushah* may be but one of the *tefillah* blessings, but it certainly maintains its own stubborn integrity in the mind set of those who pray it. And *havdalah* is still *havdalah*, with clearly distinctive rules and customs, folkways, and meanings, even if we say it in the same blessing format as the other categories we have been discussing.

So Jochanan has opened for us a wholly new area for liturgical research, not the sorting of prayers according to literary form (as Heinemann, entrenched in his literary bias, would have it), but according to categories, each one entailing its own field of meaning for worshipers engaged in praying it.

I have spent some time on Jochanan's pithy remark for two reasons. First, as I said at the outset of this chapter, I am engaged in establishing the role of categorization in the way we apprehend reality, leading up to the argument that *havdalah* functions as a presentation of the Jewish category system. I began by discussing categories of scholarly approach that function to mandate specific *Gestalten*—to return to Polanyi's useful term—and to prevent others. I have now introduced yet another instance of pregiven categorization of experience, this one being a very early system of liturgical order that mandates that the world of prayer will be viewed in certain predetermined ways rather than others. Texts will be forced into the conceptual and experiential framework of blessings, prayers, sanctifications, and separations. The world of prayer, like the world of scholarship, depends on structural constraints enforced in advance on the relevant world of experience: by those who pray, in one case, and by those who study, in the other.

But even if the reader were to remain unconvinced by this treatment of *havdalot* as one of the rabbis' primary liturgical categories, there would still be good reason to take careful note of Rabbi Jochanan's dating them in the age of Great Assembly. I will still claim that *havdalah* functions as a presentation of the Jewish categorization of reality, and this claim regarding its cultural function is independent of the question of its liturgically ontological status relative to the other prayer forms listed by Jochanan. But it is important that we establish the fact that *havdalah* is old enough to be reflective of that elementary Jewish categorization of reality, and according to Rabbi Jochanan, this is indeed the case, since it derives its existence from the age of the Great Assembly, the early era that predates any rabbinic conceptualizations of experience.

So, having encountered two sets of categories, scholarly disciplines that define knowledge and liturgical material that determines worship experience, we now turn to a third instance in which a pregiven grid of reality functions to imprint a certain preconceived order on the world. I will argue that there exists an axiomatic systematization of all experience that Judaism fixes on the raw world of sensory data. *Havdalah* serves to demarcate these primal categories, and to maintain them.

It would be relatively straightforward now to explicate the elementary Jewish categorization of reality that *havdalah* represents, if our sources contained only one *havdalah* text. We would then be in a position to look at it, and to cite the categories it presents as the categorizing scheme in question. But more than one text exists. The three that we have already seen (those labeled A, B and C), that is to say, those which have survived and are in common use today, all describe equivalent differentiations between (1) holy and profane, (2) light and darkness, (3) the Sabbath and the six days of work, and (4) Israel and other peoples. But the talmudic discussions of *havdalah* describe additional conceptualizations of essential differences. Before claiming that the particular *havdalot*—that is, separations—that our contemporary rites contain are the sole rabbinic terms for differentiating the universe into oppositions, we must survey the alternative schemes to which that same rabbinic Judaism testifies. We will then have to justify our selection of our current rite's set of binary opposites as representing more than just historical accident, the wording that has reached us by, as it were, evolutionary caprice.

The crucial discussion containing early alternative formulas for *havdalah* occurs in the Babylonian Talmud (Pes. 103b–104a).[17] Though our purposes do not require a complete analysis of the passage, at least its partial untangling will reveal the fact that more than one *havdalah* version existed and will indicate some of the wording of some of the variants no longer in use. This is one of those cases to which I alluded earlier, an instance equivalent to a psychologist's recapitulation of a patient's dream or an anthropologist's reiteration of an informant's account of kinship rules, where, as liturgist, I am constrained to try the reader's patience as I quote my own raw data. The analogy is apt in more ways than one: all three of us—psychologist, anthropologist, liturgist—have no choice but to translate the source, thus losing something of what the original tradents saw in it, and we must all restructure it into the terms in which our own craft is patterned, in a way, we hope, that we see something equally true but nonetheless absent from the originator's intent. I will avoid the temptation to analyze it more extensively than necessary, but we do need to recognize its testimony to the existence of more than one set of binary opposites being cited within variant *havdalah* texts in the second and third centuries. That realization will then force us to ask how we can have the effrontery to promote our own received version as the one to which we should attribute the singular importance of containing the elemental binary oppositions of Judaism.

To simplify analysis, I have divided the originally undifferentiated source into sections (A, B, C . . .), which correspond to what I take to be separate pericopes strung together by the editor. I have inserted my own remarks in brackets to facilitate comprehension and retrospective reference in my discussion of the text. Within each pericope, I arbitrarily number consecutively (i, ii, iii . . .) the separate statements into which the editor has cast the account. When multiple sets of binary oppositions are listed together, I have numbered them with Arabic numerals. Finally, wherever our standard set of oppositions is referred to, I have italicized it to facilitate recognition.

[A] (i) He [Rava—fourth-century Babylonia] began by saying "[Blessed art Thou . . .] who divides (1) *holy from profane*, (2) *light from darkness*, (3) *Israel from [other] peoples*, (4) *the seventh day from the six days of work.*" (ii) [Rabbi Jacob bar Abba, who was visiting him at the time] asked, "Why do you say all that? Didn't Rav Judah [third-century Babylonia] say in the name of Rav [third-century Babylonia] that the *havdalah* of Judah HaNasi [the Mishnah's editor, end second-century Palestine] consisted solely of '. . . who separates *holy from profane*' "? (iii) He [Rava] replied, "I follow the logic of Rabbi Oshaiah [disciple of Rabbi Judah HaNasi] as reported by Rabbi Elazar [ben Pedat, third-century Palestine], to the effect that if you want to stipulate only a few 'separations' you should say no fewer than three, and if you want to say many, you should say no more than seven." [This constitutes the first of several principles enunciated here; we can refer to it later as P1.] (iv) "But you have said neither three nor seven [but four]," he [Jacob bar Abba] objected. (v) "True," came the reply, "but [the last one] *'between the seventh day and the six days of work'* is a synopsis of the concluding eulogy [which follows, so is not to be counted as anything but an anticipation of that conclusion, and having no status in its own right]. After all, Rav Judah said in the name of Samuel [second-century Babylonia, a contemporary of Rav], 'When you say *havdalah* you should include an anticipation of the concluding eulogy just before the eulogy' " [another principle, P2].
[B] The Pumbeditans include a synopsis of the introduction just after the eulogy. [There now follows an excursus on the consequences of the Pumbeditan custom.]
[C] (i) Let us consider the statement of Rabbi Elazar in the name of Rabbi Oshaiah: "If you want to stipulate only a few distinctions, you should say no fewer than three, and if you want to include many, you should say not more than seven." (ii) Doesn't this contradict the statement by *tannaim* [rabbis before the promulgation of the Mishnah, whose opinion is taken as probative in talmudic discussions] that " . . . [in saying *havdalah*], those who are fluent can say many separations, while those who are not can say only one" [P3]? (iii) The *tannaim* were divided on the matter, as we see from the fact that Rabbi Jochanan [second-century Palestine] said, "Descendants of holy people recite one, but the people at large are accustomed to saying many." [There now follows an excursus identifying who the descendants of holy people are.]
[D] (i) Rabbi Joshua ben Levi [third-century Palestine] said, "In saying *havdalah*,

you should mention synopses of those distinctions cited in the Torah'' [P4]. (ii) An objection from tannaitic sources was raised to this, for the *tannaim* said, "What is the order of *havdalah*? It is ' . . . who separates (1) *holy from profane*, (2) *light from darkness*, (3) *Israel from [other peoples], and* (4) *the seventh day from the six days of work*; (5) the unclean from the clean, (6) the sea from dry land, (7) upper waters from lower waters; (8) priests from Levites, from [other] Israelites' '' [I later refer to this lengthy series as "the long *havdalah*''];[18] you conclude with a eulogy referring to 'the order of creation'; others say, ' . . . who wrought creation.' Rabbi Yose the son of Rabbi Judah [second-century Palestine] said, "Conclude with: ' . . . who sanctifies Israel.' '' Now [in opposition to P4] the distinction between sea and dry land [(6) above] is not written in the Torah. (iii) Then perhaps "between sea and dry land'' should be deleted. (iv) Then you have to delete also the reference *"between the seventh day and the six days of work* [(4) above]'' [since it too is not specified as a *havdalah* in scripture]. (v) But [recourse may be had to P2] *"Between the seventh day and the six days of work''* is merely an anticipation of the concluding eulogy [so does not count]. (vi) In that case, however, you would be unable to count it in making up the total number of references, and would have fewer than seven [i.e., 8-2=6, in default of P1]. (vii) So you have to count "between priests, Levites, and [other] Israelites'' [(8) above] as two distinct clauses: "between Levites and Israelites,'' as it is written, "At that time, the Lord differentiated the tribe of Levi'' (Deut. 10:8), and "between priests and Levites,'' as it is written, "The sons of Amram were Aaron and Moses; but Aaron was differentiated so that he might be sanctified as most holy'' (1 Chron. 23:13).

[E] (i) With what eulogy does one conclude? (ii) Rav [third-century Babylonia] said, " . . . who sanctifies Israel''; Samuel [Rav's contemporary] said, " . . . *who separates holy from profane.''* (iii) Abaye [fourth-century Babylonia]—though some say it was Rav Joseph [Abaye's older contemporary]—denounced this ruling of Rav. (iv) It was taught in the name of the *tanna* Joshua ben Hananiah [turn of the second century, Palestine], "Long life is granted to one who concludes, ' . . . who sanctifies Israel, and *separates between sacred and profane.'* '' (v) But the law does not follow him.

[F] (i) When Ulla [late third-century and early fourth-century Palestinian who settled in Babylonia] visited Pumbedita, Rav Judah said to Rav Yitzhak his son, " . . . Go and observe how he makes *havdalah.''* He did not go himself, but he sent Abaye. When Abaye returned, he [Rav Isaac] asked, "What did he say?'' He responded, "He said, 'Blessed is God who divides *holy from profane*' and nothing else.''

This talmudic passage contains many diverse strata only loosely woven together by the editor. But if we ignore the synchronic structure enforced by that editor, we can see that we have a collection of statements reflecting diverse practice, some as old as the pre-200 tannaitic era; a series of principles, most of them adopted after the fact to explain the practices; and all of this condensed into a literary style of presumed argumentation in which diachronicity is ignored. If we assume no necessary homogeneity of wording in early Jewish liturgy, we have no trouble digesting the disparity of practice; similarly, if we accept even the rules as individually arrived at by specific authorities to explain their practice, or even by later generations as ex post facto explanatory devices for wording they inherited, we have no trouble with different rules for different sets of words. Only if we take the position of the Talmud itself and assume that rules by different rabbis living hundreds of years apart must be in harmony, are we struck by a problematic: that is, the apparently irresoluble contrasts in inherited traditions. [D] for example, cites what I have called "the long *havdalah*" as an objection to P4, in that P4 demands only scripturally based differentiations in the *havdalah* formula, while the long *havdalah* contains two clauses without such biblical basis. P2 is cited in return as a means of relegating one of the offending formulas to the category of an anticipatory clause that need not follow P4, but then it is maintained that the resulting benediction lacks sufficient clauses to satisfy yet another rule, P1. All of this has a great deal of relevance to the literary structure of talmudic argument, but none whatever to the unveiling of actual practice in the early centuries, the object of our concern here.

That practice, however, is evident, in part, from the raw stuff of which the argument is composed. [A] tells us that around the year 200, Judah HaNasi cited only the dichotomy of holy/profane, a practice still in use as late as the third century (see [F]). Our own standard practice of mentioning (1) holy/profane; (2) light/darkness; (3) Israel/other peoples; and (4) Sabbath/weekdays is known at least as early as the time of Rava (early fourth century); however, these may be the unspecified terms of differentiation that lay behind the rule of P1 (i.e., to say between 3 and 7 clauses), which Rava himself quotes in the name of Rabbi Oshaiah (early third century); and it is striking that even in the long *havdalah*, which is tannaitic and therefore pre-200, our four divisions not only occur but occur together in our own order, as if they were known then as a standard text to which four more terms were then added.

There are many reasons to grant these four terms priority, if not in chronological development of *havdalah*, then at least in terms of significance for understanding what it is that *havdalah* means to say. To begin with, it is evident that our talmudic passage has undergone considerable editorializing, so that some of the variants mentioned may not have been actual practices, but mere literary conceits. The only obvious competitor to our practice is the long *havdalah*—it probably was in use, since the term used to refer to it is *seder*, or "order," and that term is used elsewhere to mean a distinct order of prayers[19]—but as we just saw, even it is built on our four terms, which occur as the first ones within it. Our eulogy, which reiterates the substance of Judah HaNasi's entire benediction, is one of several eulogies recalled here, but it adequately sums up what I take to be the essential dichotomy of all the other terms, holy/profane.

We are in the same situation as students of myth, who discover a seemingly infinite supply of any given myth's versions, and wonder which of them they are to analyze as the "real" myth. As in the case of liturgy, traditional approaches to myth have tried philologically to unearth the "original" text, as opposed to later falsifications of it. Since myth exists only in oral versions, however, the normal literary methods of historical analysis and comparison must ultimately prove disappointing, just as they do with prayer, which, the form-critics taught us, also arose in oral form with an abundance of alternative formulations. As we are in the process of discovering some underlying message that the *havdalah* communicates despite variations in its specific wording, we may profitably cite from Lévi-Strauss, who has discussed the identical difficulty regarding the structural analysis of myths.

The multiplicity of versions of a myth is a problem to which Lévi-Strauss returned time and time again, beginning in 1955, when he applied to myth linguistic categories like *langue* (the sum total of possible utterances in a language), *parole* (the specific set of utterances in any instance), and phoneme (the smallest sound a social community can differentiate). With remarkable suggestiveness, he concluded, "It is as though a phoneme were always made up of all its variants. . . . [Thus, with regard to myths,] our method eliminates a problem which has, so far, been one of the main obstacles to the progress of mythological studies, namely, the quest for the *true* version, or the *earlier* one. On the contrary, we define a myth as consisting of all its versions."[20] By 1964, he had completed the first volume of his magnum opus on a science of mythology, and he raised the question again, this time with regard to mythic accounts from different peoples.

> Someone may question my right to choose myths from various sources, to explain a myth from the Gran Chaco by means of a variant from Guiana, or a Ge myth by a similar one from Colombia. But structural analysis—however respectful it may be of history and however anxious to take advantage of all its teachings—refuses to be confined within the frontiers already established by historical investigation. On the contrary . . . myths from widely divergent sources can be seen objectively as a set.[21]

Thus, any given myth's structural message is decipherable from any one of its versions, a principle enunciated finally in a somewhat different fashion, in Lévi-Strauss's Massey Lectures of 1977:

> Science has only two ways of proceeding: it is either reductionist or structuralist. It is reductionist when it is possible to find out that very complex phenomena on one level can be reduced to simpler phenomena on another level. . . . And when we are confronted with phenomena too complex to be reduced to phenomena of a lower order, then we can only approach them by looking to their relationships, that is, by trying to understand what kind of original system they make up.[22]

The structuralist approach is the "quest for the invariant, or for the invariant elements among superficial differences."[23] Like a myth, early prayers abound in superficial differences—of wording. But a closer analysis reveals a syntax of prayer by which specific worship units, whatever their wording, were regularly combined according to rules regarding the way they were juxtaposed with other worship constitutents, so that the essential message that transcended the specific choice of words was clear. Like other prayers, *havdalah* too can be found in various versions, but the differences are superficial, in that all versions point to the basic diadic opposition in the system of culture we call Judaism.

That basic diad is the dichotomy between holy and profane, which itself may be reflected in the structuring of time, or of society (Sabbath/weekdays; Israel/other peoples); it may be combined with a secondary symbol of late Roman times (light/dark); or it may be stated baldly (holy/profane). Together these terms make up at least the only versions of the *havdalah* that have survived as actual instances of practice. The sole exception, the long *havdalah*, contains these, and if the additions to it do not add to the essential message that *havdalah* provides, they do not on that account detract from it either. That message is the essential cultural distinction of holy/profane: it is the categorization of reality into two disparate realms that I take to be the rabbis' ultimate *a priori* characterization of human experience; and it is *havdalah*'s function to ritualize that *a priori* experiential grid. To appreciate that function, we turn away from the more traditional textual discussion that has occupied us in our quest for early wording, and toward discussions in the social sciences on the phenomenon of cultural categorization.

It is by now commonplace to say that we experience reality through preconceptions of how the world is structured. But even the commonplace deserves being said once in a while, especially as we tend to forget it. Wittgenstein notes how impossible it is for the nonreligious person to contradict the religious. Putting himself in the position of the latter, he concludes:

> I think differently, in a different way. I say different things to myself. I have different pictures. . . .
>
> [In attempting to contradict a religious person] I give an explanation: "I don't believe in . . .", but then the religious person never believes what I describe.
>
> I can't say. I can't contradict the person.[24]

The words "different pictures" are critical here. We work with different pictures that we take for granted, and with which we order experience. The question of how we arrive at these structuring pictures has plagued philosophers and scientists, who have advanced a predictable variety of solutions, but the fact that we operate with them is unquestionable. As a working hypothesis regarding their function, I quote from Lévi-Strauss:

> The thought of so-called primitive societies is shaped by the insistence on differentiation. . . . Now on the theoretical as well as the practical plane, the existence of differentiating features is of much greater importance than their content. Once in

evidence, they form a system that can be employed as a grid is used to decipher a text, whose original unintelligibility gives it the appearance of an uninterrupted flow. The grid makes it possible to introduce divisions and contrasts, in other words the formal conditions necessary for a significant message to be conveyed.[25]

Or, as Mary Douglas puts it: "Culture . . . mediates the experience of individuals. It provides in advance some categories, a positive pattern in which ideas and values are tidily ordered."[26] "Categories," note. Wittgenstein's "different pictures" are composed of Lévi-Strauss's "divisions and contrasts," which place things in advance into Douglas's "categories." Certainly our language plays a major role in this—the most significant role according to some.[27] Certainly too, rituals are not unimportant. With rituals, we reinforce the categories that our culture takes for granted. Particularly in her study of the cultural role of dirt as unclassified matter, Douglas has shed light on this categorization. She studies rituals of purity and impurity, to demonstrate that "Ideas about *separating*, purifying, demarcating and punishing transgressions have as their main function to impose system on an inherently untidy experience."[28] Modern Western cultures are under the misconception that our elaborate care to dispose of dirt and debris or to avoid pollution in food or the environment is explainable by the high level of scientific sophistication we have attained. We presumably recognize that pollution makes one sick, so we try to avoid harmful bacteria. "Backward" cultures, on the other hand, are said by us to order their lives according to some sort of primitive ritualism. "Are our ideas hygienic, where theirs are symbolic?" asks Douglas. "Not a bit of it: I am going to argue that our ideas of dirt also express symbolic systems and that the difference between pollution behavior in one part of the world and another is only a matter of detail."[29] Douglas summarizes: "If we can abstract pathogenicity and hygiene from our notion of dirt, we are left with the definition of dirt as matter out of place. This is a very suggestive approach. It implies two conditions: a set of ordered relations and a contravention of that order. Dirt, then, is never a unique isolated event. Where there is dirt there is system."[30]

So Douglas too is concerned about, as she calls them, the "basic categories" that culture "provides in advance" in order "to mediate the experience of individuals."[31] Rules about impurity, she holds, are actually rules about categorization of experience, or, to be more exact, rules about dealing with those things which do not fall easily into the categories. They are rules about anomalies and ambiguities, things that, in the first instance, do not fall neatly into place but are caught betwixt and between, or that, in the second instance, are susceptible to two alternative interpretations as to their essential nature. Purity rules are one way of dealing with infractions in our category systems.

In addition, we generally try to do what we can to avoid infractions, and here the ritualization of those rules is useful. Every institution incorporates ways to reinforce the moral suasion underlying its categories of experience and then feels morally justified in punishing those who mix categories. Summer camps, for example, divide counselors, who are usually of college age, from their camper wards, who may be only a year or two younger, by different levels of privilege, different status rights, recognized places for their beds within the large bunks, and so on. Between male and female campers, or between male and female counselors, a certain amount of sexual activity is condoned, even encouraged; but counselors who get involved sexually with campers lose their job. A more blatant example of sending a clear warning about categories and then punishing offenders who mix them up is our culture's attitude toward homosexuals. People must be male or female, not both. A less serious instance of the same category class is those elementary schools which still maintain separate boys' and girls' playing areas. Woe to the boys and girls who are caught playing together.

Some of our rituals, though not those specifically under investigation here— notably, rites of passage in the human life cycle—are intended to maintain the integrity of the individual categories out of which and into which people pass. Margaret Mead has demonstrated the dangers of cultural denigration of these rites, a practice that results in ambiguity between statuses.[32]

Institutionalized reminders of essential category systems are particularly nec- essary in minority cultures whose members share also another, and therefore a competitive, set of categories, i.e., the one preached by the majority culture. All religions are such minorities in contemporary America, and one notes with regularity attempts by the clergy to introduce their own specific sets of distinc- tions at times that promise captive audiences: weddings, funerals, and, of course, holy days that still bring people to church or synagogue. Indeed, one characteris- tic of new liturgies since the Enlightenment is that they are composed so as to contain many reminders of these religious categories, lest the worshipers be taken in by the competing claims of secular modernity.[33]

Now we understand *havdalah*. *Havdalah* is the ritualized reminder of the Jewish system of categorization. It arose in the very period of Jewish history that posed a threat to a stable Jewish system of ordering reality, with the arrival in western Asia of a series of majority cultures such as the Babylonians, the Per- sians, and the Greeks. All three of these cultures posited different categorizations than did ancient Israel. The first proved less dangerous on the whole, since it was promptly overturned by the second. But both Persians and Greeks left an indeli- ble mark. Jewish culture fought successfully to retain its independence but was forced nonetheless to integrate a good many elements of these two host cultures.

Most of the forms of *havdalah* that we examined earlier are really different examples of the same theme. With the exception of the long *havdalah*, which apparently incorporated a variety of biblically based references to divinely or- dered distinctions, we find only Rava's sets of oppositions (which have become

our own) and Rabbi Judah's use of a single set, which is equivalent to our eulogy
and thus an ideal synopsis of the primary theme in the body of the benediction
that it concludes. In much later times one finds some diversity, for example, the
ninth- and tenth-century geonic record of the practice of including the difference
between Israel and Egypt.[34] But on the whole, such novelty is rare; examples
thereof are optional poetic additions[35] and were not retained in the standard rites.
The paired opposites that were kept refer above all to the one basic diadic
category, the holy and the profane, and to a secondary dichotomy between light
and darkness.

This is self-evident from three of the four sets maintained in our prayer (C).
God is blessed for distinguishing between holy and profane, Israel and other
nations, the Sabbath and the six days of work. The last two sets are the holy/pro-
fane dichotomy applied to Israel (the "holy people") and to time, the Sabbath
being normally known as *Shabbat Kodesh*, or the "holy Sabbath." The first pair
is the underlying distinction itself, which is repeated as the summarizing eulogy
at the end. The only pair that does not fall naturally within this holy/profane
dichotomy is light and darkness, and this would seem to be a function of the
ritual situation, since *havdalah* is recited *at sunset*.

Both distinctions reach back to biblical roots. The difference between holy and
profane occurs regularly throughout the Bible as probably the single most characteristic criterion for judging reality. It seems to be built into the Bible's account
of Jewish experience to the point where it is used as an oft-repeated explanation
for the Jewish way of life in all its specified commandments. Jews are to do this
or that because God is holy. They are a holy people. Their society is structured
with holy places and holy ministers. Time is divided according to its degree of
holiness.

But light vs. darkness is also present, being particularly evident in the creation
narrative of Genesis 1. It may be that this dichotomy entered Jewish consciousness as a result of the general religious environment to which Jewish culture was
exposed, first in Persian civilization and later under Hellenism. Persian Zoroastrianism, after all, was constructed on the light/darkness dichotomy, and Judaism entered the Persian orbit only after Zoroastrianism had become the official
Achaemenid state church. In Hellenistic society, this contrast of light and darkness was ubiquitous. It entered Jewish liturgy elsewhere too, being found to this
day in the first blessing before the daily *Shema*, which is falsely characterized in
the secondary literature as a blessing on the theme of creation but really should
be seen as a benediction thanking God for separating light from darkness.[36]

But insofar as we search for an opposition that is distinctively Jewish, we must
return to the holy/profane diad. Light vs. darkness may have been used by Dead
Sea sects to differentiate themselves from others, but it was not so used by that
form of rabbinic Judaism which became paradigmatic for Jewish civilization and

religion as we know it today. Thus, at that moment when the holy people left its holy time to mix with nonholy peoples in nonholy days, they reminded themselves of the essential dichotomy that underlies the Jewish experience of reality.[37] And, since that time fell also at the moment when day became night, the secondary distinction, that of light and darkness, was included. Moreover, interestingly enough, even on weekdays the very same phrase, "who divides light from darkness," is inserted into the evening blessing of the *Shema* known as *ma'ariv aravim*, while the parallel morning blessing praises God for creating light.[38] Thus even the everyday times that typify the light/darkness dichotomy received their own rehearsal of the appropriate primary distinction. For the end of the Sabbath, though, along with the light/dark diad (which naturally applied at the end of the Sabbath day, as it did for all days when dusk set in), the opposition between holy and profane was relevant. So, insofar as *havdalah* is viewed primarily as a ritual to demarcate the conclusion of the Sabbath, it is the categorization of holy/profane, not light/dark, that constitutes the primary binary distinction of Judaism.

We have now almost reached the end of our analysis. By asking questions drawn from studies of human culture, we have defined the *havdalah* benediction, culturally, as the ritualistic means by which Judaism's categorization of experience is rehearsed and thus transmitted through the generations. But it happens that this understanding of *havdalah* as a ritualized rehearsal of the Jewish categorization scheme may do more than explain the *havdalah* benediction (C) alone. It provides a comprehensive framework in which the later addition of songs and poems (C3) appears to be due to other than fortuitous circumstance. Many Jewish rituals have attracted such accretions through time, and there is no reason that we should either expect or demand that they be integrally related to the body of the ritual that they accompany in any but the most tangential way. On the other hand, if a given ritual fulfills a particular social function, it may be that the additions it attracts will demonstrate a certain affinity of theme or tone with it.

We saw above that a favorite part of the ritual, which, however, was omitted from some prayer books because, strictly speaking, it was not a "text" demanded by the ritual, is the welcome to Elijah the Prophet, who is expected to arrive at *havdalah* time. This seems to be a genuine folk tradition, its origins lost to us, its continuity independent of editorial decisions regarding the inclusion or exclusion of the text that accompanies it. A second element that shares the character of being a folk tradition is the act of conjuring demonic forces on Saturday night. Present Western rites have done away with this ancient practice, but for centuries it was usual, and echoes of it still remain, albeit in vastly disguised form. We can end our analysis of *havdalah* as a "Case of Categories" by defining the role of these two folk additions to the *havdalah* ritual.

Again, it is anthropology that provides the theoretical conceptualization necessary to convert these two prayers into items intrinsically related to a categorization ritual. We noted above that *havdalah* is recited at precisely that time when the oppositions it contains are in danger of confusion. Light is becoming darkness; Sabbath is changing to weekdays; Jews, as members of "the holy people," comfortably secure in the synagogue or the home, their holy places, are about to emerge into the wider world of the "other peoples," just as they enter unholy time as well. To use the terminology introduced by Arnold van Gennep and then developed by Victor Turner,[39] these are situations of liminality. From this perspective, *havdalah* is recognized as a rite of passage from holy to profane.

Cross-cultural studies indicate that in such instances, the recognition of the movement from one of the two basic categorical realms to the other is commonly accompanied by the perception of a certain danger. One must cross the divide that separates these two opposites, a sort of no-man's-land in which no rules can possibly apply, because rules as such are applicable only to one of the two categories, which, by definition, do not hold in the chasm that separates them from each other. As Turner aptly phrases it, "Every normal action is involved in the rights and obligations of a structure," but it is precisely the absence of that structure, and thus "normal action," that marks liminality.[40]

This description should be taken as more than a theoretical postulate arising out of the anthropological imagination. Students of Jewish liturgy, after all, are well aware of many explanations of rituals as deriving from some presumed angelology or primitive mind set that is postulated on no grounds whatsoever, other than the subjective perception of the researcher regarding the way things must have been in ancient or medieval times. (The studies of Jacob Z. Lauterbach come readily to mind.)[41] If we are to explain accretions to the *havdalah* ritual as responses to the danger associated with liminality, we should demand documented evidence that danger is actually apprehended by peoples of other cultures who find themselves without the surety that comes from the clear application of a set of social rules; when, that is, the normal categorization of experience is questioned.

Fortunately, there is no lack of empirical evidence to demonstrate this liminality hypothesis. Douglas devotes an entire chapter to substantiating her theoretical position that "if a person has no place in the social system and is therefore a marginal being, all precaution against danger must come from others."[42] Moreover, the dangers to be feared in such interstitial statuses are those which "are not powers invested in humans, but inhering in the structure of ideas."[43] Danger to humans caught between categories derives from the very existence of a social world dependent on categories. One must take care to protect oneself in such situations.

Certain of our liturgical additions to *havdalah* clearly display such efforts to protect oneself at a moment of danger. The first example to which our literature attests is the conjuring of angels. A full text can be found in the ninth-century work *Seder Rav Amram* and is common to all manuscripts thereof.[44] It was accepted early in France, appearing in the eleventh-century *Machzor Vitry*; in Provence, cited by the twelfth/thirteenth-century author of *Hamanhig*; and in Spain, first under the eleventh-century imprimatur of Isaac ibn Giyyat, and later in the fourteenth-century code, the *Tur*.[45] The texts are not always the same, though they are largely so.

There appear to be two distinct parts to the prayer. The first is the actual conjuration. Because it is a spell, it is somewhat difficult to arrive at a translation with absolute certainty. But the essential procedure is clear enough. The worshipers call upon Putah—(?) other texts say Purah—the angel of forgetfulness, to remove their foolish hearts and cast them upon a high mountain.[46] This is to be accomplished through the power of certain holy names, which vary according to the recension. There then follow biblical examples of heroes who were granted success in life, notably Noah and David. Finally, either part or all of Psalm 121, which asserts that one's help comes from God, is recited.

The second section is a separate literary unit. It begins with "Our God and God of our forebears," a normal introduction for a new prayer, but not for the continuation of one already begun. Also, unlike what precedes it, its themes can be traced to the Palestinian Talmud.[47] It has nothing to do with angels or incantations. Still, it asks for a good week in which the evil designs of others will be thwarted. *Machzor Vitry* adds a significant paragraph to this text, calling upon God for good luck (*siman tov*) three times.[48] This is probably where Moses Isserles got the idea that recitation of Bible verses (C1) is for good luck.

Clearly, *havdalah* participated in something of the magical. We know of many magical texts and practices in Jewish folklore and have even uncovered entire manuscripts in which angels are invoked or magical names used. Indeed, inhabitants of fourth-century Antioch believed Jews were particularly adept at warding off evil, and the use of amulets and such certainly did not decrease in medieval central Europe.[49] But our normative liturgical texts, those, that is, that were preserved by the official tradition, generally omitted blatant superstitious elements. It is surprising, therefore, to see Amram include the entire ritual. The subjective sense of the first paragraph is difficult to ascertain with any certainty, but its inclusion only at *havdalah* is enough to support the hypothesis that normal expectations were set aside temporarily then—so much so that angelic (or demonic) intervention in the affairs of humans could be expected.

As for the second paragraph, it shares with the first a determination to call on help from outside powers, just as Douglas predicts.[50] The beneficent power is God, not an angel, and the danger is projected onto those, in general, who harbor evil intentions. The whole thing is set in the context of magical behavior, the "good luck" reference—*Mazal Tov*—probably still being intended in its original and literal meaning of "a good astrological omen."

The greeting of Elijah deserves more space than we can give it here. It should be seen as part of a veritable "Elijah cult" that entered Jewish ritual in the centuries following the arrival of this millennium, and is probably related to millenarian thinking among Christians at the time, who anticipated the Second Coming.[51] The content of the expectation, then, was similar in both religions, whose adherents firmly expected messianic deliverance.

Elijah was greeted by Jews at three particular occasions: *havdalah* time, the Passover eve seder, and the occasion of a circumcision. Demonstrably, all three are examples of liminality. *Havdalah* we have discussed. The seder rehearsed the Exodus from Egypt but was presented to medieval worshipers as a night of watching (*leil shimurim*) for a similar deliverance.[52] This very term, *shimurim*, incidentally, implies liminality with all its attendant dangers, as we see from a talmudic adage that identifies the times and statuses in question: "Three [categories of] people require watching (*shimur*=the singular nominal form of *shimurim*): the sick, brides, and grooms. Others add, the midwife, the mourner, and students of Torah who study at night!"[53] We have illuminated Haggadah manuscripts that plainly show Jews expecting to be carried off on Elijah's ass to Jerusalem.[54] We should view this as the movement from one order of reality to another, salvation from this world of woe to the glory of the messianic age. Circumcision represented the admission of a child into the covenant, van Gennep's initiatory rite of passage.

More interesting than the liminal situation, however, is the nature of Elijah who enters it; for Elijah fulfills the requirements of the liminal or marginal personality whom Turner describes as a favorite character in rituals based on being betwixt and between.[55] From biblical times on, Elijah is the wild man who fits into no categories and follows his own code of conduct. He appears before the mighty King Ahab to demand justice. He champions God's might in a miracle contest with the priests of Baal. He flees into the desert and is fed by friendly birds. He works miracles wherever he goes. He is almost not of this world, having no fixed abode, no friends, no predictability; when he dies, he flies up to heaven in a flaming chariot.

Postbiblical lore builds on this imagery.[56] Elijah remains the support of the oppressed, and thus the harbinger of the messiah. He appears suddenly and unexpectedly at banquets and gatherings, often in costume or complete disguise. He is the Jewish trickster who lays bare the foibles of the mighty.

Turner could have had Elijah in mind when he wrote the following passage:

> Many writers have drawn attention to the role of the court jester. Max Gluckman (1965) for example, writes: "The court jester operated as a privileged arbiter of morals, given license to gibe at king and courtiers, or Lord of the manor." Jesters were "usually men of low class."
>
> Folk literature abounds in symbolic figures, such as "holy beggars," "third sons," "little tailors," and "simpletons." . . . We have all read of the homeless

and mysterious stranger . . . who restores ethical and legal equilibrium.
All these mythic types are structurally inferior or marginal.[57]

Turner emphasizes the moral stature of these types, since in this particular discussion he wishes to demonstrate a particular feature of the social form he calls *communitas*, that being the leveling of class differences and the equality of all, a perfect morality in which no one has the power to abuse another.[58] But *communitas* itself is none other than the polar opposite of social structure. It is the absence of categories. It is *havdalah* time, the ideal occasion to expect Elijah, who comes in disguise, berates the mighty, moves freely back and forth from heaven to earth and even the Garden of Eden, where, we will recall, he sits under the Tree of Life recording Israel's good deeds.

We should now summarize our analysis of *havdalah*. Surveying first philological investigations of *havdalah*, we tried to reconstruct early texts and alternative readings. But we then moved to the realm of anthropology and linguistics, building a case for cultural categorization schemes that order experience. This led us to see *havdalah* as Judaism's primary ritual for rehearsing its categories. By considering the nature of liminality, the absence of structure, we were able further to see the relationship of two later accretions to the ritual, particularly the greeting of Elijah, the quintessential Jewish marginal man.

The point of the chapter, however, as far as methodology is concerned, was to demonstrate an example of the kind of additional questions one might ask if one refuses to be limited by a literary bias. Clearly, this sort of reconstruction is not amenable to the same sort of rigorous demonstration that can be applied to the philological studies dealing solely with textual reconstruction. But worship is not a text; it is human behavior. The study ought to aim at Geertz's "construction of a construction" of the reality that worship communities assume. It is time we supplement the literary model of liturgical study with a new one.

I say "supplement" not "replace." Our findings in no way invalidate those of other methodologies, which quite correctly make available to us scientifically accurate reconstructions of ancient texts. But a holistic perspective rounds out the picture, concentrating on the liturgical ceremony as it really was practiced, the ritual field itself, rather than on some words that eventually found their way into written form.

These words of prayers, however, came finally to be characterized as different rites, and the next question we must ask is whether the classification of rites ought not to be reconsidered as a question of social structure too, rather than one of literary form and content.

THREE

Rites

A Case of Social Space

Liturgists commonly speak of a "rite," meaning by that word something quite different from what anthropologists or sociologists mean when they use the same term. The latter use the word to describe a discrete item of human behavior; the former mean a liturgical tradition: the Ashkenazic or the Sephardic services of prayer, for example, these being the two broadest categories of which we speak today. On the face of it, both liturgists and social scientists seem to know exactly what they mean by a "rite." But in fact, there is more than a little confusion regarding the word. Social scientists are not unanimous on the difference between a rite and a ritual, for example, and much work still must be done before we will be in a position to classify rites according to some universally acknowledged system that discriminates among them according to type or function. Liturgists seem to be far more precise in their discussions of rites. Yet, even that outward certainty masks a good deal of confusion regarding what it is that makes rites different from one another, and why we should bother investigating those differences in the first place.

As with so many things, the study of liturgical rites goes back to the pioneering work of Leopold Zunz. His interest, it will be recalled, was the unfolding of the Jewish spirit through time, the unraveling of the Judaic genius, parallel to the Germanic uniqueness that Zunz's contemporaries Fichte (1762–1814) and Herder (1744–1803) were discovering. He moved to Berlin in 1815, only five years after Fichte had become rector at the university there, eight years after the latter's epoch-marking *Reden an die Deutsche Nation*, and in the wake of Germany's 1813 movement for independence. Liturgy itself was of only minor importance in Zunz's quest. But since the sixth century, probably even earlier—though Zunz himself dated it closer to the seventh or eighth—there lay poetry embedded in the liturgy, and poems were highly regarded by the Western world of letters to which Zunz owed allegiance. Indeed, with the possible exception of philosophy, it is hard to imagine a more esteemed vehicle of cultural expression,

46

according to the aesthetic canons of nineteenth-century German scholarship. So Zunz worked feverishly at classifying the accomplishments of Israel's liturgical poets.[1]

His first efforts necessarily lay in deciphering the basic liturgical rubrics, and he dedicated one chapter of his magnum opus on preaching to this end. Remarkably, in some twenty-five pages, he raised—and answered, though not always correctly—most of the preliminary questions that would occupy scholars for the next hundred years. He published his findings in 1832.[2] Twenty-seven years later he turned finally to his real interest, the poetic additions to his people's liturgy. He was to write more than one book on the subject, but the treatise that concerns us here is Zunz's pioneering description of Jewish rites.

Theoretically, one can collect all the manuscripts of Jewish prayer that have ever been written, and apportion them, like so many cards, according to any differentiating system one chooses. Zunz's primary differentiating factor was the selection of poetry to be found in each manuscript. So when he was finished, he had a series of manuscript piles, so to speak, each pile containing those documents which had in common the inclusion of certain poems and the exclusion of others. Each of these he called a rite. For Zunz, then, a rite is a literary category. Such a differentiating system makes all the sense in the world for a university library, perhaps, which must decide how best to shelve books and manuscripts in its collection. The question is, whether it also has direct relevance to the actual act of prayer.

That it did have such liturgical relevance was and still is taken for granted.[3] The manuscripts were prayer books, after all. So Zunz turned to a consideration of what it was that separated the piles from one another. Presumably, the differences in poetic taste were not arbitrary. More was involved than mere random selection from an available pool of poems. One determining principle leaped out at Zunz, and it has remained unquestioned by the generations of liturgists who have succeeded him. It is geography. Quite obviously, the different selections of poetry correlate with the geographic distribution of Jews in the world. Thus, an arbitrary selection of data—liturgical poetry—was matched up with geographic preference for specific specimens of that poetry, each resulting subset being identified as a separate rite to which the relevant geographic adjective was applied for identifying purposes.

The next step was the comparison of rites, or, more precisely, the comparison of poetic preferences displayed by the different piles of manuscripts. Familial similarities resulted in the positing of lines of influence from some piles to others. By the time the process of cross-referencing was completed, Zunz had arrived at a description of cultural influence through the ages, whereby some rites were said to be direct descendents of others. There was something to this claim, certainly. He had indeed established a chain of literary dependency, demonstrating that preferred literary idiosyncrasies of one country's prayer texts could also be found in those of another.

As Zunz saw it, there were originally two rites, the Babylonian and the Palestinian. Their influence was felt in diverse ways upon two primary rites of western Europe, Ashkenaz (or Germany) and Sepharad (or Spain). But the broad dichotomy between Ashkenaz and Sepharad is so general as to be almost meaningless. To take the former, for example, it is true that the prayer books emanating from Germany are unique in enough significant ways to justify their being classed together with one another and apart from those of Spain, but even within that class, one finds important subcategories. The so-called Ashkenazic rite, which has survived among most American Jews hailing from Europe, is actually a Polish variation known technically as *Minhag Polin*. The original German rite whence it derives was practiced in cities along the Rhine and carried to Poland by Jews who emigrated there, in small numbers as early as the thirteenth century, and in large measure by the middle of the sixteenth. But even this Rhineland Rite (the *Minhag Rinus*) is not original to Germany. It has its roots in Italy and in France, and one must posit the prior existence of independent French and Italian rites, which themselves can be broken down further. In France, we hear of rites unique to Avignon and Carpentras, for example, both of these being relatively minor in significance, compared to the major influence effected by the school of Rashi and his students in eleventh-century Troyes and Vitry. Italy too must be seen as an amalgam of many independent rites, varying with geographic locale. But in sum, Zunz drew a picture of literary-liturgical creativity springing up country by country, as Jews migrated throughout Europe. From two original streams, the Babylonian and the Palestinian, there emerged eventually two other great traditions corresponding to the Franco-German world on one hand (Ashkenaz) and the Iberian peninsula (Sepharad) on the other.

While form-critics have questioned Zunz's philological hypotheses regarding the existence of original texts of prayers, they have not found it necessary to argue against Zunz's basic categorization of liturgical rites according to geographical provenance. Figure 1, a sort of liturgical flow chart, is taken from the work of Joseph Heinemann;[4] it demonstrates the health of the geographic model one hundred and nine years after Zunz's original categorization.

Heinemann makes two innovations in the model. He adds the significant body of scholarly data that have accumulated since the publication of Zunz's work in 1859, and he distinguishes between relative degrees of influence that one rite is said to have upon another by labeling the dependency as direct, indirect, or minor. The three most important examples of new data are the Egyptian rite (*Genizah*), Saadiah Gaon, and *Seder Chibbur Berakhot*. By looking for a moment at each of these cases, we shall be able to see how researchers who

Figure 1

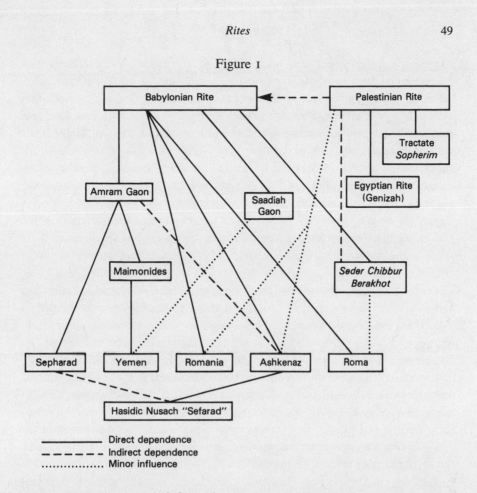

uncovered startlingly new information managed to fit their discoveries into the existent Zunzian model, and we shall learn the extent to which the model is or is not capable of assimilating new data.

By far, the most significant liturgical find in the last hundred years has been the Genizah fragments uncovered in an attic of the Ezra Synagogue in old Cairo. Though the cache of documents was known and even seen by a handful of researchers in the eighteenth and the nineteenth centuries, it was generally not made available to scholars until the end of 1896, when Solomon Schechter managed to remove about 100,000 pages to Cambridge. Among the leaves were many liturgical snippets, some of which he published two years later.[5] Scholars were quick to recognize the gravity of the find, and by 1911, Israel Lévi, Israel Abrahams, and Ismar Elbogen had supplemented our knowledge of the newly discovered liturgical fragments sequestered for centuries in Egypt. The most thorough early treatment of the subject came in 1925 from Jacob Mann, who concluded that the texts derived from a Palestinian community whose synagogue must have been in Egypt: so he entitled his article describing them "Genizah

Fragments of the Palestinian Order of Service."[6] Some scholars, like Louis
Finkelstein, have treated the Genizah fragments as if, being Palestinian, they
were the original, and therefore the most accurate, texts of the early years when
Jewish liturgy was being formed.[7] Others, of the form-critical school, are loath
to treat them as any more authentic than what has come down to us by the more
traditional route, via Babylon.[8] At any rate, the significance of the Genizah for
the Zunzian paradigm of rites is that it allows us to flesh out the hypothesis of an
early Palestinian liturgy that was an alternative to the Babylonian one. Until the
Genizah, we had barely any information regarding this alternative. We were
dependent on random reports by medieval witnesses regarding differences that
had once existed between the two major ancient centers of Jewish life. Now there
were actual documents validating Zunz's hypothesis beyond anyone's wildest
dreams.

On the other hand, technically speaking, the cache had been found in Egypt,
not Palestine. Despite Mann's conclusion that Egyptian Jewry was divided in
ritual matters into Palestinian and Babylonian communities, the Genizah representing the former,[9] Heinemann labels it "Egyptian rite," dependent directly on,
but not to be equated with, the Palestinian prayers. The confusion in terminology
is important, because it underscores the problem of depending on a geographical
taxonomy. Few seriously doubt that the documents represent the ancient Palestinian alternative to Babylonian practice. It happens, however, that by chance,
they were miraculously saved in Cairo, as opposed to Tiberias or Jerusalem.
Only fixation on a geographical nomenclature in the narrowest sense results in
the application of the title "Egyptian."

Such labeling of fragments according to their place of discovery does not
necessarily provide useful knowledge about them. In fact, the opposite may be
the case. We would only be adding to our confusion if we were to conclude that
there existed by the tenth century (the approximate date of some of our fragments, that is) an Egyptian Jewish community, sufficiently self-conscious of its
place of settlement as to have created its own rite in contradistinction to Jews in
Palestine. To express guarded hesitation at the wholesale equation of *all* the
fragments with Palestinian liturgy would be one thing. To label them all "Egyptian" because they were found in Egypt is another.

We know, for example, that Palestinian Jews found their way to Spain as well.
Were we to find a similar liturgy hailing from Spain, would we call it Spanish?
Certainly not. The hypothetical Jews who prayed with Palestinian customs in
Spain would be quite far removed in liturgical preference from other Spanish
Jews who had already developed their own rite; and, on the other hand, very
close to "Palestinians" praying in Jerusalem and Cairo.

Seder Chibbur Berakhot was also the discovery of the indefatigable Solomon
Schechter. Upon hearing of its existence, he copied it by hand from a Turin

library, before that building was consumed by fire, in 1894. Zunz, who had an uncanny ability to identify documents and their authors, ascribed it to Menachem ben Solomon, the twelfth-century author of the midrash *Sekhel Tov*. In 1930, Abraham I. Schechter proved this was indeed the case, and placed the book in historical context as being the earliest example of Italian liturgy, a forerunner of the particular subcategory known as the Roman rite.[10]

The latter Schechter's methodology too was determined by his acceptance of Zunz's model. He was inextricably bound to think in geographic categories. Thus, he explained Italian liturgy by assuming it must be Babylonian or Palestinian or both. By comparing his document with what he knew of Babylonian material, he extracted everything that differed and gratuitously labeled it as Palestinian. Once again, however, we should ask ourselves what he was explaining. Either he was right or wrong. If wrong, clearly he was explaining nothing at all. But even if right, he was simply arbitrarily linking up two geographic areas on the basis of certain fragments of shared text. At most, he was making a statement regarding the process of literary redaction on the basis of labels that may or may not have corresponded to actual Palestinian or Babylonian communities. Were there "Palestinian" Jews in Italy during or prior to Menachem's day, in the same sense that there were "Palestinians" in old Cairo? If so, in what sense were they "Palestinian," and how did they share a "Palestinian" identity with our hypothetical "Palestinians" in Spain?

Finally, we can look at Saadiah Gaon. Saadiah is one of three boxes in our chart that carry the names of the authors of books rather than a title or a geographical locale. Though buried in the Bodleian Library since 1693, this tenth-century authority's prayer book remained unpublished until 1941.[11] Saadiah straddled the two worlds of Palestine and Babylonia. Born in Egypt, he lived much of his life in the Holy Land and later moved to Bagdad, where he was elected gaon, leader of the major academy of Sura. He wrote his book while in Babylonia, so Heinemann draws a heavy line of direct dependence from the Babylonian box. Does this explain Saadiah, however? A minor objection ought to be that Saadiah's Palestinian origin resulted in his electing to preserve many Palestinian customs in his book. To call it Babylonian just because he wrote it there does no justice to the fact that this great gaon combined the two rites with which he was familiar. But even if we were to draw another line to the Palestinian box, would we really explain Saadiah? Would it not be equally logical to draw the line to the Genizah-Egyptian rite box? Saadiah came from Egypt. The point is that the geographical taxonomy does not explain what we most want to know. Our interest in Saadiah is not *whether* page three of his prayer book, say, or a poem for Passover, perhaps, follows Babylonian rather than Palestinian custom, but *why* it does so and what its inclusion implies.

What we really want to know in all three cases is how new rites come into being, what new rites signify in terms of the people who use them, at what point in history we can expect liturgical creativity, and so on. Concentrating exclusively on literary parallels between works arbitrarily labeled according to the country in which they were found amounts to liturgical reductionism of the worst order.

The "geographical" method approaches what has been described by Gregory Bateson as a "dormitive hypothesis." His description is worth quoting at some length.

> Molière long ago, depicted an oral doctoral examination in which the learned doctors asked the candidate to state the "cause and reason" why opium puts people to sleep. The candidate triumphantly answers in dog Latin, "Because there is in it a dormitive principle (*virtus dormitiva*)."
>
> Characteristically, the scientist confronts a complex interactive system—in this case, an interaction betwen man and opium. He observes a change in the system—the man falls asleep. The scientist then explains the change by giving a name to a fictitious "cause," located in one or the other component of the interacting system. Either the opium contains a reified dormitive principle, or the man contains a reified need for sleep, an adormitosis, which is "expressed" in his response to opium.
>
> And characteristically, all such hypotheses are "dormitive" in the sense that they put to sleep the "critical faculty" . . . within the scientist himself.
>
> The state of mind or habit of thought which goes from data to dormitive hypothesis and back to data is self-reinforcing. . . . If we admit that opium contains a dormitive principle, we can then devote a lifetime of research to studying the characteristics of this principle. . . . Many of these questions . . . will lead on to derivative hypotheses no less dormitive than that from which we started.[12]

Dividing rites into geographical piles according to the literature they have in common is such a dormitive principle. It is endless. An infinite number of people can look eternally at the many pages of manuscripts that constitute our libraries, and continually reconfirm the fact that certain wording sometimes reappears and sometimes does not. Other than formulating neat piles of manuscripts to which new specimens can be added, it is not clear what we accomplish this way. We have not even proven the question of literary influence. Books do not influence other books; the people who write them do. And in most cases, we have no idea who wrote what or when. Furthermore, the lines themselves are often questionable. Who is to say, for example—to return to Heinemann's chart—whether Maimonides ought not to be linked to Yemen only via Saadiah? The former lived in Egypt in the twelfth century, and even though he had his own close ties with Yemenite Jews with whom he corresponded, he certainly knew already of Saadiah's prayer book that preceded him by more than two hundred years. Who is to say which of the three—native Yemenite custom already dependent on Palestinian precedent, Saadiah, or Maimonides—influenced which? But most of all, this method ignores the essential characteristic of a liturgical rite—that it is liturgical. The real question that should concern us is why and how people formulate different rites in the first place, and this we shall never learn from multiplying comparisons of manuscripts, or cataloguing the latest find of yet another version of this or that poem.

Zunz himself was well aware of this. Though he did not attempt a sustained and systematic explanation of rite formulation, he did stop from time to time in his cataloguing of liturgical differences to note a few of the factors that went into the process. By the time he was finished, he had isolated six causes, which deserve our attention here.

1. Geographic isolation. We have already seen that geography played the major role in his cataloguing system. Zunz reasoned that Jews in a new geographic locale would inherit a common tradition but would necessarily alter it over time.

2. Cultural diffusion. Jews would tend to borrow beliefs, customs, and institutions prevalent around them in the non-Jewish world. His example was the addition of a godfather at the circumcision ceremony, which he thought was modeled after the church's baptism ritual.

3. Reflection of historical events peculiar to one area rather than another. The Crusades, for example, would be experienced by Jews in the Rhineland and give rise to elegies that would not be paralleled in Spain.

4. Personal example. Personal predilections of revered rabbis would be emulated, until some of their private practices became public.

5. Censorship. Several centuries after their composition, old liturgical formulas might be seen as morally offensive or potentially injurious to the relationship between Jews and their host culture. Jews themselves would censor out the offending line. Alternatively, at times, censors representing the host culture itself would see to it that an offending line was expunged.

6. Human error. Before the sixteenth century, mistaken manuscript copies were accepted as authentic, or authentic ones were copied incorrectly by scribes. After that, printers ground out multiple copies of books based largely on erroneous sources. They frequently combined fragments of manuscripts, patching together bits and pieces from different sources, printing half poems alongside whole ones, mistakenly transposing lines, and so on.

Zunz's list is a good one. By and large all his factors correlated with geography, however. Items 2–5 all exist differently in different locales. The Crusades occurred in the Rhineland, but not in Portugal, for example; censorship of the Counter-Reformation was common to Germany and Italy, but not to the Balkans.[13] Reverence for personal example marked German Jewish life during the fourteenth to the sixteenth centuries particularly[14] but does not seem to be as prevalent there in the eighteenth and nineteenth centuries. The printing press made available large numbers of books that transcended national boundaries, but even with this development, different communities accepted different printed editions and with different degrees of alacrity; certainly before that, scribes in Spain, for example, were long known to have practiced care for detail, while those in France did not,[15] so error too could be correlated with geography. Little wonder, then, that Zunz adopted a geographic taxonomy for his catalogue of Jewish rites.

But Zunz was only partially correct. Though at the time his interpretive scheme seemed to explain all the data, now, with the benefit of hindsight, we can see that it did not. The clearest example of difficulty is Reform liturgy. The Reform movement grew up in Germany. Its very first decisions were liturgical.[16] According to the Zunzian system, Reform Jews are German Jews and should, therefore, be classified within the category of the Ashkenazic rite; and so they were. But Reform Judaism moved to America, and its liturgy developed here to the point where it is misleading to assume that we exhaust the essential elements of Reform worship by declaring it to be Ashkenazic. True, it is more Ashkenazic than it is Sephardic. But actually, it is neither, and should not even be analyzed within the confines of an "Askenazic-Sephardic" dichotomy, which once was a reliable mirror of two societies composing the bulk of European Jewry, but which now reflects nothing at all in terms of the American experience. It might be objected that we can still preserve the geographical nomenclature by calling Reform liturgy the American rite (a title once actually advanced, as we shall presently see). Unfortunately, that will not work either, since, as it happens, American Reform liturgy now has much in common with that of the same movement in Great Britain.[17] Moreover, a Portuguese translation of the American Reform Passover Haggadah is used officially by Reform Jews in Brazil,[18] a country that is linguistically Sephardic. The Reform movement, then, is the case par excellence of a liturgical tradition that defies geographic definition. Zunz could not have known about it in his day, of course, as Reform then was limited largely to Germany, and its liturgy was still a liberalized version of the Ashkenazic rite used in Orthodox synagogues there.

But even Zunz might have noted the curious fact that in one of his instances, he had to have recourse to a novel word, "nusach," rather than "minhag," which is normally utilized to express our English "rite." The case in point is "Hasidic"—usually called "Nusach Sefarad"—which appears at the bottom of Heinemann's chart. This is the rite that characterizes Hasidic communities, those tracing their religious practice back to certain reforms begun in eighteenth-century Poland and said to be dependent on the liturgy that characterized the Lurianic brand of Kabbalah, a mystical system that thrived in sixteenth-century

Palestine. As Heinemann's chart explains, Nusach Sefarad is not really "Sepharad" at all, but an amalgam of "Sepharad" and "Ashkenaz." Its proponents were consciously adopting certain Sephardic features within the overall structure of their Ashkenazic liturgical heritage. But it could hardly be called "Minhag Sefarad"; there already was such a thing: Sephardic liturgy itself. Nusach Sefarad appeared to be Sephardic only from the perspective of those Ashkenazic Jews who either fought against, or otherwise paid particular scrutiny to, the inclusion of Sephardic customs. It really deserved a name totally devoid of geographical considerations. The simple geographic scheme of things was breaking down. Contrary to the simplistic double line of influence contained in Heinemann's chart, a rite cannot be both Sephardic and Ashkenazic at the same time, unless of course, it has entered a realm of classification that goes beyond geography.

Zunz's error was the confusion of geographic and social distance. The real determinant of similarity or difference in the rites people use is the extent to which they identify together socially, so that they project social distance between themselves and others.

The differences among rites reflect different ways that worshiping communities see themselves vis-à-vis others. Thus, for example, all Jewish liturgy is generally the same, since all Jews see themselves as standing in the line of tradition that began at Sinai, and outside of whatever alternative religious traditions the various host cultures may proffer. The Genizah fragments from Egypt match up rather closely with the other examples of Palestinian creativity, such as those Palestinian choices adopted by Saadiah, because the Palestinian cultural influence was strongly felt in both instances. People living in any of the many areas of settlement that surrounded Palestine, and who were nurtured by its culture, saw themselves as Palestinian in identity. *Seder Chibbur Berakhot* does indeed have a mixture of Palestinian and Babylonian traditions, since Italian Jews borrowed from both ancient centers of Jewish authority. Yet they built anew on their own, thus beginning what would eventually stand out as a novel Italian rite, as expressive of Italian Jewish identity as the old Babylonian and Palestinian rites had been expressive of the people who once used them there. Later, Italian Jews settled in Germany and adopted French Jewry as their younger cultural wards. After all, the eleventh-century savant Rashi of Troyes, in many ways the founder of French Jewish culture, studied with Judah ben Yakar of the Rhineland. No wonder an Ashkenazic rite common to France, Germany, and Italy developed. With it, these Jews expressed no accidental geographic bond, but a social one. And when they moved eastward to Poland, they altered it just enough to fit the new identity change necessitated by a new environment, without, however, doing violence to the fact that they still largely identified themselves as Jews of German origin. Witness their language, which changed also to incorporate Polish and Russian expressions but still remained the old Judeo-German jargon, manufactured once by the merging of medieval German and some Hebrew.

The same tale can be told regarding the Sephardic rite. Sephardic Jews today usually trace their heritage to the Mediterranean. After expulsion from Spain in 1492, or after a brief extension of time allowed some of them in Portugal, these Jews resettled elsewhere. Jews had already been exiled from France, so the northern route across the Pyrenees was not a welcome one. Some traveled as secret Jews to Holland, where the Protestant revolution resulted in their reassertion openly of their Judaism. Others migrated directly by sea to the burgeoning Ottoman empire and founded new Jewish colonies in Palestine, Asia Minor, and so on. These latter Jews did not long keep up a working knowledge of Ladino (medieval Spanish and some Hebrew combined). They assimilated into the culture of the Arabic world and changed their identity to the point where many barely thought of some presumed ancestry in Spain. Socially, the distance between their generation and their Sephardic origins was enormous. As a consequence, they adapted themselves to the rites of the surrounding areas: the Yemenite rite, for example, or the rite we call "Aram Tsova" (Aleppo). As time went on, they participated in the evolution of these rites, which were gradually internalized as their own. Today, Sephardic Jews intent on rediscovering their ancient heritage still sometimes refer to these liturgical expressions of Jews in Arabic lands as Sephardic. This can hardly be because Sephardic Jews originally from Holland or England, but now resident in New York or San Francisco, see themselves as inhabiting the same geographical locale as Jews in Yemen. But they do identify as Jews hailing originally from Spain. They *perceive* their *original* heritage as Sephardic.

The case of Jews who hail from Judaism, but who are no longer Jews, is instructive here. As examples, let us look at Samaritan, Karaite, and early Christian liturgies.

Samaritan liturgy is entirely biblical. By the time of the *tannaim*, the Samaritans had long become schismatic. Rabbinic and Samaritan liturgies really have nothing to do with literary preference or with geography. Both rabbis and Samaritans viewed the Torah as equally sacred, and they lived together. Their contrasting styles should be understood as betraying contrasting definitions of self.

The same is true of Karaite liturgy. These sectarians denied rabbinic legislation and produced liturgies from the eighth century on. The first of these, the liturgy of their nominal founder, Anan ben David, scrupulously avoids rabbinic customs, since Anan's entire platform was founded on a vigorous positing of social distance between Karaites and Rabbinites.[19] By the thirteenth century, however, both Rabbinites and Karaites found that they held a structurally similar minority status in Byzantium, where they were both treated in much the same way by their Christian host culture. Under these circumstances, they were constrained to narrow the social distance between each other. So by the fifteenth century, the liturgy of their illustrious leader Elijah Bashyazi, displays the *inclusion* of rabbinic blessings, and even candle lighting for the Sabbath (!), this latter practice being perhaps the most outstanding point of difference between Karaites and their rabbinic foes in earlier centuries.[20]

We have a similar case in early Christianity. Jesus, still a Jew, operates within the Jewish liturgical system of his time. But by the time of the Church Fathers, ardent insistence on social distance between Jews and Christians results in radically altered liturgy. In fact, the relative preference for or aversion to Jewish paradigms that we find specific Fathers in patristic literature displaying, should be viewed as witness to the extent different church leaders distanced themselves socially from the Jewish group whence they sprung. By contrast—and not unlike Jews and Karaites in Byzantium—religiously serious Christians and Jews in America today often find themselves similarly treated as minorities vis-à-vis dominant American secularism, and even, if some theorists on American religion are correct, compared to the regnant form of American civil religion, which, for example, relegates Christmas to a national holiday of little or no specifically Christian impact. So religious Christians and religious Jews have narrowed the social distance between themselves, with the result that their liturgies are remarkably similar. Despite obvious theological differences, rabbis, priests, and ministers give parallel sermons on the same subjects, often with the same message, while their worship contents display a similar choice of biblical psalms, rendered together with popular selections from modern poetry, and melodies that can hardly be distinguished as Christian or Jewish. Indeed, on American Thanksgiving, we have even gone so far as to pray together.

Finally, both difficult cases mentioned earlier, Nusach Sefarad and the Reform liturgy, can be explained by social distance. As already mentioned, the originators of Nusach Sefarad were Ashkenazic Jews who had chosen deliberately to borrow alternative Sephardic traditions, rather than generally accepted Ashkenazic ones. That is, the Hasidic Jews who founded this new amalgam of Sephardic and Ashkenazic custom were themselves Ashkenazic, even though the mystical community whence they borrowed their doctrines had been founded by Spanish emigrés. Hence, on one hand, their decision to blend the two elements of their newly found identity into a new rite expressed the positive fact that they felt equally close to both aspects of European Jewish culture; but on the other hand, negatively speaking, it erected barriers of social distance between themselves and the traditional Ashkenazic authority structure against which Hasidism was rebelling.[21]

Reform Judaism too makes perfect sense in this framework. Originally, Reform Jews saw themselves as German Jews who, however, differed from others, in that they had experienced the new vistas offered by the Enlightenment. But they were proud citizens of that German society which had granted them an exit visa from the ghettos in the first place. So they saw their Reform liturgy as German Jewish, or Ashkenazic in essence. Reform Judaism never prospered in the land of its origin. From the beginning, German society was structured such that all Jews were legally included within an established, official community synagogue. They were not free to found alternatives.[22] Moreover, in the wake of the Napoleonic debacle, central European reactionary regimes encouraged an atmosphere in which liberal religious reform became increasingly difficult.

So committed Reform Jews moved elsewhere, primarily to the United States, which offered both economic opportunity and religious liberty. Immigrant generations still saw themselves as cultured Germans rather than as untutored Americans, but it was only a matter of time until some of the later, American-born, generations forgot their German origins and concentrated instead on what really set them off from their European parents: their freedom to espouse reform. Socially speaking, then, Reform Jews today share a great deal with their liberal colleagues in England and Brazil. No wonder they also share a liturgy in what must be seen as an evolving family of Reform rites still in embryo.

But Zunz did not inhabit the twentieth-century world of mass communications and instant mobility. In his day, it still was the case that social distance generally coincided with geographic distance, so that the *accident* of geography appeared to him to be the determining factor, even though it was not. The real cause behind novel rites is a community's decision to see itself as descendant from a particular community of the past, on one hand, yet independent in its own right on the other. The first factor is expressed through the rite it inherits and upon which it builds. The second can be seen in the ways it goes about constructing its own unique definition of self, through the way it decides to pray.

In sum, rites look like literature to people who are trained in the study of books. But to the people for whom the rite is a living reality, literature is an irrelevant category. Geography too is only an apparent determining consideration. The real factor making for ritual differentiation is social, not geographical, distance. Through the way a community prays, it defines who it is, whence it comes, and how it chooses to express its own individuality. The division of literary remnants into geographical piles should be supplemented by observing the liturgical activity of people expressing their religious identity.

The liturgy of Reform Jews, to which we have already briefly referred, provides an excellent case in point. Instead of treating this liturgy as literature, we would do well to chart its development against the background of a new identity structure demanded by the entry of the Jew into the modern world of Western culture. We can narrow the focus even more to the case of Reform Judaism in the

United States, and compare, on the one hand, European-based Reform liturgy, which reflected the Jew's adaptation to modern Europe, and, on the other hand, the liturgy necessitated by a native American population of Jews whose roots in the Old World have withered to the point of becoming merely a matter of historical record. It should be clear by now that our interest transcends a philological comparison of prayer texts. It is religious identity that concerns us. So we shall avoid examining the prayers without simultaneously considering the people who wrote and prayed them. Fortunately, the people who wrote American liturgies have left us with sufficient biographical records for us to be able to piece together their visions of self, independent of the liturgical record. These former statements are not drawn from prayer books at all but are explicit statements of their authors' opinions. They will be our control against otherwise unsubstantiated claims we might have made from a study of the prayer books alone. We shall see that the liturgy of American Jews changed regularly to reflect alterations in Jewish self-consciousness. In general, with each change in the perceived social distance from others, there came also a change in Jewish liturgy.

FOUR

American Jewish Liturgies

A *Study of Identity*

It was roughly a century and a half ago that Isaac Mayer Wise, newly arrived from Bohemia, foresaw a united federation of all American Jews. To institute his dream, he founded a national lay body, which he labeled The Union of American Hebrew Congregations; a Hebrew Union College to train rabbis; and a Central Conference of American Rabbis for ordainees of the latter to belong to. Though all three bodies came later to represent only the Reform movement, their titles indicate much broader expectations on the part of their creator, who had no single movement in mind. His goal was the unification of all American Jews.

His organizational genius was matched by an intuitive recognition that American Judaism would be unlike any Jewry that had gone before. It was no mere appendage of its European parentage, but a creation *de novo*, related to, yet distinct from, its past, and worthy of such recognition as is generally accorded other equally unique Jewish societies in other times and places. He envisioned this promise despite the fact that the Jews he encountered upon his arrival here in 1846 were anything but educated. With few exceptions, he found none "who had the least knowledge of Judaism, its history and literature. . . . " "Ignorance," he reported, "swayed the sceptre and darkness ruled. As for modern culture. . . . no Jew who had recently immigrated was fitted to occupy a public position creditably." Yet, he observed, "There are life and energy in this new Judaism, whether now it be conscious or unconscious . . . I painted the future in golden hues."[1]

Nowhere was this vision of a golden age for a unified American Jewry more pronounced than in the title Wise gave to the prayer book he wrote. Traditional titles have generally been derived from the juxtaposition of several Hebrew words reminiscent of biblical citations or rabbinic allusions. Others, especially in modern times, are labeled, simply, "Jewish Prayer Book," and subtitled with the designation of the particular city or congregation for which they are intended. But Wise's title went straight to the heart of his hopes. He called his book *Minhag America*—The American Rite.[2] He and the small coterie of optimistic rabbis associated with the project fervently anticipated that the new prayer book would ultimately be adopted by every Jewish congregation in America. But Wise's conception of American Jewry as a whole new chapter in Jewish history was as premature as it was brave. Jews then, like immigrant groups generally, were in no hurry to abandon the sense of identity derived from their country of origin. As long ago as the first century, Jewish arrivals in Rome had maintained separate synagogues for Jews hailing from Rhodes or Crete or Antioch, and now, nineteen centuries later in America, Jews, as Christians, preserved their sense of security by similar ethnic clustering, which facilitated the replication of familiar modes of worship that people were used to.

So Isaac Mayer Wise's proclamation of a "Minhag America" was a conceptual leap beyond the self-image of most of his fellow German Jews who had not broken their ties to their German homeland. If economic and political circumstances had conspired to necessitate their emigration to the New World, they had not on that account ceased seeing themselves as German Jews nonetheless, albeit in America. German was still the language of discourse used in meetings and salons.[3] At German-Jewish fellowship organizations, like B'nai B'rith, events "back home" across the Atlantic were regularly discussed, so much so that many of the early wave of immigrants even returned to Europe to fight the abortive revolution of 1848. Certainly, these German immigrants felt little in common with the Sephardic Jews who preceded them here, those who had come almost two hundred years earlier via the Dutch West Indies Company to South and Central America, and then north to the colonies that would eventually be known as the United States. They were bound together not by any notions of American Jewish distinctiveness, but by their common German heritage. They were still Ashkenazic.

Even Wise could not completely divest himself of his past. Despite its lofty title, his prayer book was not particularly radical. In part this was due to a conservatism demanded by political reality. Hoping to unite disparate factions within the German Jewish community itself, Wise avoided drastic revisions. *Minhag America* is recognizable as the traditional prayer-text known as the *Siddur*. Important prayers are more or less intact; Hebrew abounds. But to that *Siddur* Wise grafted his messianic faith in universalism and the inevitability of human progress. It was not that *Minhag America* lacked sophistication—some of the textual emendations Wise made in the prayers were positively brilliant—but in terms of providing a ritual that was expressive of the new American milieu rather than the old German one, it failed. *Minhag America* may have been its title, but it fell short of its promise. It was, if anything, a prayer book for an immigrant generation, not for those immigrants' children and grandchildren who would some day identify fully as Americans and find it hard to believe they hailed from Germany at all.[4]

Thus, history was to condemn *Minhag America* to virtual oblivion. When the Central Conference of American Rabbis met to standardize a rite, that august body of rabbinic leaders, which Wise himself had brought into being, adopted as their guide not *Minhag America* but another book of prayer called *Olat Tamid*,[5] the liturgical creation of another rabbi from Germany, David Einhorn. Einhorn's masterpiece was no more truly American in spirit than Wise's. But its scope and intent were far more radical. (Relative to Wise, for example, who had included the majority of traditional rubrics and considerable Hebrew, Einhorn saw fit to eliminate whole services that he felt inapplicable to modernity.)

In part the decision to use *Olat Tamid* came about because some of the guiding luminaries in the burgeoning Reform movement were extremely close to Einhorn—in two cases, even related to him. Kaufmann Kohler, then the rabbi at Temple Beth El in New York, but later to succeed Wise as the second president of Hebrew Union College,[6] was Einhorn's son-in-law, as was Emil Hirsch, the rabbi of Sinai Congregation in Chicago. Their ideological stance as reforming "radicals" was no recent phenomenon. The very year of Einhorn's arrival in America, 1855, saw Wise receive Orthodox support for his prayer-book project in return for his signing a joint declaration of unity at a rabbinical conference held in Cleveland. Wise's concession lay in the fact that the statement he signed included an affirmation of the binding nature of talmudic authority, with the result that he was mercilessly attacked by those who were shocked to find that he was apparently prepared to sacrifice his principles for religious unity. Einhorn himself emerged as the opposition leader, and, in an article in the Jewish press, he protested against "the few men" who "in the name of collective Israel set up articles of faith which deny to dissenters a place in the communion of professing Israelites." He urged that "free American Israel keep a strict watch on hierarchical movements, which would again forge its chains, though under the most charming lullabies of peace, now in the guise of dogmas, and ere long by a *Minhag America*."[7]

Thus as early as 1855, lines were drawn and sides taken. Since the formal call for *Minhag America* arose in conjunction with Wise's Cleveland "concession," Einhorn rightly feared its promulgation and continued to warn against it in dire terms. With the Civil War and the postwar industrial boom in the East, the Einhorn wing, with its many adherents there, grew stronger. Thus Wise's hopes for a unified American Jewry with its own conservatively oriented rite acceptable to all would have been difficult to achieve under the best of circumstances.

And America in the 1890s was not "the best of circumstances." It was the scene of a tide of eastern European immigrants that had begun in earnest in the last two decades of the century. The arrival of so many Jews whose life style approximated that very form of Judaism which the liberals had spent almost a century trying to modify could hardly have been viewed dispassionately by those who had come earlier. It threw into question their very self-image of Reform: a religious approach for Jewish moderns. The spectre of vast numbers of pre-modern Russian Jews inundating America elicited a severe Reform reaction, and by 1890 Wise was forced to admit the failure of *Minhag America* to win the allegiance of his colleagues.

Yet with the rising tide of immigrants, a liturgical definition of Jewish modernity could not be delayed. As president of the Central Conference, Wise issued an urgent call for some form of authorized liturgy that would reflect American Reform identity. A committee was duly elected, and a full report was prepared by the time the Central Conference of American Rabbis met in 1892. Eventually, Einhorn's radicalism, not Wise's moderation, prevailed; the resultant *Union Prayer Book*, which was published in two volumes in 1894–95, became a Reform movement manifesto.[8]

This decision shattered any hope of maintaining the flexibility necessary to develop a single liturgy for all American Jews. American Reform was fast becoming a specific movement whose standard for liturgical propriety was that pioneered in western Europe. American Reform was left with a radicalized version of German Reform in English translation. But it clearly differentiated those who prayed from it from eastern European traditionalists and even from the previous generation of German Jews who owed allegiance to Germany, not America. Reform Jews in the 1890s wanted to be perceived (and to perceive themselves) as loyal Americans committed to progress and the American dream.

In a sense, the *Union Prayer Book* was not to fail the country as much as the country would fail the prayer book. In 1881, some 90 percent of American Jews were from central Europe. By the 1890s the eastern European newcomers, numerous though they were, still did not amount to more than a meaningful minority, whose influence was limited to local enclaves of unamericanized immigrant communities.[9] So insofar as there existed any American Judaism at all, it was a direct descendent of the German model, which the *Union Prayer Book* mirrored. Its Jewish constituency undoubtedly considered it an adequate representation of their American Jewish identity, and it was therefore, by definition, an authentic American rite for them. Its only shortcoming, if it can be called that, was that it emphasized the radical wing of Reform and enshrined the ideology of the religious left just when a new and vastly larger wave of immigrants promised to expand the center. So although it was a true American rite for the majority of American Jews in 1895, it could not hope to represent the national definition of American Judaism for long. The parameters of the Judaism it defined now limited its use to a particular segment of Jews, once the majority, but now decreasingly so. It served that sector with distinction for three-quarters of a century, but it was now only the Reform movement it represented. Wise's hope for an all-American rite failed to materialize.

Once the Reform group had congealed into a movement with its own liturgical platform, the opportunity for developing a *minhag*—a rite—for all America devolved upon the center of the Jewish spectrum, whose focal point was the Jewish Theological Seminary, a meeting place for a large variety of Jews disenchanted with both left and right. The Seminary was actually a product of Reform Jews who hoped it would socialize eastern European immigrants into "acceptable" American status. The "old Seminary" as it came to be known—in contrast to the "new Seminary," which they revived in 1902 under Solomon Schechter—had in no way been oriented toward any single definition of Judaism. Its biographer, Herbert Parzen, summarized the situation by declaring it to be "abundantly definite that it did not embody a movement. In fact it was simply a rallying centre for diverse groups and individuals. . . . While it used the terms conservative, traditional, historical, to describe its conception of Judaism, it is certain that their connotations were not the same for Kohut, Jastrow, and Szold as for Morais, Mendes, and Drachman," these men constituting several of the outstanding authorities it housed.[10] But it was precisely this fluidity of position that might have permitted a broad interpretation of Judaism not specifically rooted in the individual biases of any of the men involved, but dependent on the American scene common to all of them. Parzen recalls Schechter's speaking of the Seminary as becoming "all things to all men, reconciling all parties and appealing to all sections of the community."[11] He was to speak time and time again of "catholic Israel," and in his dedication of the Seminary building in 1903, he explained,

> Our undertaking differs from every other existing Jewish college or seminary. Almost every Jewish seminary has, I believe, originated in the desire on the part of the adherents of factions . . . to control a seat of learning and study, in which the training of rabbis and ministers should proceed according to the particular religious views and tendencies of the founders.
>
> Quite differently are we situated. The organizers of the Jewish Theological Seminary of America have had only the one single purpose in view—to establish an institution which should appeal to all desiring to prepare for the Jewish ministry irrespective of the tendencies toward which they might be leaning.[12]

Though in the same address he denied the propriety of the term "American Judaism," preferring "Judaism in America," he undoubtedly anticipated the maturation of an American Jewish community that would evolve a consensus of what it uniquely was to stand for.

By the 1940s, the absence of a definitive party status was still a Seminary reality, recognized equally by those who liked it that way and those who did not. Speaking for the former, Mordecai Kaplan described Conservative Judaism as "both doctrinally and from the standpoint of practical directives . . . still inchoate and amorphous," while the opposition spokesman, Robert Gordis, lamented the twin drawbacks of "weakness of organization and absence of a clearly enunciated philosophy."[13] But however the two groups may have concurred on the reality of the situation, they differed on its evaluation.

Mordecai Kaplan had emerged as, perhaps, the most typically American Jewish thinker of the century. His influence on Seminary students was acknowledged by friend and foe alike. Primary in his religious thinking was the conceptualization of Judaism as a religious civilization, subsuming a multiplicity of equally significant religious, cultural, and ethical components. Since he posited the freedom of individual Jews to participate in this civilization in different ways, he naturally opposed any constraining definition of what counted as licit Conservative Judaism. Though Kaplan had evolved his own personal philosophy, he was loath to declare alternatives beyond the pale. They were at worst mistakes, failures in the ultimate task of protecting the richness of Jewish civilization against the encroachment of American culture. Mistakes, yes; heresies, no.

Then too, Kaplan recognized the fact that Jews participated in American civilization as well. Since he applauded its potential, he was predisposed to appreciate the commonality of Americanism that all Jews shared, no matter what path toward Judaism they selected. This acceptance of alternative routes to Jewish civilization combined with his positive evaluation of American values to help him envision a native Jewish community that might differ in important respects but would be so similar in others as to constitute a unique American Jewry. It would, in his opinion, be the height of folly to impose artificial limitations on American Jews, declaring some forms of expression licit and others not. When the issue of the Seminary's future reached a climax in 1946, he wrote: "Some of our rabbinic colleagues are of the opinion that the interests of Judaism would best be served if the Rabbinical Assembly were to use its newly won power [N.B.] for the purpose of solidifying the center group. It should bring into sharp relief the specific principles and practices that differentiate it both from the Orthodox and the Reformist group." He further estimated, "The crucial question with which we are faced at present is, shall we function as a third congregational denomination to be known as 'Conservative'—or shall we function as a non-denominational body dedicated to the furtherance of American-Jewish life as a whole?"[14]

Though Kaplan founded a separate Reconstructionist Foundation, he never ceased reiterating his vision of an umbrella Judaism common to all American Jews, in many equally authentic combinations. In fact, his own Reconstructionist Foundation was to work toward that very goal, publishing among other things *The Faith of America*, an anthology of American writings that might be drawn on for worship services marking American holidays.[15] Kaplan claimed it was the Conservative Movement's failure to provide such an umbrella structure that prompted his own institution. This was the burden of a lead editorial in Kaplan's

1928 *SAJ Review*, and it was reprinted ten years later as the introductory statement in the first edition of the *Reconstructionist*. "The Conservatives are a
religious party," it complained. "How, then, can a Conservative movement be a
unifying movement?"[16]

Indeed, it could not. But, the question was, should it? Or should it, rather,
publish its own platform, positions, and literature? By the 1940s the leadership
of the Conservative rabbinical body, the Rabbinical Assembly, opted for the
latter. As with Reform some decades earlier, what was once a broad spectrum of
opinion with the possibility of coming to represent American Jewry in all its
diversity became a movement. Conservative Judaism, like Reform, prepared a
party manifesto in the form of a prayer book. When faced with the threat of
eastern European Jews, Reform had harked back to its immediate antecedents in
western Europe. For Conservative Judaism, it was Reform and Reconstructionism, that is, the religious left, who set "unacceptable" standards of Jewish
identity, so Conservative leaders emphasized their roots on the right, their
heritage from eastern Europe. The result was a 1946 Conservative prayer book.[17]

The book's forerunner had actually been written almost a decade earlier by
Morris Silverman, a rabbi in Hartford, Connecticut, and was but one of several
such works used in Conservative synagogues.[18] It seems to have met with
considerable success, however, since an unfavorable book review in the January
1938 edition of the *Reconstructionist* drew a response by the author, who was
able to cite congratulatory letters from Conservative colleagues around the country.[19] Thus when the Rabbinical Assembly decided to produce its own religious
literature—a goal proclaimed by Gordis himself in the lead article in the very
first edition of *Conservative Judaism*[20]—the Silverman prayer book warranted
its serious consideration. It was turned over to a committee that Gordis chaired,
whence it emerged in somewhat changed form as the official prayer book of the
Conservative Movement.[21]

The considerations guiding the committee were detailed by its chairman in a
lengthy article that appeared in the movement's official journal that same year.[22]
The article was a model of honesty and clarity. It began by paying tribute to the
authors of earlier prayer books but concluded that diversity of practice ought no
longer to be sanctioned. The time had come for the movement to produce its own
authorized liturgy. Conservative Judaism would avoid the errors of Reform,
which "threw out the baby with the bath" and created services that were "cold
and uninspiring."[23] It would also eschew the path of the Reconstructionists,
whose recently published prayer book contained "patent weaknesses."[24] The
prayer book would emphasize significant issues like Zionism—it was 1946, after
all—and the chosen people concept, which the Reconstructionists had denied. It
would, in other words, shun the task of representing all of American Jewry and
emphasize the uniqueness of the Conservative position.

History had repeated itself. As with the *Union Prayer Book*, movement sectarianism had submerged the broader issue of defining American Judaism as a whole. Now the Conservative Movement, like its Reform counterpart, had its own liturgical expression of that which differentiated it from other Jewish options on the horizon.

In a very real sense, then, the self-image of American Jews can be gleaned from the prayer books of their respective movements. Their composition coincides with those times when historical circumstances favored the selection of a specific sector of the gamut of ideological alternatives as constituting the limits of acceptable Jewishness. The proliferation of meaningful alternatives thus spawned our modern movements, whose liturgical self-portraits emphasized not so much what was the same about all American Jews but what was different about one particular group of Jews who happened to be in America. There was no Reform "movement" before eastern European Jews imported their rival ethos to America, and there was no single Reform prayer book either. Only when the presence of a real alternative necessitated a clear statement of self-definition did an authorized prayer book come into being, and it proclaimed rather precisely what its compilers did not stand for, as well as what they did. Reform Judaism was revealed as a continuation of central European Jewish liberalism, in contradistinction to European "fundamentalism." It was religious, not nationalistic; universalist in concern, not particularist. It emphasized reason, ethics, evolution, and optimism. As late as 1945, the newly revised *Union Prayer Book* carried alternative readings for each of the five sabbaths of the month (there being a possibility of five only in the English calendar, note, not in the traditional Jewish one, which follows a lunar reckoning.)[25] But all readings fell within those guidelines which general consensus had defined as the outer limits of Reform.

The same process of liturgical self-definition characterized the Conservative Movement. It too was originally a nonmovement, in the sense that no clear self-definition was required. As Reform occupied the left, so Conservatism occupied everything to the right of that. But aside from some general sense of ethnic authenticity and traditional continuity, it possessed no definition of itself. The practical implications of its emphasis on historical continuity were very ambiguous. So Conservative Judaism, like early Reform, made do with a variety of prayer books, expressing, in this case, varying degrees of the Americanization of the eastern European tradition. Since American Reform had staked its claim so far to the left, a real opportunity existed for the Conservative center to assume the mantle of speaking for the vast majority of American Jews, and it was precisely this function that Mordecai Kaplan advocated. But the sanctioning of such a broad range of choices as he championed was by its very nature a denial of the right's claims to ideological certainty, and his personal theology was unacceptable even to the less extreme faction. So the Conservative Movement too emerged with no pan-American expression of Judaism but with a liturgical platform: a book whose introduction stated baldly what the Conservative Movement was not and whose content defined quite clearly what it was. True to the circumstances that gave it birth, it, unlike the Reform liturgy, offered little opportunity for selectivity. There was one service, the eastern European model on which most previous Conservative prayer books had been based, with, however, some added material (particularly on Zionism), a few ideological emendations, a modern translation, and the omission of some lengthy medieval poetry, to which nearly all parties could consent, since some of the greatest Jewish leaders of the past had proclaimed it as being truly secondary if not downright undesirable.[26]

Unlike Reform and Conservatism, Orthodoxy has suffered chronically from a lack of institutional unity. Least of all three can it even be said to be one "movement," since it has always been splintered into diverse sects and representatives; appropriately, it has generated no single prayer book. Those who define themselves as Orthodox pray from a multitude of books, ranging from the Conservative prayer book on the left to various versions of Hasidic ritual— *Nusach Sefarad*[27]—on the right. But, since many of the groupings subsumed under the general title of "Orthodox" oppose the very idea of Americanization, and since they occupy the far right of the Jewish spectrum in any event, they, least of all, could be expected to arrive at a ritual expressive of those concerns and attitudes which unite the majority of American Jews as a distinct community.

But even the Orthodox are not immune to the rule that liturgy reflects communal self-identity by establishing the proper amount of social distance between itself and others. The best example of this "modern" Orthodox world is *Siddur Lashabbat Veyom Tov; The Traditional Prayer Book for Sabbath and Festivals*, edited in 1960 by the illustrious late rabbi Dr. David de Sola Pool. And that book well illustrates the thesis presented here, not only by its success but by its initial failure as well. The book was conceived, in part, by the influential publisher of Jewish books, Jacob Behrman. By 1946 his father had already become enamored of Pool's writing style, and both father and son now reasoned that the time had come for a modern edition of Orthodox liturgy. Behrman recalls that at first he received support from a rabbinic giant of the Orthodox world, Rabbi Soloveitchik of Boston. For reasons that are not clear, however, the latter's warmth for the project cooled considerably as Pool neared the end of his work and the book came closer and closer to actual publication. What is evident, however, is that the Orthodox world was unable to unite in wholehearted support behind the volume, so that those who favored it encountered mounting opposition. Though the prayer book was published, it never did receive the public approval of many of Orthodoxy's chief rabbinic representatives, including Soloveichik himself.[28]

Thus by 1960, the American Jewish community had established two clearly observable rites, Reform and Conservative, with the series of Orthodox prayer books constituting a loosely knit third, and the Reconstructionist books by Mordecai Kaplan and his associates, a weak fourth. From the Zunzian perspective, these were all Ashkenazic. But from the point of view offered here, each should be seen as a rite unto itself, postulating liturgical equivalents of the socio-ideological structure actually existent in American Jewry. Worshipers of each rite construct their social reality transgeographically, in that each community will feel closer to certain other groups of Jews—in some cases Jews they have never met, who live thousands of miles away—than they do to Jews of another community (who use another rite) just around the corner. And of the two worlds, geographical and social, it is the latter that counts the most. Though for matters of business, an Orthodox Hasidic Jew in Brooklyn comes into contact with local Reform Jews, the real world about which he cares, yearns, worries, and selects as ultimately determinative of his life style is the social world in which Reform Jews have no place other than as interchangeable, anonymous "others" who inhabit the territory beyond an enormous social chasm. He is at home, however, with the parallel Hasidic community in England, Israel, or Poland. And they all use the same rite.

So despite the geographical nomenclature usually associated with rites—German, Polish, etc.—the essential determining factor is not geography at all, but the extent to which a community's members identify themselves as sharers of a given situation, specific to themselves. Usually, such singularity of vision corresponds to geography, but the geographical terms we use should not blind us to the fact that it is really *perceived social* isolation, not *geographic* isolation, that counts. From a shared sense of social distinctiveness, there arise the attitudes and aspirations that make for group identity, and these are the really definitive factors. The utilization of a distinctive liturgical rite is simply one of the ways participating members of a group give public assent to their status as a community. Minor changes in experience provoke new prayers, which are added to old books. Accumulated alterations in life's circumstances lead to a revised book. Major cataclysmic events make for a new liturgy of such massive alterations as to be tantamount to the inception of a new rite. Borrowed from the past, it is an amalgam of the past and the present, a true representation of the worshipers themselves.

It might be said, then, that whatever worshipers presume to say to God, they are at the same time directing a message to themselves. The very act of worship takes on the function of identifying for the worshiper what it is that he or she stands for, what real life is like, what his or her aspirations are. The liturgical medium becomes the message.[29]

The manifest content of the prayers, however, is only one of three elements that, together, constitute this message. Content has been emphasized by scholars more than the other two because a prayer's content or message naturally lends itself to theological discussion, and because when liturgical renovation seemed called for, textual omissions and emendations of content were the most simple surgery available. Reform and Reconstructionist Jews especially were quick to identify the obvious incongruity of medieval content with the spirit of modern times as the "problem" of American liturgy. But their haste in identifying unacceptable content as the culprit should not lead us to overlook the two other variables that determine the liturgical message.

The first of these is simply the structure of the prayer book: its layout, design, organization, language of instruction, and so on. The first known prayer book, *Seder Rav Amram* (circa 870 C.E.), for example, was written in the form of a legal responsum to Jews in Spain. Inserted between the prayers were lengthy extracts from the Babylonian Talmud, and detailed discussions of the legal requirements for proper worship. In fact, so extensive is the *halakhic*, or legal, commentary, that one might even describe *Seder Rav Amram* more accurately the other way around: legal discussions about prayer, with the prayers inserted within them. But the preponderance of Talmudic guidance is exactly the point of the book—what we should consider its most evident structural message—to the effect that both corporate and individual Jewish decisions were to be founded in Jewish law generally, the Babylonian Talmud specifically, and (even more precisely) the juridical interpretations of the latter made by contemporary authorities in Babylonia.

Similarly, the 1946 Conservative movement's prayer book, discussed above, and still in use in most Conservative congregations, provided a significant structural message. Its basic eastern European Ashkenazic service was structurally updated by felicitous English translations and aesthetic spacing of print. The communicative potential of the design was apparently not lost on those responsible for marketing the volume, for they placed advertisements for it emphasizing its "Attractive format: Bound in the Best Wavely Pattern Cloth." The same advertisements reserved the largest type for the book's "title," which summarized the message loudly and clearly: "Modern Traditional Prayer Book."[30] Inherent in this very structure was the message of the Conservative movement: loyalty to tradition as viewed from the purified perch of modernity.

Alternatively, consider the early Reform movement, whose acculturated perspective was reflected just as clearly to a worshiper using the 1894–95 *Union Prayer Book*. The book opened from left to right; decorum was guaranteed by labeling prayers according to who was to do what (choir, congregation, etc.), and how (silent prayer, responsive reading, etc.); the rabbi was called "minister." The language was stilted with Thee's and Thou's; the prayer titles (Adoration, Sanctification, etc.) were in English; services were labeled in Gothic print.

As for American Orthodoxy, we have already seen that the sharp-looking modern scientific de Sola Pool prayer book was ignored by a generation of

Orthodox Jews who were emphasizing (in contradistinction to Conservatism) their opposition to liturgical renewal. It was precisely the book's structural message that their self-image denied! So the book did not come into general use until "modern" Orthodoxy, as represented by New York's Lincoln Square Synagogue, for example, saw it as an ideal representation of its "renovated" Orthodox identity.[31] Clearly, worshipers who pay no attention whatever to the meaning of prayers are nevertheless able to intuit a distinctive message merely by internalizing the structural component of their prayer book.

Not least in significance in the formation of the liturgical message is choreography, the way services are conducted. The contrast between the eastern European *shtetl* and American Reform is instructive here. In the former, worship was characterized by "davening," a particular brand of *Hazzanut*, and an intimacy among peers balanced by a seating arrangement that both reflected and supported class structure. The very pathos of the singsong sound of "davening," and the "kvetch" of the small-town Hazzan reflected the misery of *shtetl* existence.[32] The small synagogues (or *shtüblech*) in which worshipers "davened" side by side, often packed together, each person apparently doing his own thing without disturbing the others, was the most intimate of services imaginable and testified to the closeness forced on the crowded Jewish communities of the Pale. But social class in the ghetto was maintained by the system of reserving seats by the eastern wall for those with status. How different all of this was from the highly decorous service in large, architecturally elaborate temples founded by the Reform movement in America! There, the organ, the German music so dependent on high European culture, or the stylized and, to some extent, Protestantized mode of worship carried a message for Jews who were part and parcel of Western enlightenment.

Similarly, the Hasidic *niggun*, American Reform's abandonment of the *yarmulke*, mixed seating of men and women—all these and a host of other details that have composed the "how" of worship in different times and places are just as significant as the meaning of the prayers themselves in defining Jewish identity, and these two elements (choreography and content), along with the prayer book's structure, have combined to present a coherent message to the worshiper of what it means to be a Jew.[33]

The liturgical Gestalt adopted by a community thus becomes a reflection of that community's search for Jewish identity. The degree to which it perceives the old liturgy to be inadequate, and the intensity of its demand for liturgical novelty, vary with the magnitude of the events that mark it off from its historical past, the size of the chasm that differentiates its self-perception from that perceived by past generations. If several generations have enjoyed relative calm, if no cataclysmic events have shaken the bonds with the past, the old liturgy suffices. Minor alterations in the community's consciousness may move the people to add a prayer or two, to alter some custom or other, or, in some other small way, to give recognition to the minor novelties that have occurred. After several such novelties, however, the community begins to feel more alienated from the inherited rite, and a more thorough patch-up job is attempted: the prayer book is revised, or a supplement is printed. And if truly earthshaking events threaten wholly to sever the community from its past, the old rite itself is thrown into question, at which point a new Gestalt begins to take shape. The first steps are chaotic, as different people search for a viable way to blend the old tradition with the new events, but finally the more successful representations of community consciousness are crystallized into a new authorized prayer book. This book will have altered all three elements of the liturgical Gestalt: content, structure, and potential choreography.

In the process, the system of relationships between new groupings characteristic of the evolving social structure will have changed. Social distances will shrink or grow as members of the newly self-defined community consider their social proximity to their neighbors. The prayer book that emerges from this novel identity and its altered scale of social distances will one day be recognized as a new rite.

We have now returned full circle and can pursue our analysis of American Jewry's current liturgical strivings. From the perspective of Zunz, it should be noted, there is not much more that could be said. To go on describing contemporary American liturgical creativity as Ashkenazic does no justice whatever to the elementary and obvious fact that *Gates of Prayer*, for example, the Reform movement's current prayer book, is more unlike the traditional Ashkenazic *Siddur* than it is like it. Moreover, it contains material borrowed from the rival Sephardic tradition, as well as large chunks of modern poetry and prose (Robert Frost, for example) which are nothing if not American.

But the other Zunzian option, discovering a new geographic rite, the American Rite, is not wholly plausible either, for the reasons addressed above: both Wise and Kaplan failed to establish an American rite typical of all American Jews because American Jews are not all the same. What we have is a spectrum of prayer practices reflecting an equal spectrum of Jewish self-identity. Rites can be correlated successfully not with a geographic but with a social reality, that being, in our case, one's perceived place on the spectrum of Reform, Conservative Reconstructionist, and Orthodox, all however—but especially the first three—subsumed under the pressing reality of the American experience.

It is precisely this American experience that has been lacking until now. Both the Reform and the Conservative rites have hitherto tended to adopt the liturgical Gestalt that past European experience identified as the proper expression of group consciousness. As far as content is concerned Reform Judaism produced an 1894–95 liturgy (*Union Prayer Book* volumes I and II) with an even more pronounced version of the same theological emendations as had been made in

Germany in the nineteenth century, while in its 1946 "Silverman prayer book" (as the official volume is popularly called), the Conservative movement retained as many traditional concepts as it possibly could, hoping to identify itself as the true heir to the Jewish legacy. Structurally too both groups chose echoes of what they knew best from their European past. The Reform movement emulated German worship patterns and the Conservative movement adhered closely to models of the Russian Jewish Pale of Settlement. The choreography, above all, remained faithful to the past. Despite some minor innovations, there was little to demarcate American Jewish worship from its immediate predecessors across the Atlantic.

But of course, this only mirrored the fact that definitions of American Jewry had focused on the particularity of specific movements. The individuality of the American Jew as a unique genus, a specific Jewish type, such as historians recognize in the Jews of Sasanian Babylonia, or the Jews of the Spanish Golden Age, had yet to be asserted.

Recent liturgical events suggest that American Jews have finally come of age. The massive migrations of the early part of the century have ceased. American-born generations have upset the initial ethnic composition of their movements. The movements themselves have settled down to the point where they no longer feel it necessary to polemicize against one another. The American ethos has become the dominant point of departure for everyone's perception of reality. And events of this century, notably the Holocaust and the birth of the State of Israel,[34] have modified everyone's Jewish perspective so as to render all but meaningless those differences in Jewish identity which loomed so large to Jews who pioneered their movements generations ago. The result is the birth pangs of an Americanization of the Reform, Conservative, and (in some quarters) even the Orthodox rites.

The first hint of this development was to be found in the proliferation of "creative services" in the late sixties and seventies. These were initiated by youth groups, who were the first to have their ties with the European past neutralized by a thorough indoctrination in Americanism. Unlike those who lived through similar periods of experimentation in the past, American Jews were imbued with a sense of democracy that seemed to allow anyone at all to write a service; and almost everyone did. American technology, with its ubiquitous duplication machines and cheap source of paper, enabled many congregations to write a service on Thursday, pray from it Friday night or Saturday, and throw it out on Sunday. Though many of the services leave something to be desired in terms of Jewish sophistication and even English style, they do, nevertheless, provide unmistakable attempts to develop Jewish liturgies that reflect American Jewish consciousness. In content, they talk about Vietnam, group sensitivity, and the expressions of American authors and poets. Sometimes they interpret the Jewish tradition even to the point of absurdity, so as to accord with values derived from the American milieu. Structurally, they use English and, even where Hebrew type is included, English transliterations, Their choreography calls for one of the most American of instruments, the folk guitar, and American folk music.[35]

The organized movements were quick to perceive the need for an authorized response. In quick succession the Reform movement published a Passover Haggadah, a daily and Sabbath prayer book, and a Holy Day *Machzor*, while the Conservative movement issued a High Holy Day *Machzor*, a Haggadah, and (as recently as 1986) a daily and Sabbath *Siddur*. Both Reform and Conservative committees are at work on further volumes. Significantly, none of these books are mere revisions of past works. They all claim to break new ground in liturgical usage. A reviewer of the Conservative *Machzor*, for example, relates that its predecessor was "to all intents and purposes the standard Ashkenazi Orthodox Prayerbook . . . and was far from representing a liturgical development along the lines of Conservative Jewish thought." How different the new *Machzor* is! "With this *machzor*, American Conservative Judaism has come of age liturgically."[36] Similarly, the Reform Haggadah, already a best seller by commercial standards, is barely recognizable as the successor of the old 1923 *Union Haggadah*, and its prayer book is so different from the volume it replaces that many Jews who grew up nurtured on the latter felt at first that the identity of their youth was being taken away. Since, by now, American Jews are thoroughly committed to movement expressions of their identity, no one still speaks seriously of a single rite for all. But the potential for an Americanization of existing movement rites, so that they and their worshipers' identities are no longer tied tyrannically to European antecedents, is at hand.

We might conclude by noting that the Americanization process is not unique to America's Jews. Liturgical renewal is the norm also among Christians of every denomination. Was it the Second World War, which shattered the last vestiges of dependence on our common European past, that propelled American religion to its proud assertion of American strength in a world where the old authority was collapsing? Or would it have happened anyway with the cessation of European immigration and the coming of age of those immigrants' American-born children? Whatever the case, it did happen, and it happened to all Americans, not just Jews, transforming our identity structures and our worship rites in the process.

This principle of the commonality of cultural influences will occupy us when we later discuss the liturgical apprehension of the numinous (chapter 7). First, however, we must confront one more aspect of religious identity, the attempt of a group to use liturgy to explain its origins, its sacred history, how it came to be what it is, and why it deserves continued existence.

FIVE

Sacred Myths

I. Premodern Jewish Perspectives

Communities do not exist in historical vacuums. People maintain more than a horizontal perspective on who they are. Past generations who no longer people the earth bodily still constitute a genuine reality in the minds of individuals who do. At the most immediate level, people, generally, recall their parents, perhaps their grandparents, and even the third generation back. But we should also speak of a liturgical extension of memory that permits worshipers to hark back farther still. That Jews, for example, choose to remember—the preferred word is to memorialize—these generations by "saying *Kaddish*," testifies to a human desire to see ourselves as the continuers of a heritage that surpasses our own meager immediate life-space (to borrow Kurt Lewin's very useful metaphor). We thus posit our continuity with a realm of reality that transcends the personal biographies of you, and of me, and of all those many anonymous others who happen to constitute the frail fabric of one single generation's picture of reality.

The prayer of a community, too, abhors a vacuum. Prayer is a cultural creation, fashioned by people who may have only a dim perception of what they are about as they go about worshiping, but who know nonetheless that their preoccupation with the "stuff" of prayer is important in their lives. Undergirding the liturgical creativity is the twofold sense that the community that worships is of supreme significance. It asserts beliefs, after all, that others deny, and it posits plans at which others scoff. Its view of the "real" reality may be a universe in which normal experience is deemed illusory or one in which it is considered real, even compelling. But in either case, religious people band together in their worship to posit what Berger and Luckmann have aptly described as an alternative to the pragmatic reality of everyday life. Their prayers describe a "finite province of meaning" that worshipers assert at the time to be the "really real," and that (it is assumed) they will faithfully superimpose on the other reality of everyday life, as they go about making decisions there.[1] Religion thus dares to make the primary definition of what reality is for its members, and it does so, primarily, in its liturgical setting.

There are at least two ways in which liturgical rituals underscore the ultimacy of these definitions. The first is the reference they make to the "ultimate" source of truth, usually the divine (which we shall explore in chapter 7). The second, and the subject confronting us here, is religious ritual's appeal to the authority of former generations. The liturgical vacuum that we abhor is the theoretical possibility that what we are doing is the mere creation of our own devices. Lévi-Strauss once remarked that "primitives" insist on explaining what they do by having recourse to the compelling fact that people have always done things that way;[2] just as Sholom Aleichem's Jews of Anatevka proclaim "Tradition! Tradition!" in *Fiddler on the Roof*. Even we "moderns" alter the usual mode of worship with trepidation. To strike out bravely in liturgical directions unrelated to the old is to declare an independence that threatens to strip away the security of knowing we are right.

So somewhere along the way, the liturgy itself is shaped in such a way as to assure us that we do not stand alone. A chain of tradition provides a lasting basis for what we do. We are linked to history, and not just any history, but sacred history. We play the role of The Next Generation in a cosmic drama going back to the beginnings of meaningful time. Our function on this earth thus takes on mythic proportions. And our sacred history can more properly be described as a sacred myth.

The word "myth" has been used so much that it is difficult to know what one means by it anymore. Definitions are surely in order. On the other hand, its very commonality allows one to use the word without worrying lest one trespass on any single serious and specific denotation that it ought properly to convey. In the sense that I use the word here, then, I intend no necessary parallelism with those usages one comes across in the study of ancient Greek literature, for example, or the anthropological or psychological considerations of Lévi-Strauss, Leach, Eliade, Jung, or Zimmer (to name but a few).[3] We may each choose our own meaning for "myth" so long as it is clearly defined, and in accordance with some order of empirical reality that others can affirm as not nonsensical from their own perspective on human experience.

By "sacred myth," I mean the subjective and selective perception of our background that we choose to remember and to enshrine as our official "history." This mythic history is recited liturgically not for its accuracy—thus differentiating it from normal historical narrative—but for its power to galvanize group identity. In this way, the liturgical community regularly reinforces its members' current vision of whence they are derived. We can speak, therefore, of the liturgical act functioning to convey a sense of the ultimate significance of the worshiping group, by providing a sacred myth.

Before looking further at liturgy as sacred myth, a prior methodological concern should be noted. All methods are attempts to find meaning of one sort or another in an object of study that is meaningless until it is studied. The traditional methods of philology and form-criticism have defined that object as the texts of specific prayers, for which they have proposed meanings within the context of either textual redaction (for philology) or *Sitz im Leben* (for form-criticism). At the end of their enquiries, one has a prayer that no longer exists as an independent entity void of meaning, but can now be imagined as being situated in the center of a theoretical circle constituting what I shall call the "field of meaning." A prayer is exposed, for example, as having a certain origin, a response to Roman persecution, let us say, so that the philologist then reconstitutes its "field of meaning" by assembling all other such prayers, as well as all relevant information regarding Roman overlordship and the nature of Jewish responses to it. Or a prayer takes on shape as one of many examples of law-court disputations with God, and the form-critic proceeds to elucidate a "field of meaning" that includes all other such argumentative texts, along with information regarding the institution of the law court, the theology of divine-human encounter, and so forth.[4] In any case, no prayer is comprehendible in its own right; it requires a context that researchers themselves assume even before undertaking their task. It is they who determine what "count" as explanatory data. They bring to bear what Polanyi calls the matters of subsidiary awareness (to which we referred above), without which we would be able to attain no focal awareness whatever of the prayers in question.[5] So methods differ from one another on the basis of what they determine *a priori* as the limits of relevance, and, consequently, on the very basic level of the sorts of fields of meaning they are capable of generating.

It is precisely the nature of their fields of meaning that ought to serve as the criterion by which methods are judged. One could, for example, classify prayers according to the number of words they contain. In fact, it is a very similar numerological standpoint that characterized the work of many medieval liturgical commentators, particularly the school known as *Hasidei Ashkenaz*, a group of German mystics that flourished in the twelfth and thirteenth centuries. By using the mathematical "science" of *gematria*, whereby the numerical equivalent of the Hebrew consonants composing a word or prayer could be computed, identically summed phrases were grouped together and then analyzed for their hidden message. Clearly, the relevant field of meaning here is far removed even from such an obvious textual characteristic as lexical proximity; in this scheme, prayer texts belong together because they add up to the same sum, and the relevant field of outside data is a system of signification in which not history or even literary style, but numeration is paramount.[6]

But the modern world of scholarship rightfully abandoned such a paradigm, not because it did not succeed in providing a field of meaning—on the contrary, it never failed—but because the "meaning" was no longer "meaningful." It had lost what Peter Berger calls its "plausibility structure."[7] We needed new

approaches capable of constructing fields of meaning that were congruent with
contemporary criteria of meaningfulness. The results of our quest were philology
and form-criticism, each of which defined a new field of meaning; and the natural
question of each is, to what extent those fields satisfy yet more contemporary
canons of relevance.

But relevant to what? Certainly every field is relevant to some prior definition
of meaning. I have argued that the two traditional methodologies are relevant to
literature. Classical philological analysis (such as Zunz's) places that literature
within the context of politics and polemics, postulating textual redaction as the
outcome of events within those realms of human activity. Heinemann prefers to
see the literature arising out of differences in ritualized conduct within institutions. But both views define meaning according to literary concerns, and—what
has not yet been said—both are subject to severe chronological limitations. That
is, the field of meaning available to philology and to form-criticism cannot go
beyond the artificial constraints of a given historical period in which the prayers
under discussion are said to have originated.

One of the benefits of organizing liturgical study around conceptualizations
that are not themselves derived from the texts being studied, is that our field of
meaning can be extended beyond the barriers of chronological time. Within a
prayer's field of meaning, there can be more than other, similar, literary units;
more, too, than the institutional life of a subcommunity in which the prayer was
originally composed. We are able to posit an affinity with other prayers written in
vastly diverse times and places, or with rituals that transcend institutional differentiation. We discover connections among diverse data that we would never
have noticed before, because we focus on similarities in the patterns of human
ritualization as such.

So far, our universal patterns have included cultural categorization and the
ritualized determination of a group's ego-boundaries, its awareness of social
space. We now turn to a third set of data that properly belongs to the field of
meaning presupposed in this study: the ritualized selective perception of historical time.

This chapter and the next, then, are a dual case study. Specifically, by looking
at the liturgical presentation of some versions of the Jewish sacred myth, we can
demonstrate the communal search for ultimacy in its roots, as we said above; but
also, we can see how a field of meaning can be enhanced simply by adopting a
meaningful organizational principle suggested by nontextual considerations.

We shall look first at the declaration of identity mandated by the Bible and
recited before the destruction of the Jerusalem Temple in 70 C.E. Our subject is a
cultic ritual known as the presentation of the first fruits. It reveals what is
probably the earliest liturgical presentation of ritualized Jewish myth known to
us. We will then see how the rabbis of the first two centuries altered the official

picture of Jewish history, developing a new liturgical carrier for it: a midrashic reinterpretation of this very biblical declaration, which they assigned to the Passover seder. By looking at later medieval liturgical creations, including a High Holy Day rubric known as the *Avodah*, the seder poem *Dayyenu*, and a lectionary cycle, we will see how the regnant sacred myth was altered further to explain diaspora conditions, and how it was frozen for centuries because of a unique conception of time. Finally (in the next chapter), turning to the post-Enlightenment, we will see that the myth was changed with the Western world's discovery of progress and its rediscovery of history; our example will be that unique child of Western culture to which we have already referred, Reform Judaism. Rounding out our analysis, we shall turn to the Reform and the Conservative movements' liturgies of today, so as to illustrate the phenomenon of a sacred myth in the process of change.

THE EARLIEST SACRED MYTH

Perhaps our earliest example of a ritual profession of sacred myth is Deut. 26:1–11, where farmers are commanded to take the fruits of the harvest to Jerusalem and there to affirm their loyalty to the covenant betwen Israel and God. The harvest served as a visible reminder that God was fulfilling the divine part of the covenantal agreement by providing the rain and attendant climatic conditions that agricultural people require to survive. From a later, rabbinic source,[8] we may conclude that first-century Jews followed this biblical command—at least, the rabbis of the Mishnah assert that they did—on the holiday of Shavuot, the festival marking the spring harvest.

The Mishnah describes this as a joyous occasion filled with remarkable pomp and ceremony. From their small communities outside of Jerusalem, people thronged together for a festive march to the capital. When the time to leave had arrived, the person in charge announced, "Arise and let us go up to Zion, to the house of the Lord our God" (Jer. 31:6). The ritual parade, replete with musical instruments, now wended its way through the rolling hills and highways, until it reached the gates of Jerusalem. On arrival there, the pilgrims received official welcome, and continued on to the Temple, where the Levites sang Psalm 30, a hymn of praise. Finally the people individually lifted baskets of selected harvest produce onto their shoulders, and, before handing them over to the priest, made the following declaration:

> My forefather was a wandering Aramean, who went down to Egypt and sojourned there, few in number; and there he became a nation, great, mighty, and populous. But the Egyptians dealt ill with us, afflicting us by laying upon us harsh bondage. So we cried to the Lord, the God of our ancestors. And the Lord heard our voice, and saw our affliction and our toil, and our oppression. The Lord took us out of

Egypt with a mighty hand and an outstretched arm, and with great terror, signs and
wonders. He brought us to this place, and gave us this land, a land flowing with milk
and honey. Therefore, I now bring the first fruits of the land, which You, O Lord
have given me.[9]

Obviously this is a selective perception of Israel's history, recited ritually. As
such, it serves us very nicely as an example of a sacred myth. To the pilgrim who
uttered it, the story was true, true in the existential sense of being as much a part
of the taken-for-granted "facticity" of experience as the day-by-day life on the
land whose beneficence it sought to explain. From the last sentence of the
declaration, we can see that it was precisely this account of their history that
moved the pilgrims to go on the pilgrimage in the first place. Until that point in
their speech, they talk to the priest, and refer to God in the third person. But
finally, having rehearsed God's wondrous role in guiding Israel, the farmers turn
directly to God and conclude (verse 10), "*Therefore*, I now bring the first fruits
of the land which You, O Lord, have given me." Sacred myths are true beyond
the claims of empirical evidence. They are true in that they represent bases for
action on the part of those who accept their binding force. The pilgrim accepts
the tale, and *therefore* presents the produce to God's representative, the Temple
priest. If we scrutinize the myth more closely, we can see how accurately it
reflects the agricultural society of which the farmer was an integral part.

Agricultural fertility, or lack thereof, ties every strand of the story together. It
begins by recalling the wandering forebears, Abraham, Isaac, and Jacob, who
traversed the land in search of a place to graze their flocks and dig their wells of
water. Appropriately, the worst scourge was a seven-year drought that afflicted
Jacob, and although the drought is not explicitly recalled here, its result is: Jacob
"went down to Egypt," where Joseph, his once-lost son, but now vizier, was
able to feed him. There, Israel (i.e., Jacob) saw no reason to leave a land of
plenty, even when a new Pharaoh arose who "knew not Joseph." The result was
enslavement and poverty once again. But God fulfilled the covenant and rescued
the people, bringing them to ultimate glory, a land flowing with milk and honey.
So Deuteronomy, whence this account is taken, describes clearly the direct
relationship between the steadfast obedience of Israel and its reward of agricultural fecundity. We cannot fail to appreciate the contrast between the beginning of the story, when "My father was a *wandering* Aramean," and the end,
when that Aramean's descendents, no longer wandering, are finally awarded
their permanent "land flowing with milk and honey," from which they will
never have to wander again.

The next few verses in the same biblical chapter (vv. 14–15) restate the
identical theme somewhat differently, in connection with another liturgical ritual, the presentation of tithes. Upon presenting their tithe to the priest, the

farmers are told to point out to God that they have fulfilled all that is requested of them, and, in return, they request, even demand, that God do likewise.

I have hearkened to the voice of the Lord my God, and done according to all that You have commanded me. [Therefore, they conclude] look forth from Your holy habitation, Heaven, and bless Your people Israel, and the land which you have given us, as You swore to our ancestors, a land flowing with milk and honey.[10]

This latter case is the same as the former, but with reverse logic. Here, the people begin with their obedience and reason to *God's* duty to renew the land, whereas, in the former instance, that of the first fruits, the connection was made the other way around. There, we recall, the people started with a historical recollection of God's magnificent maintenance of Israel, culminating in their being brought to the land, and then they celebrated their tie to the land by the fulfillment of *their* duty, the offering of some of the land's richness back to God. The reasoning is consistent in both instances, however. The earliest myth proclaims history for Israel the agricultural people, centering on a promised land that will not cease giving forth its fruit, so long as its inhabitants obey the divine mandate.

A rereading of the farmers' declaration proves revealing in terms of what is not said too. What pictures, snapshots of Israel's past, were selectively ignored, relegated to the attic trunk, so to speak, only to be rediscovered in a later age, when agricultural living had been altered by the discovery of urban success?

Incredibly enough for modern readers, the revelation of Torah on Mount Sinai is missing. Reading the farmers' story, one would never have an indication that Israel had once traveled through Sinai and received the Ten Commandments. Of course, the farmers believed in those commandments, just as they believed in the entire written Torah whence they drew the obligation to give their first fruits in the first place. But Torah per se was as yet unimportant in Jewish consciousness. Only after the destruction of the Temple in the first century would a new leadership class, known generally to us as the rabbis, convert the concept of Torah into the essence of Judaism, claiming even that it was a blueprint, equivalent to Plato's Ideas, on which creation depends.[11] It was the rabbis who would consider Mount Sinai the pinnacle of a modified sacred myth. In fact, Shavuot, the very holiday on which the farmer had once professed his agricultural interpretation of Jewish history, the day, that is, that marked the fulfillment of the covenant of the land, would eventually be made over by the rabbis to the anniversary of the Torah's revelation on Mount Sinai.

Thus the ancient First Fruit ritual and its accompanying proclamation of sacred myth perished with the Temple cult in the year 70. When the Romans destroyed the Temple and its sacrificial service, they symbolically bore witness to the passing of the biblical era itself. Jews were now in a postbiblical age, marked by a newly composed middle class, a Roman environment replete with urban cosmopolitanism, and a recently discovered sense of the worth of the individual. The sacred myth had to be redrawn.

RABBINIC CONCEPTION OF TIME

The myth was redrawn, however, in a most ingenious way. The biblical account of Israel's history, and the agricultural myth expressing it, make use of historical chronology, in that one event precedes another, each in its proper order. By contrast, the rabbinic conception of history avoids recourse to temporal accident. For the rabbis, God had established a grand plan in which history as we moderns know it is incidental. They measured historical time not by years, which are amenable to infinite successive numbering, but by eons, which are not, and of which there are only three.

The first eon corresponds to the time when the Temple was still standing. It was characterized by the Jew's ability to fulfill the covenant in its entirety. Since we have seen that the covenant then implied first and foremost the Jew's relationship to the Land of Israel, the first era was said to have been typified by full compliance with God's agricultural statutes. Unlike the other two eras, this first one does not receive one universally acknowledged Hebrew term in our early sources. But later, Maimonides described it as being represented symbolically by the Sabbatical Year (*shemitah*), and the Jubilee Year (the *yovel*).[12] Following him, it becomes convenient for us to call this first era the *Yovel*, or, if we prefer an English title, Time-Past.

The Temple's fall ended the *Yovel*, along with its characteristically idyllic circumstances of successful harvesting and cultic appearances before the priest. A new age, *Zeman Hazeh*, or Time-Now, had begun. All the commandments had now to be reconsidered and reformulated, some of them relegated to Time-Past, others reshaped for the exigencies of Time-Now. To take Passover as an example, offering the paschal lamb at the Temple, a central command of Time-Past, was no longer possible. The alternative of offering it outside the Temple, though possible in fact, was deemed illegal in theory.[13] In its place, however, Jews could observe the commandment to talk about the Exodus and to ritualize its occurrence through symbolic verbal presentation. Thus there arose our Passover seder, with its complex order of events, including, eventually, an entire book of readings, the Haggadah, to direct the retelling.

If the first epoch or *Yovel* was Time-Past, and the second or *Zeman Hazeh* is Time-Now, the third epoch, known variously as *Olam Haba* or *Yemot Hamashiach*, corresponds to Time-to-Come. The rabbis viewed Time-to-Come as the much anticipated end of Time-Now, the period in which the halcyon existence of the best of Time-Past would arrive anew. It is variously likened to the Garden of

Eden all over again, the triumph of justice and right, or the messianically induced reestablishment of the Temple and its cult, among other things. Not much detail about the exact nature of Time-to-Come is postulated with any degree of universal consensus, except, of course, that it would indeed come. In the meantime one was to settle down to fulfill the commandments relevant to Time-Now and thereby hasten the day of that coming.

Given this attitude toward time, it is not surprising that rabbinic literature has relatively little to say about the picayune details of this or that historical event. Historians today are frustrated in the extreme by the paucity of historical information left behind by the rabbis of old. They simply do not seem to have cared enough about Time-Now to have recorded its day-to-day events that we call history. Rather, they fixed their gaze on Time-to-Come, working out the minute details of the obligations inherent in Time-Now upon which the successful arrival of Time-to-Come depended. *Mitsvot* (commandments), not history, occupied their time.[14]

This blind eye to chronology marks the rabbis' redrawing of the sacred myth. The chronological succession of individual years is relatively insignificant; the normal constraints of time are absent; for the rabbis, Jewish sacred myth could draw on the enormous richness of biblical and postbiblical personalities and events, juxtaposing them according to legend and will rather than actual chronological facts. The rabbis stated this new ahistorical principle expressly: "ein mukdam ume'uchar batorah" (The events of Torah do not follow chronological succession).[15] True, in the synagogue, the Torah was read in successive weekly portions from start to finish, but this was probably due to the desire that not one word of the Pentateuch be omitted from the reading cycle.[16] The prophetic passages, or Haftarah readings, on the other hand, were freely assigned to the various Torah portions with absolutely no chronological or historical concern. One skips back and forth among the prophets from week to week, without even any necessary knowledge of which prophet one is reading or the historical circumstances he was addressing.

On the holidays, both Torah and Haftarah readings were selected according to mythological rather than chronological principles, or even according to verbal cues inherent in the lexical similarities between passages. Thus, for example, Rosh Hashanah, the day when God attends to Israel's sins and merits, was marked by reading the story of God's visiting Sarah and assuring her pregnancy with Isaac (Gen. 21); and the accompanying Haftarah passage is the parallel conception of Samuel. Yom Kippur, the Day of Atonement, included two readings: Lev. 16, which describes the scapegoat ceremony by which atonement was achieved in Temple days (Time-Past), and Lev. 20, which lists biblical incest taboos, the violation of which we may see as constituting a particularly heinous category of sin, and therefore worthy of inclusion on Yom Kippur day.

Under the influence of rabbinic liturgical legislation, a unique view of history was popularized, particularly in the holiday lectionaries. It deserves our attention, because the rabbinic sacred myth goes hand in hand with it, and, as we shall see, when modern culture forced the confrontation with history, the rabbinic myth quickly collapsed.

History, or what we shall call "historical time," takes place in the middle eon, Time-Now, or *Zeman Hazeh*. This rabbinic conception of historical time is quite different from our system, which is congruent with chronological time. Segments of chronological time (say, Tuesday or Thursday, or 2:00 until 3:00, or 1981) are all essentially the same. They are arbitrarily chosen, neutral time slots that are filled by the events that, either by chance or by prior planning, occur within them.[17] Segments of Jewish time, on the other hand, are not all the same. Times of year are not neutral vessels in which anything might happen, but recapitulations of recurrent themes and paradigmatic events that mark human existence. The synagogue worshiper who listens faithfully to the Torah and Haftarah readings reexperiences a series of existential crises that are built inalterably into specific time frames. Seasons have unique associative feeling tones, depending on the quality of their "time." The synagogue readings tell worshipers the nature of the "time," and whether one is preparing for its arrival, experiencing it, or thinking retrospectively about it.

A good example is the period from the seventeenth day of the Hebrew month of Tammuz (late summer) to the festival of Sukkot (early fall). On the seventeenth of Tammuz, the Romans are said to have breached the Temple walls; three weeks later they completed the destruction. Liturgically, this introduces the grand theme of sin and punishment (or atonement), and thus leads up to Yom Kippur and Sukkot. We are judged for our sins on the former, and (according to tradition) the world is judged for rain on the latter.[18]

Thus the three Sabbaths between the seventeenth of Tammuz and the ninth of Av present Haftarah selections that emphasize prophetic visions of doom. But the closing hours of the ninth of Av spare the worshiper from complete despair by mandating a Torah reading emphasizing God's abiding love and mercy and the eternality of the covenant with Israel. The next Sabbath presents Second Isaiah's words of comfort, spoken to Babylonian exiles following the first Temple's destruction: "Take comfort, take comfort, my people."

The lectionary for the next seven Sabbaths displays a dialogue between God and Israel, mediated by the prophets. Israel will argue that comfort is impossible in the face of such dire destruction. God will emphasize the magnitude of divine compassion. This theme blends naturally into the High Holy Day period, which arrives at the end of the dialogue. One reads equally then of human atonement and of divine grace.[19]

The Jonah story, read on Yom Kippur afternoon, typifies this message. The prophet Jonah is charged with urging the Ninevites to atone for their sins or face divine retribution. The Ninevites represent humanity at large who have sinned and must atone (lesson one). God duly forgives them (lesson two). But Jonah too represents each and every human being. In vain, he tries to flee from God's scrutiny (a restatement of lesson one, in that people must not think that they can substitute escape from judgment for sincere atonement). But God understands Jonah's human weakness. Patiently, God explains to Jonah how foolish he has been and then forgives him (lesson two).

This message of sin followed by atonement or punishment is emphasized also by the readings on the Sabbaths before and after Yom Kippur, the former even being known as *Shabbat Shuvah*, the Sabbath of Repentance, a name borrowed from the opening word of the Haftarah for the day, "Return [O Israel to the Lord your God . . .]" (Hos. 14). And Sukkot, the festival that follows Yom Kippur by only five days, builds climactically to a final restatement of this theme. The Torah reading for each of its eight days consists of a reminder of the sacrifices due to God. The service is punctuated by outbursts of *Hoshiah Na* (God, please save us!). The final Haftarah depicts Solomon harmoniously reconciling God and Israel: "Let your heart be whole with the Lord your God," he tells Israel, and, "May God be with us, as was the case with our ancestors."

So liturgically, the specificity of historical event was blurred into a series of general statements about the quality of historical time as such. We have surveyed only the liturgical reminders for one season, but the same theme dominates the liturgy of the others as well. The macrocosmic message of Time-Past, Time-Now, and Time-to-Come is reduced to the specificity of the worshipers' own personal lives: if they sin, they incur suffering; if they repent, they are saved. That is to say, the sins of Time-Past resulted in the destruction of the Temple, and thus, the onset of Time-Now, and the relationship between sin and punishment that that event revealed, becomes paradigmatic for each and every historical episode thereafter. But keeping the commandments guarantees that some day, Time-Now will end, and the grandeur of Time-Past will be reinstated as Time-to-Come.

Until modern times, this message was repeated again and again. Jews saw every historical event as fitting this paradigm. The second Temple had been destroyed on Tish'a B'av, the ninth day of Av, because of Jewish iniquity. But not just the second Temple, alone; the first Temple too had been leveled then; and the same day centuries later witnessed the expulsion of the Jews from Spain. History within Time-Now was thus repetitive; it was cyclical; it was a redundant restatement of the sorry state of affairs that ended Time-Past in the first place. It was hardly necessary, therefore, to differentiate the accidental details of each and every Ninth of Av catastrophe. From the perspective of Jewish sacred myth, one could integrate the new into the old without changing the old, since the new was just the old revisited.[20]

So the message of sacred myth throughout the Middle Ages remained largely

what it had been when the rabbis redrew it in the first few centuries: a moral
message of the meaning implicit in history. One sins and is punished. But one
atones and obeys God, and one waits for Time-to-Come.

I do not mean to imply that at *all* times between antiquity and modernity
Jewish myth remained *entirely* the same. If one looks carefully, one sees modi-
fications grafted onto the basic theme by this or that historical experience; new
glories and new nadirs alike were integrated into consciousness and expressed in
such mechanisms as synagogue poetry that could be added to the liturgy at the
relevant season. And sometimes one reads of a challenge to this model into
which all events were fitted. But overall, the scheme remained the same, as did
the paradigmatic expressions of it. History per se ended with the demise of Time-
Past and its indelible example of divine punishment, the Temple's destruction.
From then on, one sees at best alterations on a theme, the filtering of an old
message of the way things are through the medium of the latest tragedy or the
most recent example of glory.

Jewish liturgy, then, expanded mightily through the centuries, but, as has
often been remarked, there is a sort of sameness to it, an abundance of verbiage
without a corresponding degree of thematic expansion. That is because the theme
remained standard. Only the expressions of it changed. We may indeed study
these novel expressions for the richness of the metaphors into which the old
moral was cast. And just as the study of all the impressionistic painters of the last
hundred years is surely more rewarding than a study of just one of them (or
worse, a study of impressionism in the abstract as a conceptual method), so a
study of all the strata of liturgical formulations of the rabbinic myth would be an
enriching experience in its own right. But it would not alter the message common
to them all: the moral of a covenant broken by Israel, sin punished by God,
atonement and performance of *mitsvot* leading to renewed wholeness in the
messianic future of Time-to-Come.

Two examples of the sacred myth's presentation recommend themselves for
our attention. They are excellent illustrations of both the rabbinic time-scheme
and the timeless moral of Jewish history. Both received extensive liturgical
attention throughout the Middle Ages. And both form significant sections of the
liturgy today. We will return to a study of the liturgical presentations of today's
sacred myth in the following chapter, with the appreciation that derives from a
prior look at these two ritualized recitations that modern Jews inherited.

Our first example then will be the answer, given to those assembled around the
seder table, to the question "Why is this night different from all other nights?"

THE SACRED MYTH AND THE SEDER

The Exodus from Egypt had always figured prominently in the sacred myth. As
we saw above, it was central to the Deuteronomic perspective, prescribed for

recitation in that book's twenty-sixth chapter. But even one hundred years before the book of Deuteronomy was composed, the prophet Amos was already able to assume that his listeners in the Kingdom of Israel to the north would recognize the Exodus as a pivotal event in Israel's history. He used it freely as a backdrop against which to contrast political events in that kingdom. "[God] brought you out of the land of Egypt, and led you forty years in the wilderness to possess the land of the Amorite," he says (Amos 2:10). The wilderness experience is thus a determinative foil against which to judge Amos's own age, so that to know what God wants, Israel need but look to that formative period, before God's people were "at ease in Zion . . . secure in the mountain of Samaria" (Amos 6:1). "Did you bring Me sacrifices and offerings in the wilderness?" God wants to know (Amos 5:25). The chosen people are no better than the Ethiopians or the Arameans, in the eyes of God. All three are God's peoples because all had a comparable "Exodus" of their own. "Have I not brought Israel up out of the land of Egypt?/And the Philistines from Caphtor?/And Aram from Kir?" (Amos 9:7).

With the Exodus looming so large in Israel's historical memory, it is no surprise to find that the eve of Passover was established from the earliest of days as a primary opportunity to recollect the community's sacred origins. But we lack detail about pre-rabbinic times. We hear that Passover was kept by Joshua (Josh. 5:10) and then, much later, by Hezekiah (2 Chron. 30), Josiah (2 Kings 23:21–23) and Ezra (Ezra 6:19–22). But no standardized liturgical recitation is recorded in any of these cases.[21] True, the Bible says several times to make that night a time of sacred myth-telling. When children ask their elders why that night is different, they are to be told. We must assume, then, that at least since the Deuteronomic reform of the seventh century B.C.E. the sacred myth included the Exodus experience, such that on the annual anniversary of that event Israelites met in a cultic feast and recalled their origins. But no single ritualized recitation of that recollection yet existed. The earliest Passover eves were spent eating the remains of the sacrificial animal offered up earlier that afternoon (the paschal lamb, that is) and discussing the sacred myth with those in attendance in a rather unstructured and general way.

The sacrificial element in the celebration remained foremost for centuries. Even by the end of the second century, some 130 years after sacrifice had ceased, the Mishnah recalls Passover as a cultic festival, primarily, and allots but one of ten chapters to the home seder liturgy. But the Mishnah's recollection is highly unrepresentative of what was already the dominant practice of holding the entire evening's celebration at home. We saw above that Shavuot, originally a harvest festival, was transformed into an anniversary of standing at Sinai and receiving the Torah. Similarly, Passover too was altered, not in its central focus perhaps— it still remained the time of freedom from Egyptian slavery—but in its mode of presentation.

Thus while the Exodus remained primary, the seder ceremony exploring it had changed. With the new rabbinic institution came a new rabbinic memory as well. The recollection of having been freed some 1300 years before was outfitted with the rabbis' moral of Jewish history. In a variety of ways, Egypt became every enemy; Pharaoh personified every foe; God's entry into history that one time to effect salvation for Israel was seen as paradigmatic for all times, including the end of Time-Now (whenever that long awaited event might arrive). And Passover's message of eternal hope was summarized in a single phrase, applicable to history in general—*matchil bigenut umesayem beshevach*—a phrase to which we shall return in the following chapter, but which, for the meantime, we can render according to the convenient paraphrase in the current Reform Haggadah, that is, "From Degradation to Dignity."[22]

The collapse of history into a single repetitive model, of which the Exodus is paradigmatic, is writ large in the seder's symbols. The four cups of wine, for example, have been outfitted with interpretations demonstrating how history follows a single recurrent pattern. A fourth-century Palestinian account correlates the four cups with the fact that Exodus 6 employs four different Hebrew words to describe God's deliverance: *vehotseti* ("I will bring [you] out," Exod. 6:6); *vehitsalti* ("I will deliver [you]," Exod. 6:6); *vega'alti* ("I will save [you]," Exod. 6:6); *velakachti* ("I will take [you]," Exod. 6:7). Each word is assumed now to stand for a different instance of Jewish redemption. With their four cups of wine, seder participants relive these four once-distinct historical eras, each unique chronologically, but all the same in terms of their common historical pattern. Rabbinic opinion differs on the precise identification of these eras, but that very openness to difference well illustrates the fact that precisely their arbitrary leveling of historical reality allows the rabbis to eschew historical precision. Their goal is not to fill in a historical time line, but to demonstrate a new myth: Jewish history is a cycle, in which God destroys one tyrannical empire after another, Egypt, Babylonia, Persia, Greece, and finally—by extension into the future—the most recent foe, Rome, at which time all evil will have been requited, and Time-to-Come will have arrived.[23]

The new myth extending Egypt to Rome is particularly evident in the answer provided for the seder's four questions. The ritualistic inclusion of questions was itself relatively new, a practice borrowed from the Greco-Roman symposium tradition, according to which rhetorical questions were used to prompt the topic for the evening's after-dinner discussion.[24] Contrary to Jewish custom today, the number and content of the questions still varied in those early years, as did the identity of the participant asking them. Whatever they were in any individual case, these questions always fulfilled the general function of evoking the recognition that Passover night is different in essence from all other nights.

We should think for a moment of what the stock answer might have been.

Without a novel conception of history, in which diverse events centuries apart are envisioned together as part of a pattern, the rabbis might simply have summed up the biblical story itself. The Bible is clear, after all, about why this night is different. The rabbis could well have repeated the story verbatim or, at least, just chosen selectively from it, much as the farmers had done when they brought their first fruits to Jerusalem. It is precisely this strategy that the modern American Reform *Union Haggadah* of 1923 adopted. Having rediscovered history as a chronological reckoning of "fact," this modern Haggadah portrays its authors' constraint to find an answer strictly in historical terms.

But the rabbis were not so constrained. They resorted to one of their own characteristic literary genres: midrash. The very form of midrash is conceivable only from that perspective which we have been describing here. The historical events of the Bible always transcend themselves to signify a grander message applicable to history as a whole. Midrash then is an exegetical interpretation of the biblical account, designed to illustrate the latter's "real" timeless meaning. It was through midrash that the paradise of the Garden of Eden could be transformed to refer to the future paradise of Time-to-Come. Only through midrash could Elijah, David, and Miriam carry on conversations with one another as if they had inhabited one single generation and, through their conversations, reveal the essential similarities of all of Jewish history in Time-Now. "From Degradation to Dignity"; Time-Past, Time-Now, Time-to-Come; covenant, sin, chastisement; atonement, hope, salvation—these are the grand themes of the new myth, explored regularly in discourses that weave together biblical narrative and midrashic embellishment in the rituals of rabbinic Judaism. These are the themes of the myth that constitute the answer at the seder.

Of all the narratives in the Bible, the one most familiar to people at the end of the first century was the one they had recited for centuries, when they and, before them, their ancestors, brought their first fruits to the Temple priest. This is the farmer's confession that we examined above. Beginning with those forebears who wandered through Canaan and eventually migrated to Egypt, it summarized concisely the enslavement and redemption of the Israelites, and it concluded with their entry into the land of promise. That familiar ritualistic résumé was now transferred to the seder, where it constituted the basis of the answer to the questions. So this account became the core of the Haggadah, accompanied, however, by midrashic exposition.

The midrash under discussion appears in part not only in the Haggadah texts that have come down to us, but also in two midrash collections. The first, described as being of tannaitic (pre-200) origin, is Midrash *Sifre* to the book of Deuteronomy. But we find also a parallel text in the medieval compendium known to us as *Midrash Hagadol*. This latter collection dates from the twelfth century, but it is the opinion of David Hoffmann, the nineteenth-century re-

searcher of this work, that strata within it date actually to the first two centuries
C.E. He therefore isolated those earlier units, calling them *Midrash Tannaim*, and
included our Deuteronomy midrash in his collection.[25]

Full philological comparisons of texts thus utilize three main sources: *Sifre*,
Midrash Tannaim, and the various versions of Haggadah texts extant, most
especially the Genizah fragments known to us. Since philology seeks to discover
the *Urtext*, one would have hoped that by now we would be able to point to some
consensus regarding the relative age of the Haggadah midrash in question. Unfortunately, no such consensus exists.

Our standard effort to date the midrash belongs to Louis Finkelstein, who
explains it as an anti-Seleucid polemic by Jews living under Ptolemaic rule in the
third century B.C.E.[26] (Thus, for example, its accent on an unidentified Aramean
being worse than Pharaoh is interpreted as a veiled comparison between the
Seleucid monarchy, which was situated in biblical Aram, and the Egyptian
Ptolemies.) Despite the many problems with this reconstruction, to which later
scholarship has pointed, Finkelstein's solution has been practically canonized in
tertiary literature, so that it is by far the best known of all attempts to explain the
text's genesis. It reappears, for example, in the popular commentary of Nahum
Glatzer,[27] as well as in a recent Ph.D. dissertation on the music of the seder,
where it is simply assumed to be correct.[28]

Yet for most scholars today, E. D. Goldschmidt's trenchant critique has rendered Finkelstein's account barely tenable.[29] This seems an especially apt conclusion on its own grounds (which are well known and need not be reproduced
here), but especially so when one adds to Goldschmidt's analysis the realization
that Finkelstein has predated the midrashic genre of literature by several hundred
years prior to any other independently known instance of its appearance. If he is
right, our midrash would have to be viewed as the single remaining record of that
literature until some time after the turn of the common era.

Goldschmidt's alternative, however, is to see our text as an exceptionally late
post-talmudic redaction of earlier material, and I find this solution equally unconvincing. To cite but one difficulty, the Talmud does indeed contain parallel
material, as Goldschmidt demonstrates, but it is not clear (as Goldschmidt would
have it) why we should conclude that these talmudic parallels must precede our
midrashic one in time of composition. Goldschmidt's view is colored by his
insistence on treating the problem as a case of two textual (*sic*) remnants deserving philological analysis. In fact, we have only one case of text (the Talmud and
associated literary remains), and one ritual (!), an original seder practice that
only eventually is enshrined in textual format. The parallel midrashic version in
Sifre lacks some of the remarks that our Haggadah recension contains, but it does
not follow (as Goldschmidt claims) that these missing comments were not already orally present as part of the preliterary seder celebration. Similarly, the fact

that a comparison of Laban and Pharaoh (with which our text begins) is found elsewhere in written form only as late as the Babylonian Talmud does not entail our postdating the idea itself until that time; unless, of course, we assume, gratuitously, that ritual does not contain a life of its own, with its own rehearsal of oral (!) lore. Surely no field anthropologist would concur with such an assumption, which so flies in the face of every bit of evidence gathered from rituals around the world. Only philologists, mistakenly lumping all extant texts into the domain of literature, could make the error of assuming that because their written evidence is literary, they must be studying literature from the very beginning. In sum, Goldschmidt is clearly correct when he notes that the *Haggadah text* as we have it is not known to us before a ninth-century Babylonian source (*Seder Rav Amram*); but he is wrong to assume summarily that there could not have been an *oral ritual* passed on for centuries in that form, long before being recorded in writing.

When, then, should we date this lore in its original oral form? The original Mishnah passage (Bikkurim 3:6), which mandates the recitation of Deut. 26 at the time of harvesting one's first fruits, still uses the Hebrew word *korei*, this being the verb found also in Deuteronomy's own stipulation that our passage be "read." So as late as 70, but not later, the Bikkurim ritual included a mere biblical recitation without any midrashic elaboration, as, in fact, we would expect in a cultic pre-rabbinic rite. But the Mishnah's instructions regarding the seder clearly stipulate that one is to *doresh*, that is, to accompany the biblical reading with some sort of midrashic interpretation (M. Pes. 10:4). So at some time before the Mishnah's compilation about the year 200, some kind of midrash was common here. The only question is whether it was our own. Not that we may expect a single midrashic account to have been canonized yet; but by the end of the first century, the thematic progression of liturgical rubrics had largely been set, so it is not beyond the realm of probability that the midrashic ideas, if not their precise wording, for the seder account had been fixed as well. After all, nowhere has an alternative seder midrash been discovered; whatever we have consists of variations on this one. So I would conclude that though there was no single original midrash in the sense of a canonized *Urtext*, there did exist the practice of rehearsing orally the overall lessons that we now have in the diverse written forms to which the originally oral ritual was eventually reduced. Different forms of the lesson were thus ultimately embedded in Genizah fragments, and so on.

Its origin should be placed before the Mishnah's promulgation, but probably not before 70. The *terminus ad quem* derives from the inclusion of the verb *doresh* in the Mishnaic account; the *terminus a quo* is based on several facts: first, the utilization of *korei* in the pre-70 Bikkurim rite, but also the fact that the midrash is unknown to the authors of the synoptic Gospels and to Josephus, who are alike in that they describe seders known to them in the first few decades after the destruction. If the midrash was inaugurated in the last decade or two of that century, it would still not have become universal to the point where these authors (writing in various places, but not in the center of rabbinic life at Yavneh) would know of it. But a custom from predestruction days would have been common knowledge, so that we would expect these sources to record it.

Within this time frame (70–200), we can achieve no certainty, but a probable candidate for authorship is Rabban Gamaliel II, or members of his circle, since so much liturgical activity is known to have emanated from there.[30] In any case, if the dating parameters are correct, the midrash might well reflect late first- or second-century circumstances, involving the aftermath of unsuccessful conflicts with Rome, and the tasks of postwar reconstruction.

That part of our midrash seems to presuppose issues under debate in that period, is clear. Deut. 26:8, "The Lord brought us forth out of Egypt," elicits the following interpretation:

"The Lord brought us forth . . .": Not by the hands of an angel, nor by the hands of a Seraph, nor by the hands of a messenger, but the Holy One blessed be He, in His own glory, and by Himself. . . .

What we have may be an instance of the Jewish-Christian debate regarding the existence of a mediator between God and Israel in the events leading up to the revelation at Sinai. Reuven Kimelman summarizes the matter from his own perspective, the somewhat later argumentation of Origen and Rabbi Johanan, and demonstrates how central the dispute was to the determination of the relative merit of the Sinaitic covenant. He refers to "the Pauline argument in favor of the subordination of the Sinaitic revelation by virtue of its having been transmitted through angels and a mediator."[31] If his third-century protagonists are correct in predating their own controversy to Pauline days, then at least this latter segment of our midrash can be understood against the backdrop of the late first century, and the question becomes whether the rest of it also can. If so, we would be in a position to see how the sacred myth of the pre-70 farmer was adumbrated for post-70 conditions by a midrashic extension.

Unfortunately, it is the nature of midrashic text that it is never open to a single plausible interpretation. Its very success as a literary device depends on its essential nonspecificity of denotation: its ability to transcend single time frames and to juxtapose biblical and postbiblical statements without explicit identifications of the persons, places, and events to which it is referring. Precisely this inherent ambiguity underlies Finkelstein's interpretation of its message as relating to Ptolemaic-Seleucid rivalries in an earlier age. So we may not reasonably hope to achieve absolute certainty in extracting the historical midrashic reference. But we should be able to show, at least, that it is not incompatible with what we know from the late first century, and, in fact, that the midrash becomes newly intelligible in the light of first-century social, political, economic, and spiritual realities. We have already shown that to be the case with regard to the interpretation of Deut. 26:8 as implying the absence of intermediaries in God's dealings with Israel, and can turn now to the rest of the midrash to expand on that demonstration.

Not every line of the midrash deserves equal attention. We ought first to differentiate those parts whose *structure* suggests the probable presence of contextual significance from those whose structure does not. Only the former should be assumed to contain references to the time and place whence they originate.

The style in which this midrash presents itself generally obeys the following pattern. We have first the citation of a verse or part of a verse to be expounded. Let us call this scriptural text "ST." The rabbinic exegesis ("RE") to ST generally follows the verse in question, often with an introductory demonstrative pronoun, like *zeh* or *elu*, "this" or "these" (referring to the verse about to be explained, and functionally equivalent to "i.e."). And the exegesis is often demonstrated at the end of the lesson with a supportive biblical proof text from elsewhere in scripture, itself introduced (frequently) by *shene'emar*, " . . . as it is said." We call the proof text "PT." Of the three elements, our interest lies in the exegesis. It is there that the rabbis go out of their way to add explicit meaning to the bare scriptural account under discussion.

For several verse fragments, no such exegesis is present. We have instead just ST followed by PT, a verse in question illustrated by the supportive evidence of another verse. That no new information is conveyed in such a laconic communication did not prevent the rabbis from resorting to it. Midrash was a linguistic conceit with its own aesthetics of form, and the form itself is often found without a corresponding presence of content. Other formal devices are present as well. Biblical verses frequently display a string of words in apposition to one another; from the rabbinic perspective, according to which God speaks with absolute economy of utterance, each separate term in the list must have its own meaning. Routinely, then, the rabbis stop to refer each term to its own significand, not (it should be emphasized) because they have any particular lesson to teach in the isolation of these separate significands, but just because their assumptions regarding scripture entail their existence and mandate the rabbis' efforts to note what they may be. Thus, if the scriptural text includes 3 discrete terms, which we may identify in the form of ST(A, B, C), their rabbinic exegesis will necessarily assign each of them its own meaning of the form RE(A, B, C). Using the introductory marker of *zeh* (i.e.), we get:

ST(A,B,C): *zeh* RE(A,B,C)

usually cited (via a sort of midrashic law of isomorphic distribution) in its long form as:

ST(A): *zeh* RE(A)
ST(B): *zeh* RE(B)
ST(C): *zeh* RE(C)

What I wish to argue is that in our attempt to arrive at the identification of the midrashic context, all such purely formal midrashic exegeses be passed over. That is because, though purely formal linguistic operations may carry semantic messages, it is equally possible that they do not, and there is no way for us to judge which is the case. It is equally likely that the content of any one of them— i.e., RE(A), RE(B), or RE(C), in the purely formal operation of converting from ST(A,B,C) to RE(A,B,C)—is fortuitous, just a relatively mechanical attempt at filling in the formal framework with a term that qualifies for selection merely because it fits requirements of form, but not of content.

For example, Deut. 26:7 says that God "saw our affliction, our toil, and our oppression." Since the three objects of the verb "saw" are in apposition, they can be converted formally to:

1. ["Our affliction": *this* is the separation of husband and wife, *as it is written*, "God saw the people of Israel, and God knew their plight" (Exod. 2:25)] = [ST(A): *zeh* RE(A) *shene'emar* PT(A)].
2. ["Our toil": *this* is the sons cast into the Nile, *as it is written*, "Every son that is born of the Hebrews, you shall throw into the Nile" (Exod. 1:22)] = [ST(B): *zeh* RE(B) *shene'emar* PT(B)].
3. ["Our oppression": *this* is persecution, *as it is written*, "I have seen how the Egyptians are oppressing you" (Exod. 3:9)] = [ST(C): *zeh* RE(C) *shene'emar* PT(C)].

It is clear, I think, that we have only a series of formal operations here, in which nouns in apposition are assigned their own particular denotations. If we consider them each as potentially distinctive linguistic signs, we can say that the particular significands (Saussure's signifiés) are being fixed. The words *zeh* and *shene'emar* ("this" and "as it is written," literally, "as it is said") constitute formal markers to demonstrate the parameters of the phrase structure within the sentence's syntax, the former introducing the Rabbinic Exegesis (RE), and the latter prefacing the Proof Text (PT).

The three significands are worth some attention too, since from the perspective of the additional information they provide, they are by no means equivalent in quality. Only the second (B) actually provides specificity drawn from a closer reading of the biblical text: for the general term "toil" we get the replacement of "the sons cast into the Nile," a reference to an explicit detail drawn from the book of Exodus. The first term (A) adds specificity too, but this time it is *not* from the biblical account itself. Nothing in the Proof Text PT(A) points ostensibly to the Rabbinic Exegesis RE(A) at all, and the information conveyed, that is, the idea of conjugal separation, is unknown to the biblical author. The very reference to "separation of husband and wife" is sufficiently novel here and (as it stands) vague, as to evoke consternation, unless one is familiar with the rabbinic literature elsewhere, notably, the Babylonian Talmud, Sotah 12a,[32] where we learn that Moses' own father had reacted to Pharaoh's decrees concerning the ultimate death of male children by refusing to continue having sexual relations with his wife. This must be the "separation" of which the Rabbinic Exegesis RE(A) speaks.

The midrashic treatment of the third term, "oppression," is different still, in that it adds no new information whatever. One Hebrew word of debatable meaning, *lachatz* (translated here as "oppression"), is replaced by another, equally ambiguous, one, *dechak* (translated as "persecution"), and coupled with a Proof Text PT(C) that does not even contain the second term to which the first term is supposed to point.

Looking at all three (A, B, and C), we can say that, unless we attend to the underlying difference in kinds of signification attached to each term (in which A would be specific-rabbinic, B would be specific-biblical, and C would be non-specific), there seems to be no necessary logic at all to the selection, or (in this case, though not in others that customarily make up the bulk of similar midrashic word plays) even the allotment of assigned meanings here. It is as if the manifest content of this whole formal exercise were totally arbitrary, merely a necessary linguistic assigning of different significands to appositive terms.

Thus, however possible it may be that some particular lesson lies behind the identification of any single exegetical term, it is equally likely that the entire text has only formal importance, and that the exegetical identifications are arrived at through formal manipulation of linguistic structures alone, ranging from the substitution of one nonspecific term for another (in C), to the reduction of two other general terms to specific meaning, one (B) biblical and the other (A) rabbinic in origin. Even this underlying structural differentiation among the three is probably accidental. Certainly the surface "meaning" of the trifold identification is irrelevant to our purposes, since regardless of there being any structural significance underlying it, there is no reason whatever to insist that the manifest content be probed for a message to those who once read it in the early years of its invention.

So we should decide at the outset that unless we have independent evidence that suggests we should proceed otherwise, we shall limit our investigation to those instances in which the rabbinic exegesis is *not* a predictable result of the formal requirements of midrashic linguistics; we shall look instead for cases where the exegesis is an obvious and explicit interpretation that deviates from the meaning of the scripture it explains, and where that deviation is not traceable to the structure of the rules themselves. An instance of this is the identification of "The Lord brought us forth . . ." as "not by the hand of an angel. . . ." Though of course there is nothing here that would normally have *prevented* the rabbis from interpreting this verse exegetically (so that its interpretation should surprise us), there is also nothing in the formal presentation of the text that demands it either. Their interpretation was apparently freely arrived at. Moreover, it adds information that goes beyond what the text has to say, in that it evokes extraneous doctrines of angelology and divine-human mediation. If we limit our attention to other similar such lessons, we find that they are few indeed. But they are enough to support our tentative dating of the midrash in the closing decades of the first century, and thus to warrant our reconstructing it as a novel sacred myth deriving from the events of that era.

We proceed, therefore, with the assumption that the explicit exegetical comments allude to events that may not be immediately evident to us, who live almost 2000 years after their composition, but that must have been readily recognizable to those for whom they were intended: the Jewish population living through the postwar years of the first and second centuries in war-ravaged Palestine.

To make the message manifest, I have separated the biblical passage itself (ST) from the midrashic (or rabbinic) embellishment (RE). As we have said, only the latter represents the rabbis' addition or alteration of the myth. They could not change the Bible's words, but through their added interpretation, they could shake those words loose from their original context and make them stand for the broader canvas of Jewish history. So I include in the left-hand column only those parts of the biblical paragraph which were outfitted with rabbinic elaboration, and, in the right-hand column, I list the elaboration itself.

Scriptural Text (ST)	*Rabbinic Exegesis (RE)*
A wandering Aramean was my father	Come and learn what Laban the Aramean tried to do to our father Jacob. Pharaoh decreed only against the males, but Laban sought to destroy everyone, as the Bible says, "An Aramean tried to destroy my father."
He went down to Egypt	forced by the word of God
And he dwelt there	This teaches that Jacob our father did not go down to settle permanently in Egypt, but only to settle there temporarily.[33]

Now compare the story as it appears in the two columns. The straightforward biblical version describes an unnamed ancestor or ancestors who came from the land of Aram, east of the Jordan River; after several years of bedouin-like travel through the area's deserts, they arrive in Egypt. That, in fact, is a reasonably accurate personified approximation of Israelite prehistory, the memory of its origins.

The midrashic version is more convoluted. The first and most complex clue is the strange introduction into the tale of an entirely unrelated biblical personality, Jacob's father-in-law, Laban. Though Jacob came from Aram, so too did Laban, so the midrash (for reasons yet to be described) identifies the Aramean in the sentence "My father was a wandering Aramean" as none of the patriarchs at all, but as Laban. Moreover, as the midrash understands it, the words "my father" and "Laban" do not even refer to the same person. And the verb "wandering" has been deliberately misread according to a pun in the original Hebrew, so that instead of "wandering," we have "tried to destroy." In algebraic notation:

My father [A] was a wandering Aramean [B]
    that is, A = B

which is inverted, so that it becomes

An Aramean [B] tried to destroy my father [A]
    that is, B (action against) A

in which B = Laban, and A = Jacob.

Our myth has thus been altered so as to begin with a recollection of Laban the Aramean, who disliked his son-in-law Jacob so much that he sought to kill him. The remarkable fact about this new identification of the Aramean as Laban is that it seems at cross-purposes with the night dedicated to remembering Pharaoh and Egypt, not Laban and Aram.

Why did the rabbis go to such lengths to identify the Aramean as the culprit of the story? Laban is certainly no hero in the bare biblical account, but he is hardly worse than the mythic arch-foe, Pharaoh. However, the rabbis obviously wished to portray him that way here, so they invoke the interpretive capacity of midrashic exegesis to apply the circumstances of their own day to their understanding of the sacred myth. Before turning to those circumstances, however, we require further analysis of Jacob's role in it.

As we get to Jacob, then, we note first of all that his willing rush to Egypt in order to flee the famine on one hand and to rediscover his long-lost son Joseph on the other goes unrecognized and even denied in the midrash, which knows nothing about the biblical Jacob, who went down to Egypt because he was hungry, or of his lost son Joseph, who invited him there. We are told instead that he went only because God forced him to do so through some divine decree. And, though he obeyed God's word, he went only to settle temporarily. Again the rabbis take remarkable liberties with the biblical account. The reality is that Jacob and his sons settled permanently in their new home, filled as it was with plenty, and close as they were to the administrative manager of the largesse, their own kinsman who arranged for them to have ample supply of excellent farming land. As for the divine word that Jacob heard commanding him to overcome his scruples about going to Egypt, the Bible mentions no such word and no such scruples. Why then does the rabbinic version of the Haggadah's answer cast Jacob in the role of hesitant immigrant to Egypt?

The answer to these conundrums can be seen through the recognition that the ritualized rehearsal of liturgical myth fulfills the function of interpreting history for those who celebrate the ritual. Out of the raw data of experience, it selects what matters from what does not. Often, however, there is a given facticity to one's own contemporary experience that cries out to be fit into the myth; for the myth purports to be the meaning of what is. The farmer's myth of Deut. 26:1–11 could explain many vicissitudes of the centuries, but not the destruction of the Temple. So the midrash to that myth can be viewed as part of a larger rabbinic effort to generate a myth that could give meaning to the Temple's demise, as well as to the spiritual and physical emptiness that accompanied it.

The war of 70 had been devastating in more ways than one. The farmers in the northern sector of the country, the Galilee, were to incur their greatest losses only later, in the rebellion of 132–35; but even in 70, it was in the Galilee that the rebellion against Rome had been initiated, and where the Romans had taken quick and severe steps to nip the rising revolt in the bud. The Galilee was the first major territory to fall under the Roman counterattack, with the predictable result that the food supply of the rest of the country was cut off. For three years thereafter, the Romans besieged a starving Jerusalem, and when the war was finally over, the country as a whole suffered from a general famine. Agricultural workers were in short supply now, as many farmers once recruited into the rebel army were missing or dead. The land itself had not been farmed successfully for years, great chunks of it having lain fallow, its farmers away at war, and whole plots wasted by the ravages of marauding soldiers.[34]

The long-range spiritual malaise occasioned by Rome's destruction of the Temple should not be underestimated. But in the immediacy of the war's aftermath, decline of food productivity was the most severely felt crisis, to which at least one ready solution was emigration to countries free from the terrors of war. The ideal new home would be a place in which a long tradition of Jewish settlement bode well for waves of new immigrants coming from economic hardship abroad.

No better haven could have been offered than Egypt, the land from which the Jewish people had once escaped. Since the time of Alexander the Great, Egypt, like Palestine itself, had fallen into the Greek orbit and assimilated Greco-Roman cultural influences by slow but steady osmosis. So considerable was the Jewish population at one point that Jews established their own temple at a local shrine in the vicinity of Leontopolis.[35] The largest city by far was the trading mecca of Alexandria, and in it, by the first century C.E., fully two quarters were full of Jews, Josephus citing their population at seven and one-half million![36] Legend would later declare that the largest synagogue ever erected in the ancient world had been in this same Alexandria; it was so large, said the tales, that ritual signals to stand, or sit, or say "Amen" had to be given by someone waving a banner from a wooden dais (*bimah*) in the center of the room.[37] And fact it was, not just legend, that Alexandria in the first century was the home of outstanding Jewish cultural achievement, including, for example, the philosophy of Philo.

This outstanding city of the diaspora has not received its due in Jewish history books, because of a later sacred myth that selectively perceived the diaspora in such a way as to give priority to other centers of Jewish learning, particularly the one that was just barely under way in Parthian Babylonia, but that would pick up velocity after 135 and eventually achieve prominence under the Sasanians. This Babylonian Jewry traced its ideological roots to Palestine and the Mishnah, and bequeathed successfully to posterity its claim to be a continuation of that brand of Judaism we now call rabbinic. Jews in Egypt, on the other hand, were to achieve prominence more for their Philonic-like exegesis patterned after Greek rhetoric and philosophy. But centuries later, when Jews finally defined who they were, it was rabbinic, not philosophic, Judaism that triumphed. No matter how important philosophy might have been at certain junctures in Jewish history, philosophy was plainly second to rabbinic law and was pursued within the context of rabbinic assumptions about reality. Thus, the major letters, texts, memoirs, and literary works generally that were handed down throughout the centuries were rabbinic in the first instance, and Babylonian in the second. It eventually became common for Jews everywhere, even in Egypt itself (then going through a renaissance under Moslem suzerainty) to imagine that Jewish authority had passed naturally from the second-century Palestinian rabbis to Babylonian continuers. When one spoke of the beginnings of the diaspora, therefore, one remembered proud days in Babylonian academies, while passing over equally significant times in first-century Alexandria.

But in the aftermath of the war against Rome, Alexandria was an ideal diasporan community,[38] and in this context, the midrashically modified version of the story of Jacob became exemplary. He too had suffered from a drought. And he had left the Holy Land with barely a thought, pursuing his own personal welfare. Was that attractive opportunity to be pursued with equal alacrity by Palestinian Jews in the first century? Many Palestinians answered in the affirmative, quickly deciding to exchange the war-ravished family homestead for a new life in Alexandria.[39] But Palestinian rabbinic leaders, intent on rebuilding their society at home, looked with disfavor on emigration. It was this opposition to abandoning the Land of Israel that the midrashic commentary to Deut. 26 portrays.

Lest you think Jacob went down to Egypt willingly, even in the severity of the seven-year famine, went the story now, learn that he agreed to leave the Holy Land only because God forced him to. And even then, he intended only to sojourn there for a while, never to settle in Egypt permanently. Jews reciting this account on Passover eve were thus informed that their obligation lay with the rabbis of Palestine, rebuilding the glory of God's intended homeland for Israel, not escaping temporary worldly ravages for the equally worldly luxuries of places like Alexandria.

More amazing still was the myth's perception of Pharaoh, whose description, we will recall, actually compared favorably with a certain Aramean who sought in vain to destroy all of Israel, Pharaoh's evil intent having been directed only at the death of males. Why should an Aramean, not Pharaoh, figure as the villain of the tale, especially on the night of the Exodus from Pharaoh's Egypt? Here, the answer lay in the Hebrew word for Aramean, *'Arami*. In Hebrew script of the time, the word would have appeared consonantally as 'RMI, with the vowels being supplied by the reader. Regularly, as part of the midrash exercise, Jews were invited to read their unvocalized scriptural verses with a creative supplying of vocalization other than that actually intended. In this case, the rabbis were reading 'RMI not as *'Arami* but as *R'omi*, "a Roman."[40] The message was, then, that worse even than Pharaoh was the evil Roman emperor who hoped to wipe out the Jews completely. But he only intended it. He failed, as Laban failed, and as all enemies would fail, if Jews would only remain faithful to their covenant with God.

Jews now viewed their history in terms of a repetitive motif that remained constant throughout Time-Now. It would someday end, but only with the ultimate victory of Time-to-Come. Pharaoh had failed; so too had Rome. God would someday reward hope, patience, and faithfulness by bringing final redemption. Passover eve was now outfitted with a satisfactory response to the question "Why is this night different?": It was different because on it God entered history to display divine salvation, to end the cycle of slavery due to sin, and to bring about deliverance born of steadfastness. As God redeemed on this night 1200 years ago in Egypt, so too would God redeem again on this night some time in the future.

In sum, in the wake of the Temple's fall, Jewish practice had developed a novel ritual with which to mark the anniversary of the Exodus. Within it, Jews expressed a new sacred myth. Gone was the simple chronological précis of an agricultural people searching for land and crops and eventually finding the Promised Land flowing with milk and honey. Gone too was the cultic obligation of offering produce and animal sacrifices on an altar. Instead, Jews expressed a moral to encapsulate the message of all their history, even the Roman destruction of the Temple. In place of offerings, Jews were asked to hope, to pray, to believe, and to work for the reconstitution of their land in those glorious days that were sure to come when Time-Now gave way to Time-to-Come.

It should be admitted here that the reconstruction of the Haggadah's midrash lacks the certainty of other instances of sacred liturgical myth to be cited in this and the next chapter—and necessarily so, since the text is composed in the somewhat equivocal communication style that is typical of midrash. The rabbis never state explicitly what their midrashic meaning is. Scholars must reconstruct first the context, and then the specific historical allusion, if there is one. Even when we know the earliest appearance of a text, we are still usually not sure we know when to date the composition of a given homily in it. But the explanation offered here is at least compatible with what we know of the late first and early second centuries, and dating our midrash then is at least as logical as any other suggestion in the literature, even though, to be sure, the first *written* record of the *entire* passage is as yet undocumented before the ninth century. But it is not an early *text* that is argued here, but an early *ritual*, the lessons of which are only later transferred to a variety of parallel written textual carriers, ranging from the relatively "incomplete" second/third-century midrash *Sifre* to the "complete" ninth-century *Seder Rav Amram*, that being the earliest appearance of our standardized Haggadah variant.

At any rate, three things, intertwined but separate, are being claimed here; they should not be confused, since a refusal to accept the above interpretation of the midrash in all its detail—as an outcry against emigration after the war of 70, that is—does not negate the validity of the other two points at issue.

First, we have the dating and the interpretation of the midrash, which, as I say, is no more than probable. Second, and more important, however, is the recognition that even though its style varies considerably from the farmer's profession on one hand, and the liturgical examples yet to come on the other, the midrash nevertheless can be understood to *function* identically with the others: all are examples of myth, selective perceptions of sacred histories encoded in liturgical ritual such that participants acknowledge the sacrality of their people's trek through time. Even if one denies the specific meaning of the seder myth that I have proposed here, I hope, at least, that the function of this midrash as liturgical myth is acceptable. One should at least concede the functional similarity between the pilgrim in Temple days affirming the biblical contents of Deut. 26 and the seder participant perhaps a century or so later doing the same thing with the rabbinic explanation of that same biblical passage.

Finally, there is the third point, which, in terms of certainty of demonstration, is somewhere between the other two. I have claimed not only that the midrash is a myth revised by the rabbis to fit their time, and that the specific stimulus for that revision was the war and agrarian failure that followed, but also that the general perspective of their myth went beyond history to postulate a cycle of sin-punishment-atonement-redemption. Rather than history, we have a moral of history here, an interpretive grid to explain all events in Time-Now. The cycle was instituted with the fall of the Temple, and it will end with the coming of the messiah. The myth, then, is both historical, in that it explains the Temple's demise and anticipates the apocalypse, and nonhistorical, in that everything that happens in between is forced into a mold that presupposes the insignificance of what we normally take to be historical evidence.[41]

This third claim was supported first by our discussion of the liturgical lection-ary, and now, by the collapse of normal historical perspective in the symbolism of the seder's four cups of wine, as well as by the midrash that likens Egypt and its Pharaoh to Rome and its emperor. But, as I have said, insofar as midrashic style necessarily encodes ambiguity, the last-mentioned claim cannot be made with certainty.

Fortunately, midrash did not become the favorite vehicle for liturgical com-munication. In fact, the appearance of midrash with as central a liturgical func-tion as we find in the Haggadah is almost an anomaly. Of course, the very term for the liturgical work in which it is so centrally embedded testifies to the fact that the book itself is similarly anomalous, in that it is a "Haggadah," from *lehagid*, "to tell," that is, a ritualistic mechanism for telling a tale, in which it follows that the rabbis' prime means of tale-telling, midrash, would figure prominently. But we are not dependent on the midrash to prove our point. We have ample other evidence (beside the lectionary that we have already looked at) to demon-strate that with the rabbis, the moral of a repetitive historical cycle replaced history itself as the liturgical sacred myth. Two medieval compositions demon-strate this clearly.

THE MIDDLE AGES: *DAYYENU* AND *AVODAH*

By the end of the second century, the sacred myth in midrash form constituted a dramatic-liturgical answer to the question of why seder night differed from other nights. As time went on, this answer was outfitted with a more detailed re-collection of events in Egypt, not just to recall the "facts" of Israel's first and paradigmatic salvation, but to explore in all its fullness the phenomenon of deliverance itself, such deliverance being the final reward promised by the myth.

So the midrash was expanded. In time, it was outfitted with a preface based on a talmudic debate between two third-century *amoraim* regarding the significance of the concept of degradation, in the thematic motif "From Degradation to Dignity"; and even this preface was expanded yet further by a variety of texts, both old and new, some transferred to the liturgy from literary sources that had been recorded centuries before, but that were now rediscovered as appropriate commentary on the expanding Haggadah narrative.[42]

The tale was enlarged in the other direction as well, by a series of addenda tacked onto the *end* of the midrash. The "original" midrash had stopped with the claim that God alone brings deliverance, and then with a reference to, but not a complete listing of, the plagues that deliverance from Egypt entailed. Various words in the final biblical verse that was being expounded (Deut. 26:8) were understood to refer laconically to those plagues, so that without actually naming them, the midrash could conclude, "These [i.e, the relevant biblical words] are the ten plagues which the Holy One brought upon the Egyptians in Egypt." I cite the text below, dividing it into three convenient sections, using terminology in keeping with the analysis above: ST, Scriptural Text; RE, Rabbinic Exegesis; and RE[1], a subsection of RE, its conclusion.

(ST) "The Lord brought us out of Egypt with a mighty hand (*yad chazakah*) and an outstretched arm (*zero'a netuyah*); with great awe (*mora gadol*), signal acts (*otot*) and wonders (*moftim*).''

(RE) [Each two-word phrase or reference in the plural signifies two plagues.] Thus: "mighty hand" (*yad chazakah*)—two; "outstretched arm" (*zero'a netuyah*)—two; "great awe" (*mora gadol*)—two; "signal acts" (*otot*) [plural form, signifying the minimal plural]—two; "wonders" (*moftim*)—[plural again, so] two.
 (RE[1]) These are the ten plagues that God
brought upon the Egyptians in Egypt.[43]

Sometime before the ninth century, however—we do not know exactly when it was—it became customary to specify the ten plagues referred to in the conclusion (RE[1]) and to attach the list via a brief superscription, "And these are they:" (*ve'elu hen*) in such a way. as practically to erase the seam between the earlier conclusion and this later addition to it; so that it now appears as if the entire passage, including the list and its superscription, is original to the midrash, whereas, in actuality, the midrash once ended without the list of plagues, so that the latter constitutes the first of the two major addenda under discussion here. (In the full citation that follows, I have rendered the addition in italics, without, however, lending it a separate lettered denotation, so that its smooth transition from RE[1] is evident.)

(ST) "The Lord brought us out of Egypt with a mighty hand (*yad chazakah*) and an outstretched arm (*zero'a netuyah*); with great awe (*mora gadol*), signal acts (*otot*) and wonders (*moftim*)." . . .

(RE) [Each two-word phrase or reference in the plural signifies two plagues.] Thus: "mighty hand" (*yad chazakah*)—two; "outstretched arm" (*zero'a netuyah*)—two;

"great awe" (*mora gadol*)—two; "signal acts" (*otot*) [plural form, signifying the minimal plural]—two; "wonders" (*moftim*)—[plural again, so] two.

(RE[1]) These are the ten plagues that God brought upon the Egyptians in Egypt. *And these are they*:

1. Blood (dam)
2. Frogs (tsefardeia)
3. Vermin (kinim)
4. Flies (arov)
5. Cattle disease (dever)

6. Boils (shechin)
7. Hail (barad)
8. Locusts (arbeh)
9. Darkness (choshekh)
10. Death of the firstborn (makat bekhorot)[44]

Some people even followed that enumeration by including older (second-century) material that had once been composed without connection to the seder ritual but that discussed the plagues and could therefore be incorporated here as further enlargement of the growing Haggadah text. Continuing where we left off, we thus have:

1. Blood (**dam**)
2. Frogs (**tsefardei'a**)
3. Vermin (**kinim**)
4. Flies (**arov**)
5. Cattle Disease (**dever**)

6. Boils (**shechin**)
7. Hail (**barad**)
8. Locusts (**arbeh**)
9. Darkness (**choshekh**)
10. Death of the Firstborn (**makat bekhorot**)

Rabbi Judah, using the Hebrew initials of the ten plagues, composed three words as an aid to memory:

DTSK, ADSH, BACHB

Rabbi José of Galilee says: You can prove that, after the ten plagues in Egypt, the Egyptians suffered fifty plagues at the Red Sea. About the plagues in Egypt the Torah tells us that "the magicians said to Pharaoh, it is the *finger* of God" (Exod. 8:15). But at the Red Sea the text reads: "Israel saw the great *hand* with which the Lord performed against the Egyptians, and the people revered the Lord: they believed in the Lord and in his servant Moses" (Exod. 14:13). Now, you may say that if by one *finger* of God the Egyptians were made to suffer ten plagues in Egypt, they must have been made to suffer fifty plagues by the *hand* of God at the Red Sea.

Rabbi Eliezer says: You can prove that every plague that God inflicted upon the Egyptians in Egypt was equal to four blows, for it is written: "He sent upon them his blazing anger, wrath and fury and trouble, a band of messengers of evil" (Ps. 78:49). Now, since each plague was composed of 1) wrath, 2) fury, 3) trouble, and 4) a band of messengers of evil, they must have suffered forty plagues in Egypt and two hundred at the Red Sea.

Rabbi Akiba says: You can prove that every plague that God inflicted upon the Egyptians in Egypt was equal to five blows, for it is written: "He sent upon them his blazing anger, wrath, and fury and trouble, a band of messengers of evil." Now, since each plague was composed of 1) blazing anger, 2) wrath, 3) fury, 4) trouble, and 5) a band of messengers of evil, they must have suffered fifty plagues in Egypt and two hundred and fifty at the Red Sea.[45]

The sacred myth was being expanded in bulk, if not in essential content. Its message of timelessness remains. It is so unconcerned with contemporary history that the only way to date the additions is to infer the latest possible time at which they may have been composed from their earliest appearance in manuscripts. Upon reading the various medieval commentaries to the Haggadah, one is similarly struck by how impervious their authors are to the historical process. With almost no exceptions, they can afford to ignore history because the myth on which they comment is by definition not history at all, but the metahistorical pattern of history. The events of the authors' own time, however turbulent, could safely be ignored as merely the latest dreary instance of Time-Now, which would eventually pass away.

There is no thematic alteration in this Haggadah myth until post-Crusade Europe, and even that is an alteration not so much in theme as in emphasis and metaphor. Under the influence of the pietistic atmosphere that gripped European society with increasing fervor from the eleventh century onward, and, more specifically, of the heightened expectations for a Second Coming that seized Christian eschatology in the wake of a completed millennium, Judaism too became more conscious of the promised end of days. Time-Now might end with a personal messianic appearance, which, for Judaism, implied Elijah. So, as we already saw, we now witness Elijah's appearance in Jewish liminal rites, including the seder. The seder's climax now occurred after dinner rather than before, with the door being flung open to admit Elijah, and, with him, the messiah. Attendant liturgical declarations invited the destruction of persecuting foes and implored the miraculous return of Jews to Jerusalem.

For our purposes, however, the most interesting Haggadah alteration is the second major addendum to the midrash, the stratified discussion of the plagues (which we have just surveyed) being the first. It is the poem *Dayyenu,* our next example of sacred myth. Here we see a mature rabbinic mentality at work, constructing a conceptualization of Israel's biblical history that no longer omits Sinai and Torah and is explicit about the wrenching significance of the Roman destruction of Jerusalem and the Temple.

Dayyenu is a popular favorite today. Its simple refrain, *Dayyenu* ("It would have been enough"), is taught in synagogue schools and sung at most seders. Fortunately for today's Jews, it is the Hebrew rendition and its accompanying melody, rather than the English, that holds the popular appeal, since the English message would probably be considered at least outdated, and perhaps even offensive to most modern Jewish minds.

Dayyenu posits a list of wonders wrought by God during the Exodus. Line by line, it recounts the miracles performed during the Jews' flight to freedom. Its litany-like structure is ideal for expressing a mythic view of Jewish history, since each line projects an independent verbal picture, and their totality, an album.

God has bestowed many favors on us.

1. Had he brought us out of Egypt,
    And not punished the Egyptians,   *Dayyenu.*
2. Had he punished the Egyptians,
    And not castigated their gods,   *Dayyenu.*
3. Had he castigated their gods,
    And not put to death their firstborn,   *Dayyenu.*
4. Had he put to death their firstborn,
    And not given us of their wealth,   *Dayyenu.*
5. Had he given us of their wealth,
    And not split the Red Sea for us,   *Dayyenu.*
6. Had he split the Red Sea for us,
    And not led us through it dryshod,   *Dayyenu.*
7. Had he led us through it dryshod,
    And not engulfed our foes in it,   *Dayyenu.*
8. Had he engulfed our foes in it,
    And not sustained us in wasteland,   *Dayyenu.*
9. Had he sustained us in wasteland,
    And not fed us with the manna,   *Dayyenu.*
10. Had he fed us with the manna,
    And not given us the Sabbath,   *Dayyenu.*
11. Had he given us the Sabbath,
    And not brought us to Mount Sinai,   *Dayyenu.*
12. Had he brought us to Mount Sinai,
    And not given us the Torah,   *Dayyenu.*
13. Had he given us the Torah,
    And not brought us to the Land of Israel,   *Dayyenu.*
14. Had he brought us to the Land of Israel,
    And not built the Temple for us,   *Dayyenu.*

How much more so, then, should we be grateful to God for the manifold favors that he conferred upon us: He brought us out of Egypt, and punished the Egyptians; he smote their gods, and slew their firstborn; he gave us their wealth, and split the Red Sea for us; he led us through it dryshod, and engulfed our foes in it; he sustained us in the desert for forty years, and fed us with the manna; he gave us the Sabbath, and brought us to Mount Sinai; he gave us the Torah, and brought us to the Land of Israel; he built the Temple for us, to atone for all our sins.[46]

What pictures were included, then, in this ritualized medieval album of Jewish history? Of the fourteen lines,[47] or separate pictures, offered in the prayer, the first four deal with the Exodus from Egypt: how God wrought judgment on (1) Egypt and (2) its "gods"; how the Egyptian overlords were (3) plagued and (4) forced to subsidize with their own purses the Israelites' escape to the desert. So far, these events are perfectly compatible with the earlier First Fruits myth of the farmers. They too had expressed thanksgiving for the miraculous release of their forebears from slavery. Similarly congruent with that view is a fifth line (13), which describes entering the Promised Land. The last line too (14), a profession of thanks for establishing the Temple as the institution to forgive sin, would have elicited a nod of recognition from the pilgrim offering First Fruits in the first century.

But the other eight lines (5–12)—more than half the prayer as we now have it—would have echoed oddly in that pilgrim's ears. Not that their content would have been utterly unrecognizable—it comes from the Bible. But in their selective perception of Israel's history, first-century pilgrims had learned to pass over these items. Only now, with the rabbinic version of the myth, were these particular pictures of the past recovered (some of them, from virtual oblivion) and made primary desiderata in the expression of Israel's saga.

In three lines, we read how God (5) split the Red Sea, (6) brought Israel through on dry land, and (7) drowned the Egyptians. The Red Sea experience had emerged in the rabbis' thinking as particularly paradigmatic of God's salvation. They had inserted it in the daily worship service twice, morning and evening, in the section of prayer known popularly as *mi khamokha*, that being the final section of the benediction entitled *Ge'ullah*, "Redemption."[48] But God also (8) sustained Israel in the desert, (9) providing manna there, and this constituted *Dayyenu*'s next affirmation.

Another line (10) is given over to one specific commandment, the keeping of the Sabbath, to which the rabbis attached particular significance. As we saw above in connection with *havdalah*, various midrashic tales connected the coming of the messiah with keeping the Sabbath. Finally, in two separate lines, *Dayyenu* sings (11) of God's bringing Israel to Mount Sinai (12) to receive the Torah. This is the culminating event for rabbinic theology, a clear departure from the pilgrim's biblical myth, which omitted Sinai and Torah from consideration.

There is no reason to assume that all medieval Jews understood enough Hebrew to comprehend their liturgy in its entirety. But, unlike the daily or Sabbath worship services, the seder was frequently conducted not only in Hebrew but in the vernacular as well.[49] It is probable that by then the veiled midrashic reference to Rome (in the original midrash) and the despoliation of the Land of Israel centuries before went unrecognized, but the myth as a whole was clear enough. *Dayyenu* too presented Jewish history as an instance of "Degradation to Dignity." Out of terrible bondage Jews had been released by plagues and wonders. But they had at last been privileged to approach Sinai, receive Torah, and erect a Temple to guarantee atonement.

The rest of history, from 70 onward, was Time-Now, warranting no specific description. Everyone knew that the Temple was gone, destroyed by Rome on that fateful day of the Ninth of Av. During the calendrical march of Time-Now, life was in limbo, awaiting the restoration of the sacerdotal system in Time-to-Come. This was the burden of prayer after prayer recited in synagogues, and stated most eloquently in the middle blessing of the *Musaf Tefillah* on those occasions when the Sabbath falls on the New Moon:

> Long ago You formed Your world, finishing Your work on the seventh day . . .
> Lord our God, lovingly you gave us Sabbaths for rest and new moons for atonement.
> But *since we sinned before You, we and our ancestors, our city was destroyed, and
> our Temple laid waste* . . . so we can no longer perform our obligations there. May
> it be Your will . . . that You bring us up joyfully to our land, and plant us within our
> borders, and there we shall offer before You our obligatory sacrifices.[50]

What could be clearer? Jewish history still revolved about the Temple, just as it had when that edifice still stood. But now the Temple was gone. So Jews were to pray for its return; and, in the meantime, they were to guard well the Torah's commandments that were given at Sinai, the breach of which had been responsible for their Temple's destruction in the first place. But salvation would someday come. God had intervened in Egypt and again at the Red Sea, so reward was guaranteed for those who waited faithfully. So as Jews finished their seder in the Middle Ages, they cried out at the end, "Next Year in Jerusalem."[51] Perhaps by next year, Time-to-Come would have arrived.

Shortly, we shall see that Jews today also express a sacred myth as part of their seder. They too answer the question "Why is this night different from all others?" The answer in today's liturgies varies greatly from that of those rabbis who inhabited the hundreds of years between the dawn of the first century and another dawn, much later, of the modern age. It expresses a new conception of time and integrates a modern consciousness of history. Particularly in this century, Jews have grown aware of the heaviness of history! And this burden of contemporary events had to be given expression in equally contemporary mythic consciousness. But before we look at today's permutations of the sacred myth, we have to explore one more means by which Jews have expressed the traditional one. I refer to that unique liturgical creation known as the *Avodah*.

THE *AVODAH*

Liturgically, the word *Avodah* is now used with at least two related connotations. First, it is the title for the seventeenth benediction in the *Tefillah*, in which capacity it is recited three times each day.[52] The rubric was already known in pre-70 days, and is cited as part of the ceremonial events surrounding the offering of the daily *Tamid* sacrifice in the Temple.[53] Our sources provide no details regarding what it consisted of in the Temple context, but the term is used congruently there, since *avodah*, generally, denoted the sacrificial service of the priests. From there, apparently, an *Avodah* benediction was devised for synagogue recitation, and (as Zunz already noted)[54] it was one of six *Tefillah* blessings known so well by early Tannaitic times that it is assumed in the Mishnah to be recognizable by its technical title. As we have it now, the *Avodah* benediction is a stratified composition that betrays theological expectations both before and after the Temple's destruction. A brief consideration of both perspectives will enable us to grasp the centrality of the cult in pre-70 thinking, and then the alteration of that mentality, which the Temple's demise necessitated, and which we see reflected in the new sacred myth of the rabbis. For purposes of analysis, critical Hebrew words appear in parentheses, and what I take to be the post-70 stratum is bracketed.

(1) Be pleased (*retsei*), Lord our God, with Your people Israel, [and with their prayers (*bitefillatam*). (2) Return the sacrificial service (*avodah*) to the Temple precincts (*devir beitekha*)]. (3) Accept willingly [and with love] the offerings of Israel [and their prayers] (*ve'ishei yisrael* [*utefillatam be'ahavah*] *tekabel beratson*). (4) May the *Tamid* offering of the sacrificial service of Israel, Your people, be acceptable (*utehi leratson*) to You. (5) [May our eyes behold Your return in mercy to Zion. Blessed art Thou, O Lord, who returns His presence to Zion.]

What we have is not one prayer, but two, distinguished as such by Elbogen, who listed also a sampling of the variety of formulations typical of the diverse rites.[55] The earlier one, clearly pre-70, presupposes a daily cult in which a *Tamid* is offered for the purpose of being accepted by God. (Standard translations render *tamid* here as an adverb [always, or regularly], but the pre-70 context of this stratum of the benediction makes it equally likely that we have the actual proper noun denoting the sacrifice here.)

The regular verb associated with this cultic offering is *retsei* (be willing!, take pleasure in!, be pleased with!) or its nominal form, *ratson* (will, pleasure). If we look at the additions, we discover that the third sentence contains a patent redundancy in its inclusion of both *beratson* (willingly, pleasurably, with pleasure) and *be'ahavah* (with love). The verb *tekabel* (receive) can take one of them, but not both, at least not as the Hebrew syntax now stands. So I bracket *be'ahavah*, and include it along with *utefillatam* (and their prayers). We thus find that the cultic object of divine acceptance is *ishei yisrael* (the offerings of Israel), characterized as being received by God *beratson* (willingly), an idea that the next sentence (4) also repeats, now more specifically, in that a particular offering, the *Tamid*, is cited, but again with a qualifying adverb built from the noun *ratson*, i.e., *leratson*. Added to this cultic notion (in 3) is the further plea that prayers also be acceptable to God, not, however, *beratson*—for words built on *ratson* are characteristic of the literary stratum describing the sacrificial cult—but *be'ahavah* (with love), this being the preferred adverbial phrase in the later stratum dealing with prayers. We see a similar addition of *ubitefillatam* (and with their prayers) in sentence 1, without, however, any adverbial accompaniment. In no sentence does prayer appear as the sole object of the petition.

To the extent that prayer was at all relevant to the cult, it was purely as a concomitant to the sacrifices, which were the real concern. Prayer was added to our benediction only after sacrifice was rendered impossible, and, as our blessing makes crystal clear, the ultimate goal of classical rabbinic worship was the reestablishment of sacrifice once again. Prayer is relevant, then, only to Time-Now; for Time-Past, as for Time-to-Come, it is sacrifice that belongs. Thus *avodah* (as the cult) constituted the dominant conceptual focus even after the Temple was destroyed, since its reinstitution was what one prayed for, above all else, as the characterizing hallmark of Time-to-Come.[56]

The cult was tied intrinsically to doctrines of sin and atonement. That its principal function was later seen, in fact, as the forgiveness of sin is clear from the *Dayyenu*, which says explicitly that God provided the Temple "to atone for our sins."[57] And it is equally evident from the mountains of discussion in rabbinic literature, and even from the Bible itself, which details the many offerings that are owed by those who have sinned against God.

But describing the Temple only in terms of sin is to get a one-sided view of the ancient Israelites' conception of their covenant with God. A covenant has both positive and negative aspects. Those parties who fail to live up to their end of the agreement are in a state of default, that being the same as sin, if the party to whom one owes the obligation is God. But it is equally possible that the human party to the covenant may have fulfilled what is demanded, in which case it is God who must demonstrate compliance. That was the burden of the ritual admission cited earlier by the farmers bringing their tithe. They stated explicitly that they had followed the tithing procedure to the last letter of the law, and openly demanded from God that God bless them in return.[58]

So the Temple was seen as the focus not of sin and atonement per se, but of the covenant, the breach of which constituted sin, and the return to which came through atonement. God and Israel met ritually in *avodah* to reenact their mutual pact. True, where Israel had failed, offerings of atonement intended to rectify the relationship with God were in order. But at the same time, those who had acquitted themselves honestly of their duties must have thronged to the Temple to receive reassurance that God would grant rain and fertility for crops, animals, and even their human families, as the tithing farmers also demanded.[59]

In either case, the opportunity to reestablish mutual covenantal trust was an awesome day for reckoning and rejoicing. Those who had not sinned would be reassured of their reward, and those who had erred would be forgiven. The only place—I emphasize the word "only"—the *only* place where that reconciliation was deemed possible in the pre-rabbinic mentality was the Temple in Jerusalem; the only people who could assure it were the priests, most particularly the High Priest; the only acts that would achieve it were cultic; and the most significant time when all this occurred was the Day of Atonement, Yom Kippur.

After 70, the cult was by no means forgotten. Though technically it now belonged only to the idealized worlds of Time-Past (just ended) and Time-to-Come (as yet unrealized), it could still be pursued secondarily in Time-Now by means of *Avodah* as synagogue and home worship. Worship as prayer service was thus consciously patterned after the cult,[60] and provided with ample opportunity to recall the actual sacrifices, now defunct but some day to be restored. We already saw this ritualized recollection in the *Avodah* benediction of the daily *Tefillah*, for example, but it was more centrally displayed on the annual occasion when the cult's covenantal role had been prominent: Yom Kippur. We thus arrive at the second rubric for which the name *Avodah* is pertinent: a series of lengthy poetic compositions for Yom Kippur day.

These poetic compositions perpetuated the memory of the sacrificial system at its most lavish. They were, however, not composed immediately after the Temple's fall in 70 but were written several centuries after that, and based on earlier memories carried elsewhere in rabbinic literature. With abundant detail, the tannaitic authors in the late first and the second centuries had recorded their own recollection of the Yom Kippur spectacle, much of it already expanded by the imagination of generations who had never actually seen the cult themselves. It was these images of former greatness on which the poets were able to draw for their own epic descriptions of the cult in Time-Past. I have chosen not to cite here the *Avodah* poetry in all its detail; it will suffice to recapitulate briefly the description of the *Avodah* ritual that is carried in the Mishnah and that was transferred, often verbatim, to the poems in question.

As the Mishnah reports it, the High Priest had prepared exclusively for this event a full seven days before it arrived. When the day finally did come, the Temple courtyard was packed to overflowing with those intent on witnessing the acts destined to reconcile them with their God. They saw the High Priest bathe himself and change clothes four times: first golden finery, then linen, then white, and then back to gold again. Lots were cast to determine which of two animals would be sacrificed on the altar, and which would have a crimson ribbon, indicative of Israel's sins, tied around its neck, and then be cast down a precipice as a scapegoat. "Though your sins be red as scarlet," the prophet had announced, "I will make them white as snow."[61] People could not easily forget the priest's circumambulation of the altar, his dashing of the sacrificial blood against the altar's base, his confessions for his own family and person, and then again for all of Israel; and above all, perhaps, his entry surrounded by incense to the innermost room in the Temple, the Holy of Holies, whence he would emerge with all due haste after a short prayer for Israel's welfare. This speedy exit, we are informed, in a blatant testimonial to the awesome nature of the Yom Kippur ritual, was so as not to "terrify the Israelites" by a more protracted absence. Whether accurate or not, this is what was recalled by those living a generation or two after the Temple's fall, and what they faithfully recorded in the Mishnah.[62]

It was this and similarly early rabbinic memories that now entered the liturgy in poetic form, influenced, apparently, by the poetic renaissance in the Eastern church, and a coincidental golden age of synagogue poetry (in Hebrew, *Piyyutim*). The *Avodah* was only one poetic form of many, but it is one of the earliest. Yose ben Yose (fifth to sixth century?) is the first of three Byzantine Jewish poets who make up what we call the classical period of *Piyyutim*, and his *Avodah* poems remain to this day typical of the genre. We have also an anonymous *Avodah* that predates Yose. Both the work of Yose and of his unknown predecessor set the style of all *Avodah* poems in the future, so that later examples followed identical canons of form and content.

All those *Avodah* poems speak at length of the once-existent priestly cult insofar as rabbinic records recalled its functioning on Yom Kippur. This recollection is introduced by a biblical verse explicitly stating the atoning function of the priestly ritual and interpreted by the rabbis to refer directly to Yom Kippur, Lev. 8:34: "As has been done this day, so the Lord has commanded to be done: to make atonement for you." But this verse and its following description of the Yom Kippur Temple service form only the second of two parts to the poem. With but one exception (a twelfth-century *Avodah* by Moses ibn Ezra), all *Avodah* poetry begins not with the cult but with history. The Yom Kippur *Avodah*, then, presents us with our next prominent example of the rabbinic version of the sacred myth.[63]

As we would expect, God's establishment of the cult is central to the *Avodah*'s view of sacred history. It begins with the account of creation, but then moves swiftly through the high points of the biblical narrative until the election of Aaron, Moses's brother, as High Priest in the tabernacle worship that marked the desert wanderings from Egypt to Canaan. But the entire biblical period is viewed here as a process designed to produce a Temple. So the narration now skips to the functioning of Aaron's progeny many years later in that very Temple, and it is here that we encounter Lev. 8:34, and Part Two of the poem, the recollection of the lavish priestly rite that had once marked the Day of Atonement.

The synagogue service knows of other *Piyyutim* too that utilize descriptions of history to lead up to their central focus; for the festival of Shavuot, for example, or for the specific genre of poetry celebrating God's saving grace as symbolized in the gift of rain or dew. And there, history is utilized for different purposes. In the latter, for example, biblical events demonstrate human dependence on dew and rain, either literally or symbolically, in terms of their salvific qualities. In the former, history leads to Sinai, where Torah was revealed. So we cannot maintain that the rabbis saw history *only* in terms of a preamble for the Temple. Indeed, we saw earlier that they deliberately added Sinai to the myth; just as they used rain and dew elsewhere to symbolize salvation in terms of bodily resurrection. But all our "historical" poems have in common the fact that by modern standards, they are not historical at all. In all of them, history is limited in scope to Time-Past. The calendrical cycle determines whether it shall be Temple, Torah, or rain that is celebrated, but whatever the focus, history merely leads up to it, after which the worshiper regularly prays for deliverance in Time-to-Come.

The *Avodah* deserves our attention more than the other poetic instances of utilizing history, because the Temple's destruction and ultimate reestablishment best symbolize the mythic structuring of time into past and future eras, and because the grand themes of sin and atonement, which are implicitly conveyed in the others, are more clearly and explicitly stated here. Moreover, it presents the same myth as the liturgy of *Dayyenu* and the *Musaf Tefillah*, which we looked at above; so we are justified in viewing it as inherent to the liturgy in general, not simply as an outgrowth of Yom Kippur. We have devoted this attention to the *Avodah*, then, because it demonstrates so clearly the extent to which the rabbinic sacred myth did away with history completely, substituting instead the meta-historical message of sin, which ended Time-Past; atonement and pardon, which will some day bring about Time-to-Come; and the utter insignificance of Time-Now, except as an epoch in which one pursues God's will in expectation of eventual deliverance.

SUMMARY

Before turning to Reform Judaism and the nineteenth century, we should summarize this repetitive but consistent message carried by the rabbinic sacred myth. Throughout the long years stretching from the rabbinic conceptualization of reality when the Temple fell, until the dawn of the Enlightenment, Jews gathered for their ritual life in synagogues, where they intoned pages and pages of prayers, all with the same meaning. Time-Past consisted of a trek from Egypt to Sinai to Promised Land to an established Temple cult. When Israel sinned, Time-Past gave way to Time-Now, with its many vicissitudes and tragedies. On Passover, Jews rehearsed this myth by recalling slavery and freedom, along with God's gifts in Time-Past, any one of which "would have been enough"; and (since the Middle Ages, at least), they ended their seder by looking to "Next year in Jerusalem," when Time-to-Come would be born. On Yom Kippur, with its accent on atonement, it was the moral message of the myth that was voiced, in an *Avodah* that blithely forced sacred history into a mold of sin and suffering, atonement and redemption. This message was reiterated also in Haftarah cycles surrounding the Ninth of Av, and in prayer after prayer uttered on more regular occasions, such as the middle benediction of the Sabbath–New Moon *Musaf Tefillah*, quoted above.

But the nineteenth century called this traditional myth into question. As Jakob Petuchowski summarizes, this was

> . . . because nascent Reform Judaism, child of the emancipation, found no existential meaning in the concept of "exile." Diaspora existence, for Reform Judaism, was not punitive exile on account of Israel's sins, but rather the inevitable consequence of Israel's glorious mission to be a "light unto the nations." With the concept of "exile" thus banished from its theology, Reform Judaism also had to revise those liturgical expressions which linked diaspora existence to Israel's sins.[64]

Petuchowski surveys German reformers' attempts to do away with these expressions, and notes in passing how the notion of exile differentiated early Reform ideologues from their contemporaries who were formulating a rival Zionist perspective. "If the former no longer found any meaning in the concept of 'exile', the latter was very much obsessed by it."[65] His characterization of the chasm between the two movements is absolutely accurate, to be sure. But on another level, both religious reformers and Zionist visionaries were in substantial agreement: their common rediscovery of history—the recognition that Time-Now, no longer relegated to theological insignificance relative to Time-Past and Time-to-Come, had to be understood in its own terms.

Jews were reevaluating the significance of history for several intertwined reasons. First, like everyone else in nineteenth-century Europe, they were entranced by the romantic era's emphasis on the *Volk*. They were discovering their own historical uniqueness as a discrete people by laying bare the details of their own development through the ages. Second, freed from the morass of medieval ghetto existence, Jews like Zunz were attending universities where they were discovering the new sciences of history and philology, which could then be applied to their own literary heritage in ways to which we have alluded in these pages. Third, modern science had demonstrated the doctrine of progress, so that history could be viewed as having its own inherent pattern that is revealed only in the flow of events hitherto ignored; messianism was inherent in history itself. Finally, and most practically speaking, they hoped that a thorough study of the changing fortunes of the Jews might demonstrate the appropriateness of granting the Jewish people full rights of citizenship. It was this final hope that separated reformers from Zionists, the former declaring the end of "exile" and thus the beginning of "at-homeness" in modern Europe, and the latter pronouncing such a declaration illusory. What matters here, however, is the realization that both Reform Jews and Zionists had turned to history to achieve their ends. Both were convinced that Time-Now held meaning, and both dedicated themselves to a zealous effort to work within history to ameliorate the status of the Jew.

Not unsurprisingly, a new sacred myth of Jewish history had to be manufactured. The medieval message would not do. What the myth had now to reflect was change within Time-Now, not changelessness throughout it. If anything, Time-Now emerged as the single era most demanding of attention, since it was the stuff of which human history is made, and, realistically speaking, Jews wanted civil rights in the universities, salons, concert halls, and legislatures of living, historically bound human societies.

Of the two factions, Zionists and religious reformers, it was the former that broke most decisively with its normative rabbinic past. The Zionists' new myth is clearly encoded in their own rituals, particularly the Passover seders that even the most ardent secularist Kibbutz societies continued.[66] But for our purposes, a study of Reform ritual will prove most instructive. Reform Jews, after all, proclaimed their continuity with religious tradition and, as a consequence, composed liturgies that invite comparisons with their medieval prototypes.

SIX

Sacred Myths

II. After the Enlightenment

THE SACRED MYTH OF CLASSICAL REFORM JUDAISM

The new sacred myth for Reform Judaism is evident particularly in its new Haggadahs and *Avodah* rituals, but not there alone. Reform ideology did not limit its proponents to a literal translation of traditional liturgy; on the contrary, Reform editors believed themselves duty-bound to devise new books with novel paraphrases of old prayers as well as creative texts that had no precedent at all in tradition.[1] Since these same authors spoke for the very vanguard of acculturated Jews most attuned to the nineteenth century's rediscovery of history, their prayer books abounded with pictures of the modern Jew's perspective on that history.

The most striking facet of Jewish history that called for integration into the myth was the diaspora, now reaching fruition (as the authors saw it) in rapid progress toward enlightened European society. Hitherto, the centuries of diaspora life could be subsumed under the category of "exile" and then ignored as part of Time-Now, which, by definition, commanded no attention to detail; particularly forceful reminders of life in "exile" could be compressed into the old theological mold of sin and punishment and then allocated a day of remembrance, usually the Ninth of Av. The events of Time-Now, if remembered at all, were only subsumed under the cyclical view of Jewish history, according to which the same pattern of events simply recurs until Time-to-Come. This was plainly unacceptable to modern Jews, however, whose aspirations within European society dictated that their sacred myth provide a positive lesson regarding the diaspora, not a negative one. They needed an acceptable rationale for the creation of a diaspora in the first place. No longer could the Temple be seen as the pinnacle of Jewish religiosity, its destruction viewed as punishment for sin, its absence during Time-Now painfully bewailed. Obviously the Temple had fallen, but that fall had to have some consequence beyond supplying a paradigmatic demonstration of the eternal Jewish sin-and-punishment cycle, and a root metaphor of cultic restoration in Time-to-Come.[2]

The rewriting of history through ritual is pervasive in early Reform annals, but particularly evident in the work of Reform leaders who migrated to America and freely adapted their novel perspective on Jewish history to the realities of life that greeted them here. Illustrative of their effort is the pioneering work of Isaac M. Wise and David Einhorn, two rabbinic writers of prayer books in nineteenth-century America, whose work we have already surveyed generally in chapter 4. As we saw there, Einhorn's volume even became the dominant model for the authoritative Reform prayer books, the 1894–95 *Union Prayer Book*, Volumes One and Two.[3] In what follows, we shall explicate the sacred myth of their liturgies, with the preliminary caveat that we are not engaged simply in an academic exercise. We are discussing the way generations of American Jews were taught to see their history, and hence themselves.

Isaac M. Wise viewed his past with considerable pride. His version of Jewish history appears most strikingly in a prayer composed for the morning of Rosh Hashanah.[4] He begins on familiar ground, postulating a golden biblical age of "our pious ancestors," Abraham, Isaac, and Jacob. The height of Israel's ancient past, though, is "the everlasting covenant of light and truth" entered into at Sinai. God "consecrated Israel to be the bearer of heaven's gift to man, divine and immutable truth. God gave us the law and sent us His prophets to guide the children of man on the path of truth and righteousness." Wise recalls how the first Temple was destroyed because Israel "rebelled against God's will," and how Ezra returned from a short exile in Babylonia "to read the law to the people of Thy covenant." There then followed "all the dark centuries of human perversion," when God watched over Israel so that Jews survived, even though "mighty empires and proud nations vanished from the face of the globe." God's plan was that Israel might be preserved to "witness the progress of truth and light, the triumph of justice and freedom," this latter age being ushered in here, in nineteenth-century America.

To some, nowadays, this sort of vision may seem trite. Others will comment that it contains nothing of novelty. But the fact is that Wise effected a glorious marriage between the traditional rabbinic myth and the new nineteenth-century one. Wise no more wished to spend time on the details of the Middle Ages than did his traditional rabbinic contemporaries who still denied his nineteenth-century historicism. And both parties also saw a happy consonance between the hope of humanity and the fulfillment of Israel's dreams. Also, insofar as they agreed on the essential goodness of ancient biblical days, they can both be seen as not yet abandoning at least that aspect of Judaism's premodern time scheme. They were also alike in stressing the centrality of Torah (what Wise calls "the Law") and even in their blindness to the existence of any women in Israel's history. (The Jewish past is made of Abraham, Isaac, Jacob, Joseph, Moses, Ezra, and "the children of men," says Wise.)

But significant alterations have slipped into the familiar story. Though looking the same on the surface, the time scheme has been altered substantially. For the rabbis, Time-Now included all time until the coming of the Messiah, whose advent was still awaited in the distant future. Wise believed in no personal messiah, but he was a firm messianist, advocating a messianic age that would result from the strivings of humanity in the very enlightened era through which he was living. So the prime novelty of Wise's temporal order consisted in this: he translated Time-Now as "the Middle Ages" and Time-to-Come as the perfect world order, *which he thought he and his generation had already begun to usher in*!

He also glosses over the cultic element in "the Law." The rabbis knew that the covenant on Sinai included more than a little obligation to sacrifice. From their forebears they knew too how central the cult had once been to Israel. And we have seen that they explained the Temple's demise while holding out hopes for its rebirth in Time-to-Come. Meanwhile, they read about sacrifices every morning in their liturgy, and maintained lengthy descriptions of the cult in their *Avodah* service and elsewhere. But the reader of Wise's prayer would hardly know that a second Temple had ever even existed. Wise does mention the fact that "Zerubabel proclaimed again Thy holy name on Mt. Moriah." But one wonders if Jewish worshipers even recognized who Zerubabel was or perceived that Wise's euphemistic "proclamation of Thy Holy name" really referred to bloody animal sacrifices.[5]

Wise does more than omit. He also adds some significant heroes to the story. The most outstanding ones are Zerubabel, whom we have already noted, and Ezra. Both were leaders in the generations of the return, the former being among the first emigrés out of Babylon in the sixth century B.C.E. and the latter organizing Jewish life in the reconstituted Judean state roughly a century later. Zerubabel's role in Wise's narrative is his restoration of worship, this being the compromise Wise was willing to make with recognizing the reestablishment of the Temple.

Ezra was even more important. Ezra "read the law" to the people, thus reminding the returning Jewish exiles of their historic mission. One gets the impression that Ezra and Wise are comparable figures in the sacred myth of Wise's *Minhag America*. Both men emerge from periods of gloom, the Babylonian exile on one hand and the pre-Enlightenment "dark ages" on the other. And both will act as God's messengers to assure that the covenant goes on and God's promises are fulfilled. For Jews have a mission in Wise's scheme. They are bearers of truth, guarantors that human history will survive even the direst tragedies and rise to heights of unimaginable glory.[6]

Einhorn was a more radical reformer than Wise, and it was his conception of Jewish identity, rather than Wise's, that the Reform movement as a whole eventually adopted. But Einhorn's radical adaptation to the spirit of German (and later, American) liberalism proved no impediment to the championing of the Jewish people's mission in history. The paramount shortcoming he found in the historical myth proposed by Wise was its dearth of conceptual grandeur. So Einhorn's prayer book echoed the same magnificent message regarding Israel's role, but presented it in sweeping monumental majesty.

By adapting a vision of the prophet Isaiah, Einhorn arrived at an extended metaphor of Israel as suffering servant, destined to carry the torch of God's truth to all humanity, and thus to usher in the messianic age. With remarkable audacity, he drummed home his heroic claim loudest on the Ninth of Av. Traditionally, as we have seen, the Ninth of Av was a fast day, commemorating the paradigmatic destructive event of Jewish history; for Einhorn, however, it represented a day of hope, the Temple's destruction being part of God's plan to scatter Jews and their message to the furthest reaches of the globe. His prayer book calls for the following explicit reading on the occasion:

> However dimly and painfully our soul is moved by the recollection of the unutterable grief with which our ancestors went forth from their beloved Zion, their house, to go into the vast wilderness of heathen nations; doomed to tread the thorny path of martyrdom—in all these sore trials we recognize Thy guiding fatherly hand, a means for the fulfillment of Thy inviolable promises and the glorification of Thy name and Thy law before the eyes of all nations. Verily, not as a disinherited son, Thy first-born went out into strange lands, but as Thy messenger to all the families of man. Israel was no longer to dwell in separation from all the rest of Thy children who were languishing in darkness and folly; he was to spread abroad the stream of his salvation and become himself the carrier of the refreshing waters of healing powers. The one Temple in Jerusalem sank into the dust, in order that countless Temples might arise . . . all over the wide surface of the globe. The old priestly dignity was taken away, and the old sacrificial worship ceased, but in their stead the whole community . . . became a priest and was called upon to offer those sacrifices which are more acceptable in Thy sight than thousands of rivers of oil, the sacrifices of active love to God and man. . . . *The flames which consumed Zion, lit up the birth hour of Israel as the suffering messiah of all mankind.* Freed from the bonds of his childhood, *in martyr heroism, Israel had to pilgrim through the whole earth*, a man of sorrows . . . despised and rejected of men, to deliver by his very fetters his own tormentors, by his wounds to bring healing to those who inflicted them. When at last his great sacrifice of atonement is completely wrought, he will find his reward in seeing all men gather into one brotherhood, doing God's service in love to man. In this our hope, *this day of mourning and of fasting, hath, according to the word of Thy prophet, been turned into a solemn day of rejoicing* in view of the glorious destiny of Thy law and our high messianic mission. . . .[7]

One can only stand in awe of the majestic grace with which Einhorn dismisses a fast day that epitomized almost two thousand years of Jewish history. Traditionally, the Ninth of Av was said to be the most tragic day in the Jewish calendar. Heavy with the memory of constant disaster that was said to have occurred then, this day was marked, literally, by deep mourning for the Temple of old. Its ritual was punctuated by moanful sighs and wailing chants of Jews worshiping their way through the biblical book of Lamentations, and a series of medieval elegies. Now Einhorn displayed the incredible audacity of announcing, "This day of mourning and of fasting hath, according to the word of Thy prophet, been turned into a solemn day of rejoicing."

He was not the first to annul the fast, but he was the only one to do so successfully, and yet to be judged by history as still remaining within the Jewish fold. According to the Palestinian Talmud, Rabbi Judah HaNasi, the titular and actual head of Palestinian Jewry in the closing days of the second century, is reputed to have attempted to declare the fast at an end, but the Talmud is so amazed at this recollection of Judah's daring, that an anonymous objector in the talmudic discussion questions the veracity of the report and concludes that it could not possibly be correct.[8] In the seventeenth century, it was again annulled, this time by Sabbatai Zevi, the false messiah whose legendary fame in his own time swept across Europe from Poland and Turkey to France and Holland. His was a theological statement to the effect that Time-to-Come had arrived. After Sabbatai's death, a group of his followers celebrated the Ninth of Av with feasting, accompanied by a special liturgy in honor of Sabbatai's birthday, said to fall on that very day![9]

Einhorn's action was a similar theological statement. He would have been horrified at any attempt to compare him to a false messiah whose ideological roots lay in Mediterranean mysticism. But the analogy holds. Though no self-appointed messiah, Einhorn did indeed picture himself as ushering in the messianic age of enlightenment, justice, and peace. One wonders, in fact, just who we should identify as "the prophet" according to whose word the fast is annulled. Technically, Einhorn must be referring to Zech. 8:19: "Thus saith the Lord of hosts: the fast of the fourth month and the fast of the fifth and the fast of the seventh and the fast of the tenth shall be to Judah joy and gladness and cheerful seasons. Therefore, love ye truth and peace"; or to Jer. 31:13: "I will turn their mourning into joy, and comfort them, and make them rejoice from their sorrow." But is it possible that Einhorn is also referring to himself? Einhorn believed that divine revelation continued beyond Sinai and was available to seers of every age.[10] He was in this sense a latter-day prophet championing the cause of social justice and rational progress designed to move humanity into the golden age of Time-to-Come. He, no less than Zechariah, identified God's word as "truth and peace." Jewish tradition, however, had pushed Zechariah's prophecy to the end of days, so that the only "prophetic word" proclaiming that the projected demise of mourning on the Ninth of Av had actually arrived, belonged to Einhorn and the other Reform leaders who agreed with him.

By his annulment of the Ninth of Av, Einhorn was heralding the appearance of

Time-to-Come. Israel had suffered in God's service through the darkest days of medieval misery, but the Jewish passion for faithfulness to its mission was finally bearing fruit.

If we turn now to Einhorn's *Avodah*, we see that its sacred myth chronicles the same tale as his prayer for the Ninth of Av. Even in ancient times, he tells us, Israel was the forerunner of the truth, apprehending God's law at Sinai and building an advanced religion in the midst of heathen degradation. Since being exiled from its land for the greater glory of humanity, Israel has suffered greatly, but "Our history's lessons are indeed . . . a mighty call unto Israel ever anew to search the depths of his own self-consciousness."[11] For its own salvation, the world depends on the mission of Israel.

So Einhorn the radical and Wise the moderate concurred in the rewriting of Israel's history. They both supplied diaspora life with positive purpose. In their scheme, the Temple's fall had actually freed Jews to proclaim God's universal message to the world. Medieval misery was a sort of necessary testing period until humanity grew to sufficient moral stature to accept Israel's witness. But with the Enlightenment, that period was over. The prophetic prediction of a messianic age was about to be realized, at last.

Einhorn's reference to "the prophet's prediction" is worthy of special note! The insertion of the prophets into the sacred myth is so subtly achieved that one assumes they were always there. But they were not. The pilgrims of the first century had recited Deut. 26 without adding one word about Amos, or Jeremiah, or Isaiah, or any of the moral champions whom we simply take for granted. Nor did the *Avodah* poems deem it worthwhile to trace history as far as the prophetic age. Even the rabbinic decision to add the Mount Sinai experience did not carry with it a parallel determination to include these later prophetic keepers of the covenant. They are not even included in the traditional *Dayyenu*.

It should not be imagined that the rabbis were uninterested in the prophets. On the contrary, as we saw, they mandated regular prophetic readings in the form of Haftarah passages for every Sabbath and holiday. But their opinion of prophetic eloquence was of a piece with their denial of history. As they saw it, the prophets had nothing to say about the historical realities of Time-Now. Though their assertions had to be considered significant, the prophets were essentially just repeating what the Torah already commanded.

On the other hand, the prophets had accurately forecast the fall of biblical Israel and Judah to Assyria and Babylonia, and they were in receipt of equally authentic predictions that had not yet come to pass but surely would in Time-to-Come. These predictions of natural punishment and revival were carefully extricated from their original historical context, in which the rabbis had no interest, and connected instead with pertinent occasions in the annual calendrical cycle. Thus, for example (as we have seen), on Yom Kippur, one read the prophet

Jonah to indicate that God accepts those who repent. On the Sabbath immediately before the Ninth of Av, one read Jeremiah's vision of Jerusalem's
devastation, to set the mood for the day of the destruction; and on the Sabbath
thereafter, one read Second Isaiah's message of consolation to the emigrés in
Babylonian captivity, to show that God never abandons Israel. But in no ritualistic telling of history were the prophets admitted as real-life historical personalities, until Reform Jews decided to include them.

What role did the prophets play in the reformers' sacred myth? In a word, they
predicted the end of the Middle Ages and the coming of the Enlightenment; and,
by example, they indicated ethical behavior befitting all enlightened religious
people, whether modern Jews newly freed from the shackles of ghetto living, or
equally broad-minded Christians intent on solving Europe's "Jewish problem"
by ameliorating the circumstances that had prejudicially enforced the second-
class status of the Jews to start with. The prophets thus became a foil to the
oppressive society from which Jews were fleeing, a critique equally valid for
Jews and Christians. In the first place, Reform prayer books quoted the many
cases in which prophets spoke out against a religion of outward form, that form
being the sacrificial cult. In the second place, the prophetic religiosity that
manifests itself in the fight for a just and humane society served to remind the
European ruling classes, particularly the liberals who were already painfully
conscious of the evils of the new age of urbanization and industrialization, that
they owed their insight to the Jewish tradition itself, and that they would find the
Jews willing allies in their universal fight for decency.

As a moderate reformer when it came to liturgy and ritual, Wise felt obliged to
include much of the traditional structure of the *Avodah*, even though that decision entailed mentioning the cult and its attendant priestly activity. But he was
able to offset this emphasis on sacrifice by quoting the prophets to the effect that:

> I will not admonish thee on account of sacrifices and burnt offerings. . . . I have not
> given commandments to your parents on account of sacrifices and burnt offer-
> ings. . . . What I ask and what I require of thee is nothing except to fear me, to
> worship with gladness and a happy heart; for obedience is better than sacrifice. And
> the contrite heart is better to me than a pure offering.[12]

Similarly in the Rosh Hashanah morning prayer, where Wise explicitly states his
sacred myth, he thanks God not only for "the Law," which for him, we may
recall, was the "everlasting covenant of light and of truth," but, in the same
sentence, for "the prophets," who, together with the Law as their guide, were to
lead "the children of men on the path of truth and righteousness."[13]

Einhorn was even clearer. He too included reference to the High Priest's
function on Yom Kippur of old, his purpose being the presentation of further
support for his theology that represented all Jews as a collective priesthood

dedicated to cleansing the world of evil and sin.[14] The Middle Ages had been the time of Israel's collective atonement, and the new age was to offer reconciliation between ailing humanity at large and the one God of all. So he noted in his *Avodah*:

> All Israel is constituted the world's priestly community. . . . Ours it is to lead all mankind to the wellsprings of Thy word and thus to prepare and usher in the universal reign of justice and righteousness.[15]

But Einhorn knew this mission to be true because the prophets had said so. His image of Israel the suffering servant, which we quoted above, is taken from the book of Isaiah, after all. And the task of his own generation, he tells us again in the *Avodah*, is to bring to pass "the promise of Thy prophets."[16]

We can call this amalgam of the historical perspective held in common by Wise and Einhorn the classical Reform sacred myth. Again, I emphasize that I mean in no way to denigrate a view of history when I call it a myth. I wish only to indicate that every historical perspective is selective in what it chooses to emphasize or to omit, and that examples of these histories are encoded by religious communities as ritualized reminders for public occasions. The ritualized recitations of the myth are not meant to be objective rational calculations in the first place. They are intoned as justifications for certain values and life styles. They are epic poems of life no less than such myths as the *Iliad*. The classical reformers, like the rabbis who preceded them, necessarily formulated such a myth to explain the world they knew, as well as the world they wanted, and to mandate the requisite behavior to transform the former into the latter.

Their myth, like the one they inherited, went from the Patriarchs, to Egypt, to Sinai, to the Promised Land, and to the Temple. But unlike the medieval version, the myth did not stop there. As a foil to the concept of Temple, the prophets were inserted. And the Temple's fall was heralded as introducing the period of Israel's universal mission to all peoples of the earth.[17] The revised wording to *Dayyenu* in the 1923 *Union Haggadah* makes this point concisely and eloquently. The old version, it will be recalled, ended with God's bringing Israel to its Land, and building a Temple there to atone for sin. The 1923 Reform Haggadah adds two concluding lines to this inherited text.

> Had He built for us the Temple, and not
> sent us prophets of truth—*Dayyenu*.

> Had He sent us prophets of truth, but not
> made us a holy people—*Dayyenu*.[18]

Only one general observation needs to be added to round out the picture of the classical Reform myth. Though the old 1894–95 *Union Prayer Book* and the

1923 *Union Haggadah* incorporate the classical thinking of Einhorn and Wise, they do so with their own particular refinement of vision. When these nineteenth-century pioneers spoke of the prophetic vision of justice and righteousness, they had only the roughest notions of a particular blueprint for social action destined to bring about the golden age of the future. Civil rights for Jews was a given, of course, and general justice for all was at least an honorable corollary thereto. Certainly, Einhorn, who fled a pulpit and comfortable position in Baltimore rather than support the cause of slavery during the Civil War, testifies to the unselfish nature of his zeal for social justice.[19]

But that zeal had yet to be filled with anything beyond the truisms of a prophetic call to arms. And the prophets were still only part of the myth, not its dominant focus. Though reformers had discovered the prophetic cause, they had not converted wholeheartedly to a religion modeled almost exclusively after prophetic example. What had yet to be added to the myth was the repainting of the prophets as biblical social activists.

That step was begun in the late 1880s and was a Jewish reflection of a general religious development in America, notably, the social gospel. By then, rapid postbellum industrialization had exacerbated social ills in the burgeoning cities of the Northeast and the Midwest. Reform ideologues in New York, Pittsburgh, Cleveland, Chicago, and all the other metropolitan areas where this new Judaism was so heavily represented, were painfully aware of this age of the "robber barons" and the founding of their giant empires of railroads, steel, and oil. This was so, ironically enough, even though leaders within the Reform laity owed their position in society to their own financial connections through banking and industry to these very industrial fortunes. Yet ideologically, their liturgy explicitly favored reform. We shall see, shortly, how the 1885 Pittsburgh Platform (on which the Reform movement was constructed) could not be clearer about this stand. But evidence continues for the next several decades too. In 1909, for example, the national lay body for American Reform Jewry adopted a resolution condemning "the evil results of child labor"; in 1918, Reform rabbis met in convention to support the minimum wage, an eight-hour day, workman's compensation, and a variety of similar measures; and in 1919, Rabbis Emil G. Hirsch (Einhorn's son-in-law) and Stephen S. Wise spoke out bravely in support of workers in revolt against management within the U.S. Steel Corporation.[20]

At the same time, European Socialists were suggesting the solution of redistributed wealth and privilege. Their thinking had entered Christian theology as early as 1849, in the philosophy of Henry James, Sr. By the end of the century, popularized versions of socialism were carried to America by boatloads of immigrants whose ready availability for sweatshop labor (ironically enough) only underscored the validity of the ideas they preached. The result was a variety of

Christian groups who reinterpreted the function of religion to be the caring for a whole society rather than the winning of individual souls.[21]

For Reform Jews, hailing from European liberalism in the first place, and imbued with the doctrine of evolutionary progress leading inevitably to universal human rights, this down-to-earth doctrine of caring for the poor and protecting the powerless came as a welcome addition to the mythic role of the prophets, who had declared long ago that these very policies were the business of monarchs and privileged classes in all times and places. Surely that was what the prophet Micah had intended (Mic. 6:8) when he declared: "It hath been told thee, O man, what is good and what the Lord doth require of thee: only to do justly, and to love mercy, and to walk humbly with thy God." These very words therefore, appear in the *Avodah* of the Reform movement's first official prayer book of 1894. "Thou demandest not sacrifice, O Lord, but love with the whole heart and soul. Thou hast taught us through Thy prophets what is good and what Thou requirest from us: to do justly to love mercy and to walk humbly with Thee."[22] And to these lofty ideals were added yet other prophetic goals newly recovered from the forgotten "attic photographs" set aside so long ago when the original sacred myth had been composed. "To plead the cause of the widow and the orphan; to love and protect the stranger; to feed the hungry; to break the bonds of wickedness; to free the oppressed."[23]

These social sentiments, replete with the idealism and optimism characteristic of the heady 1880s and 1890s, had already been canonized within the Reform movement's official program. This is clear from the official definition of Judaism agreed upon at the historic Pittsburgh Conference in 1885. There, the leaders of Reform drew up a manifesto of their religious vision, and, as their eighth principle, concluded:

> In full accordance with the spirit of Mosaic legislation which strives to regulate the relation between rich and poor, we deem it our duty to participate in the great task of modern times, *to solve on the basis of justice and righteousness the problems presented by the contrasts and evils of the present organization of society.*[24]

In more felicitous language befitting prayer, it was this very declaration which entered the *Union Prayer Book*. Its sentiment would now be included in liturgical rehearsals of the sacred myth. Thus, Reform Judaism had committed itself to a view of Jewish history that differed radically from that of the rabbis in the long centuries before them, as well as from other modern movements like Zionism and secular socialism, which were attempting in their own way to come to terms with modernity by altering the perception of the Jewish past.

This new myth left an indelible mark on the Reform movement, which now put all its energy into realizing in action what the myth said in words. Through the better part of this century, educators trained their youth in religious schools, camps, and youth groups to remain true to the liberal dream. Rabbis preached and the laity lobbied on behalf of a prophetic vision that had largely been relegated to the attic for almost three thousand years. The sacred myth (this time, cited from *Dayyenu* of the 1923 *Union Haggadah*) stated the change very well. Jews were to be grateful to God, not just because they were taken from Egypt, granted the Torah, led to the Land of Israel, and given a Temple (these being inherited dogmas from an earlier age). In the end they were to give thanks because God "sent unto us prophets of truth, and made us a holy people to perfect the world under the kingdom of the Almighty, in truth and in righteousness."[25]

THE SACRED MYTH TODAY

The messianism promised in the classical Reform myth did not materialize. For all the humanitarian efforts expended by Jews and non-Jews alike in their service of the Almighty, the self-appointed saviors of the twentieth century have been other than those envisioned long ago by the Bible's "prophets of truth." It is customary to designate the Holocaust as the most shattering evidence of disillusionment in our time, and rightfully so. But the sense that Time-to-Come had not yet arrived had been growing throughout the century.

For the founding German-born Reform Jews, there was first the effect of World War One. Though pale by comparison with the Second World War, the Great War was itself a blow to the assumptions of human progress nursed by early generations of Reform Jews. Proud citizens of America though they were, many of them still looked to Germany for evidence of that cultured perspective which heralded the messianic era of history. They were at home in English, for example, but they often preferred German, belonged to German Gentlemen's clubs, founded Germanic lodges, and followed events in Germany via a German or a German-American press. A typical example of such a man was Gotthard Deutsch, who was teaching at the Hebrew Union College in Cincinnati when the war broke out. Michael Meyer describes the crisis posed for him when his assumptions regarding German moral superiority were challenged by that conflict.

> . . . Deutsch remained culturally a German. His children were taught German before they learned English, his diary until the final years was conducted in German (then, in Hebrew), and he was an active member of the local German Literary Club. When, on the eve of Passover in 1917, the United States declared war, he was so shaken that he was unable to conduct the *seder*; for six months thereafter, he could not bring himself to attend services in the College chapel.[26]

For the growing ranks of eastern European Jews newly relocated in America, by contrast, Germany's wartime role as an enemy of the United States posed no dilemma of conscience. Those already huddled in America's ghettos may have watched the unfolding conflict with interest, but hardly with surprise. Many had left eastern Europe precisely because their homes in the Polish Pale of Settlement were situated directly in the line of the German eastern front, and by the time of America's entrance into the war, they (or their families) had already suffered twice: first, at the hand of German troops advancing into Russia, and then, under Russian counterattacks in the other direction.

But these Jews from Poland and Russia were affected in at least equal measure by the disillusionment that set in with Stalin. To be sure, even western European Jews had been more than touched by the promise of Soviet Communism. As late as 1927, no less a pessimist on the human condition than Sigmund Freud still considered it prudent to temper his analysis of religious "illusion" by warning his readers:

> Let me, therefore, give an express assurance that I have not the least intention of making judgements on the great experiment in civilization [!] that is now in progress in the vast country that stretches between Europe and Asia. I have neither the special knowledge nor the capacity to decide on its practicability, to test the expediency of the methods employed, or to measure the width of the inevitable gap between intention and execution. What is in preparation there is unfinished, and therefore eludes an investigation.[27]

Whatever inchoate hopes for a breakthrough into the realm of the messiah that even Freud harbored were magnified a thousandfold by intellectuals like Arthur Koestler who joined the Communist cause avidly, only to have their hopes cruelly dashed by the recognition of the horrors of which Stalin was capable. And for every Arthur Koestler, whose name and odyssey to Communism and back again are known through literature and the arts, there were thousands of anonymous Jews, most from eastern Europe itself, who brought socialist theories and aspirations with them to America, only to discover the same disheartening information in the headlines heralding the breaking news of Stalin's purges in the thirties.

These same eastern Europeans were at that very time growing to the age when either they or their children would make up a greater and greater percentage of Reform Judaism's temple rolls, so the lingering effect of events in Russia were to have consequences of considerable magnitude for the next generation's Reform Jewish identity. Meyer reports, "Even before the Wall Street crisis of 1929, the Reform movement had begun to stagnate. From 1927 until 1929, membership . . . went up by only 264 souls while the number of congregations decreased by one."[28] This lull in religious affiliation that preceded the economic decline should be sought in the life cycle of the generation of Jews who first came here at the turn of the century. We saw above that by that time, German immigration had virtually ceased, while eastern European immigration had grown rapidly.[29] The latter reached its first peak in the years following the Kishinev pogrom of 1903, and continued strongly until arbitrarily cut off by legislation in the twenties. We also saw how, insofar as religious affiliation mattered at all, it was the Conservative movement that attracted these eastern European Jews. Many more, however, preferred no affiliation at all, whether because they were more concerned simply with the tasks of acculturation to America's economic frontier, or out of a principled decision, as often as not growing out of socialist principles. So in the late 1920s, adult American Jewry was largely made up of a generation in the last half of its life, which had arrived from Poland and Russia but either knew no religious allegiance at all or belonged to Conservative Judaism.

Their children, on the other hand, were another matter. Born during the first two decades of the century, the older members of this cohort were not to reach adulthood until the thirties. By 1927, their parents had already elected as adults not to join Reform congregations; these, their children, were still too young to choose any affiliation at all. As adults themselves, later in the thirties, they might have elected some sort of membership, but then the depression intervened. Moreover, childbearing was delayed as a result of the adverse economic conditions, so the impetus to join a synagogue in order to provide Jewish education for their children was still not a factor. In fact, we know now that the postwar baby boom was in part caused by the coincidence of these older women having children later, and their younger contemporaries (born from 1925 to 1940) having them earlier. Thus at the same time that the postwar boom encouraged couples born after 1925 to have children while they, the parents, were still young, the preceding depression had delayed childbearing for those born during the decade before, so that both older and younger couples found themselves with educable children and growing incomes at the same time: the early fifties.[30]

Precisely then did the rosters of Reform Judaism burgeon. The Conservative movement still remained the favorite religious address of these children of eastern European parents. But, contrary to what one might have predicted in 1927, when Reform affiliation was shrinking, even though the Jewish population unaffiliated with the Reform movement had grown enormously from the 1880s, when Wise still imagined that Reform Judaism would be equivalent to American Judaism at large, Reform congregations remained a close second to Conservatism. Entire belts of Reform temples soon dotted the new highway systems leading from suburbia to the inner city whence young congregants had recently come. But as heady as the Eisenhower era was for America, it could not recapture the naïve sense of messianic faith that had once gripped German Jews in the

1890s (on one hand) and eastern European socialists in the 1910s (on the other). For Jews, at least, the world had passed beyond the hope of imminent redemption. Stalin's trumped-up Doctors' Plot in 1953, to name but the most obvious of many such incidents, reminded Jews forcefully of the failure of "the grand experiment," and, of course, most significantly, Jews by now had practically been eliminated from Europe.

So it is that the events of this century have confronted Reform Jews, as stubborn facts that refuse to disappear; the optimism, the almost naïve assumption of automatic progress leading to worldwide peace just around the corner, required second thoughts. In an ironic way David Einhorn stands revealed as a false messiah, no less than Sabbatai Zevi. We shall therefore see that the "story line" of the classical Reform myth has been altered to reflect the experience of a messianic realm that did not come.

Strictly speaking, however, it would be incorrect to blame the facts themselves for the altered communal identity. One can imagine, at least, certain circumstances under which even the Holocaust, as satanic as it was, might have been integrated into the old myth, with a minimum of alteration. There are, after all, many Orthodox Jews to this day for whom the traditional myth of sin and punishment still represents all we need to know about history, and one hears their explanation of the Holocaust as divine punishment on a generation of Jews who failed to keep God's commandments. So for that segment of Jewry still loyal to the premodern rabbinic myth, even the worst example from contemporary history has demonstrated no need for reevaluation. Similarly, there are Reform Jews, members now of the American Council for Judaism, who bravely hold to the classical Reform myth, not to the extent, perhaps, of promising imminent deliverance, but in denying any significance to the modern State of Israel, and in reproducing the religious rhetoric of the last century essentially unchanged. Obviously, these two extremes encountered the brute facts of the Holocaust as much as other Jews did. But, unlike the majority of Jews, the ultra-Orthodox and American Council made the facts fit the mythic mold, rather than the other way around. It is not the events themselves, therefore, but the events *as perceived* that are the causative factor in the change of sacred myths.

Thus, for example, no major changes in the Jewish myth resulted from the Rhineland massacres of 1096, or from the decade of disaster initiated under Bogdan Chmielnicki in Poland in 1648. Each of these is an instance of widespread social dislocation with outright mass murder amounting to the decimation of entire Jewish populations. Each is reflected by the appearance of novel historical movements: German pietism (i.e., the *Hasidei Ashkenaz*) in the first instance, and Polish pietism (e.g., Maggidism and then, growing out of that, Polish Hasidism) in the second. Also, we have liturgical responses to each case, a *Memorbuch* tradition and the beginnings of a *Yizkor*, or Memorial Service, from the Rhineland, and further elegies and memorial prayers (like *El Male Rachamim*) from Poland. But neither catastrophe was sufficient to produce a rejection of the dominant rabbinic myth of sin and suffering, atonement and redemption. Thus, we should not be surprised to find that the Holocaust, however immense in magnitude, would not in itself be enough to force a rewriting of the myth's interpretive grid.

Yet the myth as carried in most current liturgies, including the Reform and Conservative movements' versions under study here, leaves us no doubt about the fact that such a reinterpretation has occurred. Its echoes sound in nearly every pronouncement of the official speakers for the Jewish community, whether in the diaspora or in Israel. It transcends synagogue ritual and pervades Jewish consciousness on all levels. One sees it in the newfound symbol of Masada, where Israeli recruits and American teenagers, both, are brought for rites of passage into adulthood; the former receive their solemn induction into the armed service of their country, and the latter are increasingly transported halfway across the world to celebrate *bar* or *bat mitzvah* at the newest shrine to Jewish continuity despite the world's enmity.[31] Prominent thinkers like Emil Fackenheim and Irving Greenberg find consonant meaning in Jewry's latest and direst tragedy, the former declaring a 614th commandment, Not to award Hitler a posthumous victory, and the latter hailing an entire new epoch in Jewish history, a Third Era of Holocaust and Beyond.[32]

The new mythology that motivates American (and Israeli) Jewry has been noted with near unanimity by one observer after another, beginning first, perhaps, with Jacob Neusner's 1973 anthropological foray into evolving American Jewish religion.[33] In 1978 (in what proved to be a prologue to his and Eliezer Don-Yehiya's full-length work on Israeli civil religion), Charles Liebman also demonstrated the extent to which traditional religious concepts have been merged in the Holocaust-Rebirth scheme envisioned by Israeli society;[34] and Jonathan Woocher finds the same justifying mythology in its American counterpart, the guiding philosophy of the overarching institution of the Federation of Jewish Philanthropy.[35]

In all the cases cited above, we find a combination of secularity and religion, and it is this amalgam of symbols from two distinct realms of discourse that deserves our attention as we try to understand why, for most Jews, the Holocaust necessitated an actual restatement of the sacred myth in a novel way. We said above that nineteenth-century German Reformers rediscovered history. The peculiar dilemma of modern men and women torn between secular science and traditional religious affirmation was evident in their very assumption that they could study Judaism from the perspective of German *Wissenschaft*, while still identifying religiously as Jews. The very history that they discovered, then, was at once both scientifically objective and religiously pregnant with meaning. What they bequeathed to posterity, and what made them different from their rabbinic predecessors, was the commitment to wed their religious vision to the hard facts of political reality that their scientific posture revealed. It was this *prior* commitment to the findings of "scientific objectivity" that distinguished them from earlier instances of generations caught in the web of disaster, for example, the Rhineland and Polish communities of the eleventh to twelfth and seventeenth centuries, whom we mentioned above. For these latter groups, historical events bore no inherently objective ontological status at all. Only the religious myth was real. And the same is true of ultra-Orthodox groups who repeat the traditional myth even in the face of the Holocaust. But this generation has been raised with a dual consciousness, in which religious symbols and scientific fact must somehow together cohere in complementary fashion. The vast majority of today's Jews, therefore, are not free simply to assimilate the horrors of the Holocaust into the previous mythic structure. Unable to deny the reality of objective history, they must alter the religious structure with which it is combined, thus redefining their sacred myth in terms equally compatible with Jewish tradition and with the objective state of a world that has known the Destruction of the Six Million.

Above all, this new myth requires a restatement of eschatological expectation, which the old Reform myth postulated as already begun. In this regard, modern Jews are no different from previous ages that witnessed failures of apocalypse. Nascent Christianity developed theologies of a Second Coming. When Sabbatai Zevi apostasized, his followers redirected their messianic hopes to the day when evil would be rooted out from within. Even the minuscule and socially isolated Lake City sect of Marion Keech, which Festinger, Riecken, and Schachter studied during the early 1950s, found that "when prophecy failed," they had to delay their anticipation of the end of time, if not deny it. These authors draw our attention to three alternative strategies that millenarian groups adopt when cognitive dissonance threatens systems of belief:

> Attempts to reduce dissonance . . . may take any or all of three forms. The person may try to change one or more of the beliefs, opinions, or behaviors involved in the dissonance, to acquire new information or beliefs that will increase the existing consonance and thus cause the total dissonance to be reduced; or to forget or reduce the importance of those cognitions that are in a dissonant relationship.[36]

Clearly, modern sacred myth-making, no less than many other commonly recognized historical prototypes, has suffered from just such dissonance. Premodern victims of dashed messianic hope had no stake in the reality of scientifically demonstrable historical data, and were therefore free to adopt the third strategy of ignoring the dissonance implied by the facts of their historical milieu. But, unlike their medieval predecessors, modern Jews have already been socialized to accept objective scientific history as fact and are therefore not able to ignore the events of their time. So they have made use of the two other alternatives. In part, they have "acquired new information or beliefs," most notably, the successful founding of the State of Israel, and a concomitant determination that a Holocaust will "never again" be allowed. In part too, they have "change[d] one or more of the[ir] beliefs," namely, the facile assumption that nineteenth-century science was the preamble to Time-to-Come, already ushered in during the social reforms of the late 1890s.

What follows, then, is the new myth of Jewish history that greets worshipers in Reform and Conservative synagogues of post-Holocaust America. It differs most markedly from what we have seen in that it represents a channeling of religious hope into the distant future. But, like its Reform predecessors, this myth accepts as equal realities historical process and transhistorical promise. In accord with Jewish tradition surveyed in the previous chapter, the sacred myth for today's Jews is found most eloquently in the rite of the Passover seder, and in the *Avodah* rubric of the Yom Kippur service. I propose describing only the former, as contained in the official Haggadah liturgies of the Reform and the Conservative movements.

But that description must be prefaced by a somewhat technical discussion of the Haggadah's motif that we encountered above: *matchil bigenut umesayem beshevach*. The phrase comes from the Mishnah, it will be recalled, where it constitutes a second-century description or characterization of the Haggadah narrative that awaits the inquiring child at the seder. As such, it has entered modern Haggadah editions in English translation. In this book, I have been following the translation that is found in the current Reform liturgy, where *genut* is called "degradation," and *shevach*, "dignity"; so the phrase would be: "[In telling the tale of the Exodus, one is obliged to] begin with [an account of] degradation and conclude with [an account of] dignity." The degradation and dignity involved are taken to mean some aspect of the sacred history of ancient Israel, which suffered the former but was delivered to the latter. One can see immediately how perfectly attuned this is to the sacred myth of today, and if it is to be claimed that our myth is really a function of contemporary life rather than an accurate transferral of an ancient mind set, one is constrained to explain how the phrase "Degradation to Dignity" came to be employed as the prime description for the Haggadah as early as the second century. But a closer look at the phrase will indicate that originally it could not have meant "Degradation to Dignity," and, moreover, that it was not even a description of Israel, but of God!

Ritualized myths see historical texts through colored spectacles. They do not simply *consciously* mistranslate or misconstrue the whole in terms of a selective perception of the parts, choosing this event or person but omitting that one (though they do that too); the colored glasses they use to observe their historical saga are, as engineers say, "soldered in"; they cannot be removed for us to get a better view of what the texts "really" say; we are often unaware of the extent to which we skew our own story.

The Mishnah, then, says that upon hearing a child's inquiry regarding the basis for the seder ceremony, one should respond "according to the level of the child's understanding. Begin with *genut* and conclude with *shevach*."[37] But what are *genut* and *shevach*? I do not mean, "What text is to be recited as *genut* and *shevach*?" or even, "What practice are the rabbis advocating here?" What I have in mind is neither a literary nor a ritual question. "From *genut* to *shevach*" is the rabbis' description of what is supposed to happen regardless of the text and irrespective of the ritual method by which that text is rehearsed. I will call it the Performative Framing of the ritual event and must, therefore, pause to recall what is meant by performative language.

The specific class of language acts called "performative" was introduced by J. L. Austin in a series of William James Lectures delivered at Harvard University in 1955 and published seven years later under the title *How to Do Things with Words*. Austin concluded his own lectures by demonstrating the shortcomings of the very term with which he had begun, but those shortcomings aside, the word "performative" has had a particular attraction for students of ritual, since if anything is a blatant performative speech-act, ritual is. In fact, many of Austin's examples are taken from rituals. In general, a performative is a sentence in which "to utter it (in, of course, the appropriate circumstances) is not to describe my doing [the event in question] or to state that I am doing it: it is to do it."[38] It is a case in which saying makes it so.

> Speaking generally, [says Austin], it is always necessary that the *circumstances* in which the words are uttered should be in some way, or ways, *appropriate*, and it is very commonly necessary that either the speaker himself or other persons should *also* perform certain *other* actions, whether 'physical' or 'mental' actions or even acts of uttering further words.[39]

Performatives do not describe, then; they accomplish; one can ask of them not whether their content is true or false but only whether their proposed action is successfully (Austin says, "felicitously") accomplished. This certainly sounds like ritual, and two of Austin's own examples from the field of ritual are "I do" (in a wedding), in which case we do not ask, "But did you really?" meaning to question the truth content of the statement, as if it were not performative but descriptive; and "I name this ship the Queen Elizabeth," in which case we would not ask, "But is it really the Queen Elizabeth?" since we know that the utterance was performative, and that, consequently, if all the appropriate conditions of the utterance were present, the very saying that it was the Queen Elizabeth made it so.

If much of ritual is performative in nature, instructions about ritual tend either

to express the conditions under which performative utterances turn out felicitously, or to capture those conditions in a technical phrase, without, however,
stipulating what they are, but instead assuming that the hearer knows them in
advance. The first case is obvious: we tell seminarians what clothes to wear for a
wedding, what tone of voice to employ for a funeral oration, where to stand at
the graveside, how to hold their hands at the benediction, and so on. The latter
case, however—what I want to call the Performative Framing—is less obvious,
but is what I have in mind here, as I try to understand the nature of the Mishnah's
laconic "Begin with *genut* and conclude with *shevach*."

By analogy, imagine instructing our seminarians about to perform their first
wedding, "Marry them"; or, for a funeral, "Bury them." The first case,
"Marry them," is a technical expression with absolutely no commonly used
general denotation other than a wedding, and it can be used here only because the
seminarians already know more or less what should happen. The details have yet
to be filled in, of course, but the instructor might well say, "Today, we will
discuss how you marry them," and then proceed to explain the details of how
such a successful act is accomplished: that one wears formal garb, asks certain
prescribed questions, refrains from joking during the ceremony, concludes with a
benediction, and so on. In both instances, the words "Marry them" serve to
frame the nature of the performative act intended, in the same way that a door
frame gives a person access to a room, determining the vantage point from which
the room will be viewed; or the way a particular type of picture frame hems in a
painting and sets it off as modern or old master. Whether I say simply, "Marry
them," or follow that up with instructions so that "Marry them," constitutes a
prologue for explanatory detail that will follow, the words "Marry them" constitute a verbal framing in that they establish in the hearer's mind the parameters
of the ritualized event to be effected by the appropriately conducted ritual or
performative action. "Bury them" differs from "Marry them" in that the word
"bury" does denote a simple physical act as well as the performance of a
religious ritual; so here, especially, the instructor depends on the fact that the
seminarians know roughly what sort of thing is to be done; they won't simply
pile some earth over the bodies.

In sum, both "Marry them" and "Bury them" are akin to Austin's examples
of performative language, not that these two instructive sentences are performative themselves, but they are preparatory to the performative speech-act, instructive of the fact that such a ritualized event should occur. To use the instructive
mode of discourse regarding performative language is to convey to the hearer not
only that something should be said, but also that it should be said felicitously,
that is, that it should be said in such a way that the saying accomplishes its goal.
The set of instructions that might follow would be designed to detail how such a
felicitous outcome can be assured, but not everything can be communicated even

there. The seminary students who are would-be performers of the instructions must be trusted with the ability to know in advance at least the general tone that should prevail during the ritual action. If one must say even, "Bury them, but with dignity" or "Marry them, without demonstrating sadness," one suspects that the listener will probably fail to perform the events in question, no matter how many of the instructions they internalize. So rituals attract to themselves specialized framing utterances, headings or titles for the acts involved, that are used as shorthand oblique references to the acts involved, and that may or may not explicitly refer to the tone or other supportive characteristics that must be present for a performative speech-act to achieve its end felicitously.

Our Mishnaic citation "Begin with *genut* and conclude with *shevach*" is such a Performative Frame. It is functionally equivalent to saying, "Now do the seder." It occurs in the Mishnaic text as a heading, under which is to be subsumed the various ritual details that constitute the successful (or felicitous) seder event. To paraphrase, we are told that when you, the seder leader, are asked about the meaning of the night (i.e., when the first ritual actor opens the night's proceedings in the appropriate ritual way), you are to go from *genut* to *shevach*, that is, "to do" the seder.

In other words, the instructions about *genut* and *shevach* are just that, instructions; they are *not* descriptions. Hence, the notion that by these words the Mishnah describes a second-century characterization of the Exodus is mistaken. The message of today's sacred myth is that the essence of the holy people Israel is to move from degradation to dignity, and that this recurrent motif of Jewish history, first encountered in the formative Egyptian slavery-to-freedom event, is ever after repeated until the latest example, our own time. This message is certainly an instance of powerful myth-making in the present, but it has nothing to do with the original intent of the phrase we borrow from the Mishnah to prove it.

Nor do the words *genut* and *shevach* even mean *Israel*'s degradation and ultimate dignity. A search for parallels elsewhere in rabbinic literature demonstrates that *genut* is a common opposite of *shevach*, and that it means "shortcomings" or "disgrace" as opposed to "praiseworthiness" or, sometimes, just "praise." Thus, for example, we find the curious admonition that one should refrain from voicing the *shevach* of one's neighbor, since that can lead only to an implication of the neighbor's *genut* as well. This advice is carried variously in two parallel recensions (on the same page, in fact), the latter of which substitutes for *genuto* (lit. "his [the neighbor's] *genut*) the word *ra'ato* (lit. "his *ra'ah*"), that is, the neighbor's evil deeds or character faults for which censure, not praise (*shevach*) would be in order.[40] So *genut* is like *ra'ah*, both being the opposite of *shevach*. *Shevach* rightly evokes praise (or is itself "praise"), while *genut* deserves rebuke.

This interpretation is borne out by the Targum to Gen. 13:14. When Shechem rapes Jacob's daughter, Dinah, and then requests her in marriage, Jacob's brothers refuse the match on the grounds that the marriage would be "a reproach to us" (Gen. 34:14). The Targum renders the Hebrew word for "reproach" (*cherpah*) as the Aramaic *genuta*. Taking this instance together with the previous example, we can see that by juxtaposing *genut* to *shevach* in their Performative Frame for the seder, the rabbis were not even talking about degradation and dignity but about unseemly behavior deserving censure and of worthy acts deserving praise.

But whose behavior is in question? Ever since the rabbis of the Talmud took it upon themselves to interpret the Mishnah's laconic reference to *genut*,[41] it has been usual to assume that we are discussing behavior predicative of Israel. Thus, one description of *genut* was slavery itself, while another was Israel's worship of idols in its early prehistory. But these later rabbis of the talmudic period no longer understood what the original Performative Frame denoted. Their alternatives aren't even in the same class of nouns, in that slavery is imposed from without and so is hardly a case of *genut*, the slaves' own disgrace; while idolatry, though self-selected, and therefore a case of *genut*, is not even part of the Exodus story (though, to be sure, it was eventually added to the Haggadah's tale, so as to satisfy the exegetical expectation that it ought to be there).[42] If however, we abandon the idea that Israel is the subject at all, our difficulties disappear.

That this is indeed the case becomes clear from a close reading later on in the same Mishnaic passage whence the instructions "from *genut* to *shevach*" are drawn. We find there a series of binary opposites, each one contrasting the state of bondage with the state of freedom. This appositive string constitutes the introduction to the *Hallel* (see below) and the benediction we call the *Ge'ullah*, "Redemption," and thus forms a series descriptive of the opposition between redemption and its absence: "[God] brought us from servitude to freedom, from sadness to joy, from mourning to festivity, from darkness to great light, and from enslavement to redemption" (*me'avdut lecherut, miyagon lesimchah, ume'evel leyom tov, ume'afelah le'or gadol, umishibud lege'ullah*).[43] Given the fact that the wording of early rabbinic liturgical formulae varied from place to place, we cannot conclude that the binary opposite of *genut/shevach* was *never* included in this benediction, but it is at least odd to find it missing here, if it is just another metaphor for the difference in state between servitude and freedom: in this case, Israel's actions that were worthy of denigration (either while enslaved or beforehand, in its act of idolatry) and its praiseworthy behavior thereafter. But it is not included. What we have is not simply one more paired opposite for non-redemption/redemption, but another notion entirely, compatible with the absence of our phrase from the benediction in question, and with its inclusion as a Performative Frame heading up the seder's instructions.

We saw above that the phrase is not in the Haggadah text at all, but part of the Mishnah's instructions for conducting a seder felicitously. Since the seder began as a tableship rite, and since much of the Mishnah's description of the ritual action necessary to promote a felicitous end to the rite revolves about the proper handling of food, drink, and appropriate accompanying statements, we should not be surprised to find that *genut/shevach*, far from being a theological characterization of Israel's history, fit for inclusion in the sacred tale of the Haggadah text (where it is absent), is really an allusion to another tableship custom, once common, but forgotten today. This leads us to a consideration of tableship customs in Greco-Roman society, in the search for a general custom descriptive of the entire evening's ritual, one that could be used as a general heading for the event, in the same sense that "burial" is a general heading for the rite of interment.

Such a custom is discussed in Stein's pilot study of the seder's prototype, the Greco-Roman symposium, where we learn that one particular form of that festive meal presented the evening's celebration in terms of the gods themselves, who were assumed to underwrite the course of history and human events. Stein is explicit in his description of this symposium format, explaining that the evening began with a sort of "roast," in which the gods were disparaged; and it concluded with a recitation of their praise.[44] Without doubt, the seder once ended that way: with praise of God in the form of the Egyptian *Hallel* (Pss. 113–18).[45] So I suggest that its beginning was perceived as a sort of rebuke, a disparagement of the Divine One who had let Israel fall into servitude in the first place. The seder was therefore characterizable as proceeding from *genut* to *shevach*. Thus the blessing of Redemption correctly omits the opposition of *genut/shevach* from its list: it has nothing to do with Israel, before and after the departure from Egypt. It is a shorthand notation for the character of the evening, which was a description of *God's* actions in history, beginning with God's *genut*, but ending with God's *shevach*.

The point I have tried to make in this lengthy excursus from my primary topic of this chapter, the changing sacred myth carried in the Haggadah, is the extent to which a new generation misreads its sacred texts, in what Harold Bloom calls "a critical act, a misreading or misprision, that one poet performs upon another, and that does not differ in kind from the necessary critical acts performed by every strong reader upon every text he encounters."[46] Designers of ritual are very "strong readers"! An original notion of an evening devoted to considering God's defects and virtues evident in the Exodus narrative gave rise to a shorthand way of referring to the seder ritual. Borrowing on Austin's suggestion that rituals are performative actions, I called the phrase as it is used in this instructive way a Performative Frame. As such, it was correctly placed in the Mishnah's instructions for the rite, but omitted from the text. It constituted a ritualistic conceit whereby the evening of the seder was fit into a pregiven mold framed as a description of God who stood behind history. It did not purport to be descriptive of Israel, but of God.

However, the phrase "From *genut* to *shevach*" has been rediscovered in our time as a convenient synopsis of the shape of history as our new sacred myth imagines Israel's destiny to have been. Thus, in the Haggadah issued by the American Reform movement, it appears as an overall description of the redemptive process, for the leader begins his/her narration of the Exodus with it.[47] In so doing, it introduces us to what has become today's dominant liturgical myth of Jewish history.

Jewish history, for the rabbis, was epochal, the present era of Time-Now being viewed as a sorry state of limbo through which historical Jewry must pass on its way from the paradise lost of Time-Past to the messianic Time-to-Come. Nineteenth-century liberal Jews rediscovered the historical detail of Time-Now, bequeathing to posterity the very science of Jewish history, along with empirical evidence that the Jewish chronicle was fully as bad as readers of rabbinic sin-and-punishment literature might have supposed anyway. But along with their denial of the concept of exile went their parallel refusal to accept the rabbinic explanatory moral. If Jews had suffered, as they apparently had, throughout the medieval period, it was because they had been chosen to play the role of suffering servant in the moral evolution of humanity: so argued both Wise and Einhorn. But Time-Now was drawing to an end. Modernity they saw as nothing less than the footsteps of the messianic age drawing relentlessly nearer. They themselves were the earliest harbingers of Time-to-Come.

Today's myth retains the discovery of Time-Now's historical detail but denies the conclusion that Time-Now has ended. In the wake of this century's repetitive demonstration of inhumanity and suffering, today's Jewish liturgy has had to find comfort within the confines of history itself. So we discover that our liturgy arranges history into a pattern, with an existential message of hope not unlike the myth of Sisyphus. Sisyphus was condemned to roll a boulder up a hill, endlessly, knowing that near the top, it would inevitably roll down again, whence he would have to begin anew. So too, Jewish history appears in our texts as a continual return of the cycle of Jewish suffering and miraculous recovery. To be sure, it differs from the Sisyphus myth in that Sisyphus's burden is never ending—comfort must be located within the task of rolling the boulder—whereas, for liberal Jews today, even though the ultimate deliverance of Time-to-Come has been pushed back beyond reasonable expectations of our lifetime, its arrival is still held out as a genuine reality. So we find our liturgy promising eventual deliverance from the cycle of suffering and rebirth, while at the same time actually glorying in the ongoing miracle of a Jewish people continually beset by historical tribulation but always rising anew to life and hope. And the continued existence of that people, particularly in its newly revived homeland of Israel, despite suffering sufficient to have destroyed it, is given explicit theological value: if not ultimate deliverance itself, it is at least a witness to the promise that such deliverance will eventually arrive.

It is this Phoenix-like resurrective capacity of the Jewish people that is described now by the phrase *migenut leshevach*, "degradation to dignity" (as it is translated in the new Reform Haggadah). Jewish history is portrayed as alternating cycles of degradation at the hands of tyrants followed by miraculous recovery of dignity, the latest such example being the Holocaust, and, in its wake, the birth of the modern State of Israel. Neither the Reform Haggadah nor its Conservative parallel leave any room for doubt regarding the theological significance of either Holocaust or State. Let us look at each in turn, beginning with *A Passover Haggadah*, the official Passover text for Reform Jews.

To begin with, this Haggadah reidentifies Pharaoh not just as an unnamed Aramean anymore, but as Hitler. The Egyptians of the Reform Haggadah's narrative reemerge here, first in the prose of Peter Fischl, who perished in Auschwitz in 1944, and then in one of the diary entries of Anne Frank.[48] The latter goes farther in that it also provides us with our message of hope, even in the face of history's cruelty, for Anne concludes that "people are really good at heart," that "this cruelty too will end, and that peace and tranquility will return again." Not that even Anne is willing to adopt the other-worldly eschatology of the rabbis. She is utterly impervious to metaphors of posthistorical redemption. A trifle naïve, perhaps—easier for us to judge, with hindsight, surely—but nonetheless a realist, Anne wishes only to draw some moral about living her life within history, not beyond it.

Realistic also is Abraham Shlonsky, whose poem "A Vow" follows the entry from Anne Frank's diary, in a translation that bespeaks the more concrete symbol of Masada: "Never again!"

> In the presence of eyes
> which witnessed the slaughter,
> which saw the oppression
> the heart could not bear,
> and as witness the heart
> that once taught compassion
> until days come to pass
> that crushed human feeling,
> I have taken an oath: To remember it all,
> to remember, not once to forget!
> Forget not one thing to the last generation
> when degradation shall cease,
> to the last, to its ending,
> when the rod of instruction

> shall have come to conclusion.
> An oath: Not in vain passed over
> the night of the terror.
> An oath: No morning shall see me
>   at flesh-pots again.
> An oath: Lest from this we learned nothing.[49]

So today's liturgical myth locates worshipers within the scope of human history, which failed to come to an end as Wise and Einhorn had hoped. The Holocaust is the latest instance of travail within that history. On the other side of things, however, we find the birth of the Third Jewish Commonwealth in the form of Israel the State. Though, like the Holocaust, the State is fully within history, it is yet symbolic of metahistory, in that if it is not ultimate deliverance of Time-to-Come, at least it is taken to signify that though delayed, Time-to-Come will at least someday arrive. From his new home in Palestine, Israel's poet laureate Chaim Nachman Bialik looked back at oppression under the czars. In this Haggadah, his words epitomize the newly found assertive temperament of Israel's founders, and the new Jew of American history, for that matter, for both are alike in their novel insistence on learning from history the lesson of "Never again." Thus, Reform Jews at their seder now read:

> We are the mighty!
> The last generation of slaves and
> the first generation of free men!
> Alone our hand in its strength
> tore from the pride of our shoulders
> the yoke of bondage.
> We lifted our heads to the heavens,
> and behold, their broadness was
>   narrow in the pride of our eyes.
> So we turned to the desert, we said
> to the Wilderness: "Mother!"
> Yea, on the tops of the crags in
> the thickness of clouds,
> with the eagles of heaven we drank
> from her fountains of freedom.[50]

If Bialik's message of this-worldly deliverance is not clear enough, it is amplified in a reading intended to conclude the Haggadah narrative and introduce the final songs. The reading appears under a rubric entitled "An Additional Cup Set Aside for the Future," thus promising a final Time-to-Come after all. In the meantime, however, our gaze is fastened on history itself, even by the Haggadah's italic preface to this reading, which informs us, "Within this service may be found texts representative of the entire sweep of our history and tradition, texts from prophetic, rabbinic and modern sources, including the Declaration of Independence of the State of Israel.'' Here, the relationship between the State and ultimate deliverance is clarified. The State is not Time-to-Come, but it heralds that day of final redemption.

> *Leader:*
> It is still dark as we pour this cup;
> But light dawns over Zion as we raise this
>   cup,
> For the day when we will tell
> Of the deliverance of all.
> We set aside this cup
> As a sign of hope,
> For the beginning of Redemption.
>
> *Group:*
> As a sign of the beginning of Redemption,
> The people Israel lives![51]

The Reform Haggadah had been in use for eight years when the Conservative movement finally published its own version of the seder ritual. But the eight-year hiatus in no way diminished the message of Israel the people, suffering and reviving. Nor was the latest example of the paradigm, from Holocaust to Israel the State, diminished in symbolic intensity. If anything, the theology is more explicit. Even in 1946, Conservative liturgy had presented the struggle for Jewish statehood in messianic terms; for example, by inserting a meditation on the theme of ''rebuilding . . . Thy holy land'' in the very section of the service that we cited earlier as an instance of the rabbinic myth of historical suffering caused by sin, the *Musaf Tefillah*.[52] Thirty-six years have not changed the Conservative movement's mind.

Conservative editors feel greater constraint than Reform editors do in maintaining the traditional text. So whereas the new myth of the Reform Haggadah often supplants the old one, Conservative liturgy presents both old and new side by side. The traditional text is printed in the center of the page, with the novel interpretations embedded in a more general running commentary and consigned to the margin; or, at times, the new message is structurally set off as a separate unit in between two traditional rubrics. In our case, we find regular references to Holocaust and the State of Israel both marginally and in a new unit that the introduction calls ''a new section . . . marking the latest milestone in the far-flung travels of our people.'' The description that follows deserves full citation, since it describes faithfully the thesis presented here. We find the new myth superbly summarized in the first three words alone; and from the inclusion of that summary in an introduction penned by the editor himself, we may certainly conclude that the formation of myth is not merely an unconscious mechanism, but is partly willed, planned, and executed by writers of liturgy in every generation.

> *Catastrophe and Consolation*: each generation must endure or witness this fateful yet all too familiar cycle. Both the Holocaust and the State of Israel are mirrored here, for they shape our own Exodus. . . .[53]

History, then, is a cycle of catastrophe and consolation, which every generation must endure. The latest instance is Holocaust to State of Israel. That, in a nutshell, is the liturgical myth in Jewish liturgy today.

Examples from the Conservative Haggadah can easily be multiplied. Recollection that "the Egyptians dealt harshly with us" prompts the recognition also of "despots through the ages" whose "satanic strategy . . . escalated into systematic persecution, mass expulsion and calculated genocide."[54] Remembrance of the first Passover, observed in Egypt so long ago, leads to remembrance of "so many Pesah evenings . . . in times of danger and duress, with bloodthirsty mobs howling at the door, amid bullets and bombs. . . . Among honored survivors of the Holocaust are scraps of paper, makeshift *Haggadot*, written by hand, written by heart, written within sight of the smoking crematoria."[55] Elsewhere, God's miracles in Egypt evoke the time "during the Six-Day War, when Israel was once more beleaguered, outnumbered, imperiled, while the world once more adopted a wary interventionist pose, [and] it seemed . . . that only a miracle could save the Jewish State. When the Israeli victory came . . . even Jewish agnostics prayed first and rationalized it later!"[56] Slavery to freedom is equated here with "Auschwitz to Entebbe in a single generation."[57] "Servants of the Lord," a general reference in Ps. 113, is accompanied in the marginal commentary by the putative speech of none other than Eleazer ben Yair, who led the Masada zealots first in battle against Imperial Rome, and then, to their own suicides.

> "Since we, long ago, my noble friends, resolved never to be servants to the Romans, nor to any other than to God Himself who alone is the true and just Ruler of mankind, the time has now come that obligates us to make that resolution true in practice." So spoke Eleazer ben Jair to the defenders of Masada in the year 73 C.E., according to the stirring docu-drama outlined by Josephus. "Let us die before we become slaves under our enemies, and let us go out of the world together with our wives and our children, in a state of freedom." For seven years, a few hundred zealots had held at bay the panoplied legions of Imperial Rome. When defeat became inevitable, they chose death by their own hands rather than dishonor.[58]

This is clearly a new view of Jewish history. Its new hero is Eleazer ben Yair, who epitomizes the Jewish people under eternal seige. All of history is contained in the contrast between Auschwitz and Entebbe, for until some distant future, Time-Now, with its cycles of catastrophe and consolation, is all we have.

Psalm 118:17 reads, "I shall not die, but live." The marginal commentary adds:

> In the aftermath of the Holocaust, Jewish survival has acquired a new dimension: a dimension of sanctity. . . . This may be an age without heroes. It is, however, the heroic age *par excellence* in all of Jewish history. . . . Nowhere is this truth as unmistakable as in the State of Israel. The State of Israel is collectively what the survivor is individually—testimony on behalf of all mankind to life against death, to sanity against madness, to Jewish self-affirmation against every form of flight from it and to the God of the ancient covenant against all lapses into paganism . . . its watchword is *am yisra'el ḥai*—the people Israel lives.[59]

As Theodor Herzl, who is quoted here, put it:

> I believe that a wondrous breed of Jews will spring up from the earth. The Maccabees will rise again. The Jews who will it shall achieve their own State. We shall live at last as free men and women on our own soil, and in our own homes die peacefully. The world will be liberated by our freedom . . . and whatever we attempt there for our own benefit will redound mightily and beneficially to the good of all mankind.[60]

So despite many differences, the two official Haggadah texts of the two largest Jewish religious movements in North America are in substantial agreement on the nature of Jewish history. What the Reform text calls "degradation to dignity" is equivalent to the Conservative Haggadah's cycle of "catastrophe and consolation." In both cases we have a story of an eternal people buffeted by history, the end of which is symbolized in the State of Israel's miraculous appearance, and in the continued vitality of the Jewish people: "the beginning of redemption" (for Reform Jews);[61] "the beginning of the flowering of our Redemption" (for Conservative Jews),[62] and even "the dawn of our Redemption" as it is boldly labeled in a special prayer for the State inserted into the latter's grace after meals.[63] The new history is made of Auschwitz, Entebbe, the Maccabees and Masada; of Eleazer ben Yair, Anne Frank, even Theodor Herzl, and of Holocaust writers whose Yiddish poetry is reproduced here in the original language that almost no one understands any more, but that symbolizes six million who died speaking it—Yiddish is, in fact, becoming a holy tongue, reserved for Holocaust martyrologies and liturgical memorials.[64]

Throughout this account I have emphasized the reality of sacred myths to the worshipers who internalize them from their liturgies. They are taught from early childhood and reinforced in sacred assemblies throughout one's life. They are not open to rational argumentation. In the sense that C. G. Jung speaks of a symbol as directing us to something deep inside our psyche, something inchoate and unamenable to the logical contours of mental structuring, we may see these sacred myths as possessing symbolic reality, and thus surpassing alternative accounts in the force of the demands they make upon us.

For rabbinic and medieval times, that myth declared the utter insignificance of Time-Now and prompted patient acceptance of this limbo-period until such time as our sins might be pardoned and the messiah might arrive. Classical Reform Jews rediscovered history, but could not free themselves from the hope that Time-to-Come would indeed come, miraculously, and in their age, for their own rediscovery of history was a sign of humanity's evolution beyond the immoral confines that prevented the realization of the messianic ideal. Israel's exile became for them Israel's mission. But now, a new myth has arisen. It is fed by the events of our time, and presented in the clearest of images to today's worshipers, in the time-honored rites of Judaic ritual and in Jewish civil religion (American and Israeli, alike).

Clearly, one of the prime functions of liturgy is the presentation of sacred myths to sacred assemblies, that through a selective vision of their past, they may learn how to plot their future.

APPENDIX

Inclusion in the Myth

The Case of Women

This chapter has dealt extensively with the sacred tale of a people as presented in that people's liturgy. A related question, so far unrecognized in our discussion, is the issue of identifying who the members of a people are. This identification is far from obvious. Society is always divided along an assortment of lines: chronological, social, sexual, racial, and so on. Not everyone physically present "counts." The sacred myth entails immediate consequences only for the sacred individuals whose tale it is, and not everyone is granted equivalent sacred status.

This academic matter has emerged forcefully in recent years with the realization that liturgy has largely been penned by men for men, so that, generally speaking, in both Christian and Jewish circles, among the categories of excluded members have been the more than fifty percent who are women. The standard myth has hitherto supported this social classification along sexual lines by emphasizing male heroes, on one hand, and by regularly speaking in masculine language, as if to indicate that the sacred tale being told was intended only for the men present. In chapter 1, we referred to the fast-day ritual in the first century, whereby a male elder addressed the men present as "Brothers" and proceeded to identify male, but not female, paradigms of human beings crying successfully to God for help.[1] We saw also how Reform Jews like Isaac Mayer Wise may have added prophets in general, or even Ezra and Zerubabel in particular, to the myth's cast of sacred characters; but they did not add women, even though at their rabbinic synod of 1845, they declared them theoretically equivalent to men.[2] Certainly the issue of masculine language, the carrier, if not the content, of the myth, was never even considered until relatively recent times. But one of the true novelties of the new liturgical myths is their decision to consider the presentation of both content and carrier in terms equally inclusive for men and women. This chapter would be incomplete without our including some discussion of the phenomenon.

A word regarding the timing and the manner in which the new liturgy came into being is in order before we begin. For reasons not wholly evident, the new liturgies of which we have been speaking are part of a much larger reform in worship styles that itself is only part of a greater revolution still in church and synagogue structure, ecclesia, theology, and sociology. Vatican II can conveniently be taken as the historic landmark for the change, but preconciliar Catholic voices had been demanding change for years, so the phenomenon of liturgical renewal (as it is known in Christian circles; Jews tend to use the word "reform") did not arise overnight. At any rate, by the late sixties, it was evident within Jewish and Christian communities that the old liturgical ways would not last. The only questions were how much would change, how fast, and directed by whom.

In the Jewish community, it was the Reform movement that felt the stirrings for change first, and it is the liturgy of this movement that we will survey here. By 1970, a committee was already at work on what would some day become *Gates of Prayer*, the daily Sabbath and Festival prayer book for the movement. A second committee was working concurrently on *A Passover Haggadah*. These were the two committees that first had to confront the feminist issues just then being raised. Since then, one can isolate four stages in the process by which committees came to terms with the challenge before them:

1. *A Passover Haggadah* (published 1974), which makes almost no concession to feminist assertions that women are excluded from the liturgy.
2. *Gates of Prayer* (published 1975), which emends masculine language for people so as to include women, but does not alter masculine references to God. It also adds women to the all-male lists of biblical heroes that constitute basic prayers in the liturgy.
3. *Gates of Repentance* (published 1978) follows the same guidelines as *Gates of Prayer* but is noteworthy for the fact that its first committee draft advocated altering masculine language for God too. At the very end, God-language was reinstated in the masculine, but only by a very close margin of decision, and against the strenuous objections of some, including the general editor.
4. Post–*Gates of Repentance*: 1978 to today. No major new prayer books have been issued since 1978, but a minor one, *Gates of Forgiveness*, intended as penitential liturgy, illustrates the trend since that time. All God-language is now either neutral—generally phrased in second-person address or, in one case, even leaning toward the feminine, in a prayer addressed to "mothering presence." The Haggadah has been reissued with its blatant sexisms regarding human beings emended. For Reform Jews, at least, the inclusion of women in the liturgical myths is taken for granted.

With this background, let us survey the extent to which women now find a place in at least one version of the liturgical myth of Jewish history.

The new Reform liturgy avoids the constant references to "men," "children of men," and the like, which characterized the liturgies of Wise, Einhorn, and the early *Union Prayer Books*. (One notable exception is a prayer in the first edition of *A Passover Haggadah*, which emanated from stage 1, above, but was altered in the revised edition of stage 4.)[3] In keeping with this position, statements of the new myth now either avoid exclusive references to "God of our fathers" (but not "our mothers"?) or include historical reminiscence of the "God of our mothers" as well.[4] Similarly, the Haggadah's "four sons" now reappear as "the four children."[5] And the version of Jewish history in the *Avodah* now notes that God created both male and female, [6] the Temple cult of old was witnessed by "men and women,"[7] and the victims of Nazi atrocity were "infants, women, young men, old."[8] Another meditation on the same historical theme reads: "In the beginning God created heaven and earth, and the earth brought forth life, and life gave birth to man and woman . . ." and later: "a vision was seen by the founders of our people."[9] The original poem from which this reading was adapted read: "and life gave birth to man," and the "vision was seen by the fathers of our people."[10] Clearly, women have become candidates with men for mythic heroism.

On the other hand, it is apparent that these books were composed in the dawning of the age of equality for women. Many long discussions were held regarding the extent to which linguistic alterations were desirable, even given the commitment of the Reform movement to remove impediments to women's attainment of equal rights. Men and women argued their cases on each side. Yet on some matters, no clear decisions were reached. The publication of the books could not wait until the revolution in women's rights might be concluded, and, with the benefit of hindsight, the editors might know the proper course of action. So it may be that living now, in the wake of what I have called stage 4, many would argue that these books do not go far enough in the integration of women to fully equal status here.

One notes, for example, that in the very same *Avodah*, it is "Abraham's descendents" that "stood at Mt. Sinai"; and that the "spark of hope for better days" is "a remnant saved by a miracle from that fire kept by our fathers always upon their altars."[11] This latter case is a translation and reworking of a poem by poet laureate Chaim Nachman Bialik. Should the authors have emended his poem in the translation, invoking not fathers but forebears, or fathers and mothers? That is what they did with the daily *Tefillah* prayer, "God of our fathers," becoming "God of all generations," or sometimes, "fathers and mothers."[12] Moreover, a reading through the entire *Avodah* reveals no women who were included in this mythic account as meriting outstanding distinction in Jewish history. They may stand with the men, but they do not stand alone as independently significant in their own right. True, here too, one is constrained to some extent by the nature of the historically received texts that form the basis for

Jewish liturgy. But one wonders whether liturgical editors of the next decade will further emend this *Avodah* to include new readings faithful to their movement's vision of true equality. Wise added Zerubabel and Ezra, we recall. Will others someday add also the wisdom of Deborah, the faithfulness of Ruth, the witness to history of Glückel of Hameln, and the like? As we saw, Anne Frank does find her way into the sacred myth as presented in the Haggadah, but she is an exception.[13] As noted above, the Reform movement has issued a new printing of its Haggadah, which promises that it emends its sexist language; and Passover of 1982 also saw for the first time a companion volume for the seder that complements the main Haggadah text by providing a compendium of readings that bear witness to the experience of women in Jewish tradition.[14] Clearly the issue is far from over.

In this regard, however, the greatest debate deals not with the human beings who cross the stage of history, but with the language used for God. The lengthy debates on this issue bring into focus the process of liturgical myth-making. It was eventually decided to retain masculine terminology for the divine, since, presumably, no modern Jew confuses the necessarily metaphorical description of God with the real nature of a supreme being. Committee members argued that it has been some eight hundred years now since Maimonides taught that the real God is beyond the power of words to describe. Yet on the other side it was noted that a subtle relationship does indeed exist between God-language and God-concept; and an equally significant bond between God-concept and self-image, since people say they are created in the image of God.[15]

Should the prayer books have altered all translations of Hebrew to read "You" instead of "He"; "Your Kingdom," or better, "Your Sovereignty" or "Realm," instead of "His Kingdom"? And what should one do with the traditional and majestic image of the Days of Awe, *Avinu Malkenu*, which translates literally as "our Father, our King"? The matter is complicated and still unresolved. As we saw above, the latest of the *Gates* series, *Gates of Forgiveness* (that is, the *Selichot* service of preparation for the High Holy Days) does in fact balance the masculine imagery with a reading addressing God in the feminine. ("Mothering Presence . . . Mother, Sister . . . Mother Present in us all, Mother Present in all presence.")[16] And at this writing, discussions are being held about reprinting all Reform prayer books with altered wording to reflect a more developed state of consciousness.

Whatever will finally be done with regard to wording is beyond our knowledge now. But the rediscovery of the mothers as well as the fathers who constitute Israel's history is a historic break with past communal consciousness, and so, a major addendum to the sacred myth that motivates Jewish existence for Reform Jews who pray from the liturgy of today.

SEVEN

The Numinous

A Problem of Recognition

We have already had occasion once to resort to the metaphor of a field;[1] there is, we said, a field of meaning that is created around a prayer text, when that text, previously meaningless, is given significance according to the canons of a given method. Method thus imposes categorization on text, by throwing it into relief against what emerge as parallel or related texts, all of which now appear as relevant entities and therefore enter the field surrounding the text that was the original object of study. Propositions describing that which binds all the texts together will similarly be included in the field. Eventually we pronounce ourselves satisfied that we have unearthed the prayer's "meaning," by which we mean we have developed a context in which the prayer makes sense, and within that context, we have a hypothesis connecting the prayer being studied with other prayers.

The nature of the field varies with the method, so that a philological field, with its emphasis on alternatively worded texts or its information regarding politically motivated prayers, will differ from a form-critical one, the latter preferring statements about institutions that generate prayer types, and contrasting formal characteristics of worship material.

Within either field, different hypotheses are possible. Generally, one accepts as a "given" the nature of the field of meaning that one's research will produce, but within that "given" one redraws the lines of influence, so to speak, putting together in ever new ways the field's "facts," which can be compared to pieces of a jigsaw puzzle.

But there is another way in which the term "field" is employed. Though related, it differs subtly. I mean the descriptions of psychological or social phenomena that characterize the writings of such theorists as Kurt Lewin or Victor Turner, for example. The two uses of "field" are the same in that they both posit a Gestalt notion of reality, whereby meaning is conferred on an object only through its many relations to the configuration of relevant objects in its "field." But they differ also. Lewin and Turner use "field" to describe what they actually observe happening in the case studies before them. So Lewin's psychological field and Turner's ritual or political field are intended as useful descriptions of what each of them is studying at the time; field of meaning, on the other hand, is a hypothetical construct stating the *a priori* circumstances under which any object is studied and classified as having meaning; it describes the conditions under which meaning is conferred on that which is observed, as well as the resulting network of facts that will be considered adequate in explaining what is seen. It is an epistemological, not an empirical, category. So, even though Lewin's definition of field as "the totality of coexisting facts which are conceived of as mutually interdependent"[2] applies equally to both usages, there are actually two kinds of fields possible, and we would do well not to confuse them. The first is the empirically observable set of relationships within which social activity proceeds, and within which its actors discover meaning. This may be a psychological field, an anthropological field, a ritual field, a political field, or any other area of human activity. The second is the set of nonempirically derived propositions regarding any of those fields that a third party determines in advance to use in describing the activity in question.

Clearly the two fields are related. My selection of a set of propositions to describe an activity (i.e., the field of meaning) will be determined by what I perceive to be the nature of the field I am studying (psychological behavior, political activity, and the like). Since liturgists have regarded their field of study as a class of literature, namely, prayer, they have preferred fields of meaning composed of propositions about texts. Since I do not see myself as studying books, I am obliged to draw a broader definition of the types of propositions I will admit as explanations for the field I end up selecting.

I should like to say that I am studying the "liturgical field." That is, there are people who find themselves in what they believe to be liturgical situations, and they then follow certain defined rules of behavior carrying out a class of activities that we call liturgical. I apply the determinative "liturgical" here in the sense in which Turner, for example, uses the word "political." He describes the Hidalgo Insurrection by defining its "political field," by which he means, "the totality of relationships between actors oriented to the same prizes or values."[3] Of course, his definition contains an implicit thesis regarding the nature of political action, in that "orientation to" implies "competition for" prizes or scarce resources. So it need not be adopted wholly by us. I cite it only for illustrative purposes. The parallel in our case is that I mean to replace a category of books with a category of human activity: the community at prayer, an activity that I understand as organized around a set of relationships between people and their neighbors, people and their holy texts, people and their God. The totality of all these relationships constitutes the liturgical field.

Of them all, it is the relationship between the worshiper and God about which liturgists have had the least to say. They have generally relegated this area to theologians. Now Christian institutions tend to give theology a dominant position in the hierarchy of studies, so that for them, there exists an abundance of theological statements regarding the divine-human liturgical relationship, but it is rabbinics, not theology, that plays the major role in Jewish studies, so that Jewish libraries are, relatively speaking, quite impoverished with regard to serious theological treatments of liturgy. At any rate, in neither case do we find many sustained attempts at a phenomenological cross-cultural description of the divine-human liturgical relationship per se, one, that is, that does not presuppose theological categories of Judaism or Christianity. What we require is a "generic" description of the means by which worshipers in the liturgical field intuit a worshipful relationship with the divine. This will vary from culture to culture and even from time to time, but a pattern common to all instances ought to be definable. We have been doing just that, elucidating patterns of liturgical activity governing other relationships in the liturgical field, the last one being the communal tracing of authenticity through time by means of a sacred myth. We turn now to the second means by which ultimacy is assured within the liturgical field: the establishment of a relationship between worshipers and God.

At the very outset we have a problem of language. It is hard to know what to call this relationship without already prejudicing our case. For the time being, I am content to use the term one meets most frequently in sociological descriptions of religion, a term borrowed from the phenomenology of religion. I mean the word popularized by Rudolf Otto in his 1917 epic, *The Idea of the Holy*: the numinous.

Otto's goal was a forerunner of what is attempted here. He wished to transcend the sterile rationalism of nineteenth-century scholarship, which had reduced religion to ethics. The very word he coined, "numinous," was an invention "to stand for the holy minus its moral factor . . . and . . . minus its 'rational' aspect altogether."[4] If religion was going to be religion, its numinous aspect had to be admitted to consciousness and accorded appropriate scholarly attention in its own right. We might paraphrase Otto's intention by saying that if worship is to be worship, the same thing is true. The liturgical field in its entirety must be accepted as a given, and explicated according to an appropriate field of meaning.

His method was appropriately phenomenological. To determine the essence of the numinous, he invites his reader to "direct his [*sic*] mind to a moment of deeply-felt religious experience."[5] Otto thought this experiment would validate his own soul-searching, in that people would thereby experience immediately " 'creature-consciousness' . . . the emotion of a creature, submerged and overwhelmed by its own nothingness in contrast to that which is supreme above all creatures."[6] Standing over against one at such moments is the *mysterium tremendum et fascinans*, the God of awesomeness, *majestas*, the wholly Other before whom mere creatures stand in utterly silent, open-mouthed awe.

Otto had internalized his academic Protestant environment and could speak with authority on the experience of the numinous within his circle. But he had also visited the east in 1910, stopping for lengthy intervals in Egypt, Palestine, India, China, and Japan. He intended his claim as a universal description of religious experience. Knowledgeable in comparative religion, then, he sought literary records of other cultures to confirm the case of German Christianity as generally true for all great religions. So, having described the phenomenology of the experience of the numinous, he marshaled considerable supportive data from world religions, even appending to his book a chapter on liturgy in which he reproduced numinous texts from the *Bhagavad-Gita*, Christian mysticism, and the liturgy of Yom Kippur.[7] Whether his claim actually does correspond in all details to a universal experience of the numinous is something to which we shall return.

Certainly it would have been recognizable to at least one other class of religious people in Otto's Germany: Reform Jews. Though Reform Judaism was by then represented in the main here in the United States, it still carried the cultural preferences that it had inherited in Europe and was plainly known by one and all as a German Jewish phenomenon. Testimonial to its acceptance of Otto's definition of the numinous in worship comes from sources as diverse as the 1810 "Proclamation . . . ," which governed the first reforms of Israel Jacobson in the Kingdom of Westphalia, and a 1964 plea by Nathan Perilman, then the rabbi of New York City's distinguished Temple Emanu-El. The Westphalian preamble describes worship as "beautiful . . . blissful . . . solemn . . . and lofty." Worship's intention is to give the individual the opportunity to "appear in the sanctuary with the intention of humbling himself before the throne of the Almighty and All-Present."[8] One hundred and fifty-four years later, Perilman concurred. He urged the Reform movement (which was then on the verge of undertaking the liturgical revisions described in part in the last few chapters) to do nothing to impede the awesome sense of dignity inherent in the classical worship pattern brought here from Germany. The service as he knew it (and loved it) "makes its own decorum." Worshipers are "spiritually exalted, emotionally touched," transported from "the vulgar and the rowdy to the noble, the stately." The "sacred and the ordinary are kept properly apart."[9] A casual reading of early Reform prayer books and hymnals turns up one text after another that Otto would gladly have added to his appendix on liturgical numinosity. A typical and commonly used piece is:

> God is in His holy temple,
> Earthly thoughts be silent now.
> As with *reverence* we assemble,
> And before His presence bow.[10]

This is Ottonian numinosity (as I will call it) at its best!

So Otto gave us a valid description for Protestant Germany of his day, and for Reform Judaism, which was so influenced by it. Only a deeper analysis will show us if we ought to generalize more than that. Since Otto used early Jewish material as examples of his experience from other cultures, singling out especially Isa. 6:3, the *Kedushah*, we should begin our deeper investigation there. We want to know how Jews in the first two centuries of our era experienced the numinous in their worship.

The stirring recitation of Isa. 6:3, "Holy Holy Holy is the Lord of Hosts," is embedded in three different rubrics of Jewish liturgy. Each is known technically as a *Kedushat Hashem*, or sanctification of the name of God.[11] The *Kedushat Hashem* is commonly called, simply, the *Kedushah*. The earliest reference to the *Kedushah* is associated with a second-century Palestinian rabbi who is addressing the issue of whether a worshiper should repeat the words "Holy, Holy, Holy . . ." along with the prayer leader.[12] From the context of his remarks, we can ascertain the fact that the *Kedushah* must already have been in existence for some time.

Philologists were quick to give attention to the *Kedushah*. Its subject matter, divine holiness, seemed appropriately religious. It is not some minor liturgical rubric, but a prominent prayer, known to Jew and Christian alike (it seems to have entered the Roman rite sometime in the fifth century, and, given its centrality in the synagogue service much earlier, its absence from such texts as Hippolytus's eucharistic canon is somewhat of a puzzle).[13] Most of all, perhaps, was the fact that its relative ubiquity throughout the prayer book provided a ready theater for philology's favorite question: i.e., of several extant examples of an ancient text, which should be deemed the original, and which seen as secondary extensions of that primary version?[14]

To these approaches, Heinemann directed his usual, and by now even predictable, form-critical caveat. "Once again, with regard to the confusing problem of the history of the *Kedushah,* it would seem that most problems can be solved by assuming the simultaneous existence of diverse traditions of prayers in different localities."[15] That is, no one form should be seen as prior to the others. This led him to a formal analysis of this benediction as one of the many blessings that constitute what he called "the fixed statutory prayers of the synagogue," as opposed to the law court or the house of study or some other institution of the time.

But Heinemann was not untouched by Otto. In passing, he noted that despite its inclusion in a benediction dealing with creation, the *Kedushah* "is not intended to relate the events of the past, but rather to inspire a feeling of 'fear and trembling', of sanctity and awe in the heart of the worshipper, i.e., they are prayers of a 'numinous' nature."[16] Later on, in emphasizing the stylistic feature of the second-person address of God in these synagogue prayers, he cites Otto and Heiler to the effect that in the numinous type of prayer, we should not normally expect a second-person stance, since "the worshipper, who is filled with a sense of awe and reverence [N.B.] in the presence of the Deity would not dare to address Him in the second person."[17] So we have come full circle. Heinemann accepts Otto's analysis fully.

The problem is that Otto—and Heinemann—are really making two claims, not one, and only the first is acceptable. The first is simply the categorization of a sort of liturgical material as numinous. That is, committed to the principle of accepting the numinous as a category within the liturgical field, they now classify the *Kedushah* as numinous; so far, so good. The second claim, however, goes further. It actually equates the numinous with certain specific feelings that Otto experienced. Since Otto could not imagine addressing the *mysterium tremendum* in the second person, it followed for Heinemann that it is strange for ancient Jews to have done so. It is this further cross-cultural judgment of the essential quality of the numinous that we have no right to make. We may not automatically apply Otto's criteria anywhere beyond the European-bred, intellectual, enlightened, upper-middle class whose members constituted Otto's Christian churches and Germany's Reform temples alike. To do so is to make the critical error of confusing the numinous per se with a specific culturally bound example of the way in which the numinous was apprehended.

What we need is a conceptualization of the numinous as it operates in liturgy—any liturgy—that maintains the existence of the numinous component without forcing it into the straitjacket of any particular cultural manifestation. To arrive at this end, we shall need some cross-cultural comparison. So let us look more closely at the *Kedushah*. It was the product of a time and place vastly different from those of the Ottonian system. We will then be able to compare two different apprehensions of the numinous and posit a framework in which the numinous of any liturgical field should be viewed.

The story behind the *Kedushah* is one of the most fascinating tales to have been unearthed in the two hundred or so years since the modern study of our liturgy began. Everyone is agreed by now that the *Kedushah*'s popularity is related to the activity of a group of mystics known as the *yordei merkavah*, or "those who go down into the chariot." But because of scholarly antipathy to mysticism, it has taken almost a century to establish the society in which they lived and the identity of those who constituted their ranks. Fortunately, this blindness to the presence of mysticism in Jewish tradition has largely been removed, so that greater consensus exists today on at least some of the key matters in question. The literature is extensive, but well known, so that a general review should suffice us here.[18]

Nineteenth-century scholarship had established the existence of the *yordei merkavah* mystics and a worship style peculiar to them. The critical set of articles on the subject appeared in 1893.[19] Their author, Philipp Bloch, isolated a set of prayers that shared certain stylistic features, assigned them to these mystics, and declared that the avowed purpose of these texts was to enable the mystics to attain a state of trance. Rhythm, repetition, sound, elaborate praise of God, without, however, burdening the mind with conceptualizations of the deity being praised: these were some of the formal characteristics that enabled the mystic to escape the fetters of mundane reality and to enter the realm of the numinous. The last-mentioned characteristic is especially significant. Words in prayer were not always intended to convey information about reality. The very reverse was often the goal. The mind was to be freed from the normal strictures of thought, so that, in the extreme instance, a trance might set in. We deal with a form of mantra. True, these mantras are not strings of totally meaningless syllables, but they are mantras nevertheless, in that otherwise meaningful words are used in meaningless ways: that is, the sentences they constitute do follow the normal rules of syntax and are thus translatable into conceptually valid statements, but their function is irrelevant to their message, and their cognitive content is not allowed to intrude upon their rhythmic affective function. Indeed, the theologically disparate concept-signifying words, *kadosh* and *barukh*, often appear interchangeably in *merkavah* liturgy, since their normal "meanings"—we would say, "holy" and "blessed"—were irrelevant to a liturgical experience that presented words for purposes of their rhythm, their sound, their affect, not their sense-values, their dictionary-defined equivalents.

More striking was the fact that these prayers were apparently recited—at least by some—after several days of fasting, and in a bodily position marked by placing the head between the knees, thus allowing the blood to rush quickly to the brain. Behind this praxis was a cosmology that pictured our world in the center, with seven heavens surrounding it. In the furthermost heaven sat God enthroned in a chariot of glory, surrounded by angels giving praise, in the very words of the *Kedushah*. Worship's task was to transport the mystics to the seventh heaven, where they would join the heavenly band of laudators.

At first, nineteenth-century scholars did not know what to do with this information. They were convinced that Judaism in antiquity was a relatively stable monolithic system, marked by rationality and ethics. This was a stereotype, of course, but it matched the imagined state of Christianity that was popular then, it too being envisioned by scholars as a unified world of rationalistic orthodoxy; it was, in fact, just such a view of his own tradition that Otto himself had been hoping to transcend in his discovery of the numinous. No one could deny that these mystics once existed, but they could be assigned marginal status in the growth of Jewish tradition and thus be denied lasting influence. Hence it was said that they were late in arriving on the historical horizon, and that they came from distant regions geographically. So both geographically and temporally, one could study what George Foot Moore would one day call "Normative Judaism" without taking into account the decidedly non-normative *yordei merkavah*.[20]

But evidence for the influence of these mystics continued to grow. As early as 1934, just seven years after Moore postulated his Normative Judaism, Scholem's studies placed mystics in Palestine in the fifth century, and twenty-six years later, Scholem admitted he had not been brave enough. They really belonged in the third or fourth century.[21] Meanwhile other scholars, like Alexander Altmann, were confirming the mystical nature of increasing numbers of prayer texts,[22] and students of early synagogue poetry were turning up clear evidence that the poets of the great classical age of Palestinian *piyyutim*—ca. fifth to seventh centuries—incorporated mystical lore and technical vocabulary in their work.[23] It became harder and harder to imagine a neat and tidy Judaism in which mysticism was only tangential.

But we have already seen, in our chapter about rites, that distance is not necessarily a geographic matter. It can be social. Thus even with the newfound discovery that the mystics inhabited the same geographical locale as "The rabbis"—"the very court of Judah the Prince," as Jacob Neusner put it[24]—scholars have managed to maintain the fiction of Judaism's development relatively independently of the *yordei merkavah*. This deft feat has been achieved by relegating the mystics to sects and picturing them as a group of interesting, if odd, people who inhabited different worlds from the leaders who composed and transmitted the "mainstream" Jewish texts. It is as if on one hand we have Judah HaNasi and the great rabbis surrounding him, meeting daily in committee to hammer out a rational conceptualization of Judaism in the form of legal disputes and moral values, while elsewhere, totally unrelated, there exist some unknown mystics bent on achieving a trance and pursuing the numinous.

In fact, there is no evidence for any such separatism. Though we know of mysticism in second-century Palestine, we are given no information to substantiate the idea that mystics constituted separate social sects. The names we have of mystics correspond to names of prominent rabbis whom even the dominant paradigm assigns to Judah's circle of rationalists. The only reason one imagines discrete sects of mystics functioning separately from the rabbis at large is that scholars have wished it so. To paraphrase Neusner's fine description above, they not only *inhabited* the court of Judah HaNasi, they *were* the court of Judah HaNasi. What we have been calling mysticism should be reevaluated as one of many normative ways in which Jews—leading Jews, rabbinic Jews—expressed the numinous in their worship. Not all, of course, and not in equal degrees—but many.[25]

It is clear, moreover, whence they arrived at their numinous imagery. Plainly, what we have is Jewish gnosticism.

To many, the idea of Jewish gnostics has seemed a contradiction in terms. It conflicted with the regnant view of the late Roman empire's socioreligious structure. Accepting at face value the official definitions of a pure and "orthodox" Judaism and Christianity bequeathed us by Jewish and Christian leaders of those early years, we were too quick to postulate self-contained societies of the faithful holding bravely to a well-known set of their own religious norms. We thus carved up the religious life of Greco-Roman society into a set of competing religions, in which Judaism and Christianity were given priority. Gnosticism then stood as another religious option (as evident from the polemic against gnostics contained in Irenaeus, Tertullian and others), which was, by definition now, plainly at odds with Judaism. Presumably, one could not be both gnostic and Jewish any more than one could be both heretical and orthodox, since the hallmark of Judaism, it was said, was its monotheistic principle, while gnosticism was, presumably, characterized by blatant dualism.

Now liturgists trotted out every proof regarding the care with which the rabbis (always conceived as a monolith) protected their religion from the gnostic threat. Like the Church Fathers, they were credited with far-ranging statesmanship. Jews were prohibited from saying "We thank You" twice in a prayer, lest people think there are two powers in heaven.[26] In a similar polemic against the gnostic doctrine of two creators, society's evil being ascribed by it to the Jewish God (of evil), Isa. 45:7, which credits God with "making peace and creating evil," was altered liturgically to say "peace and all things."[27] An apt image for the way we moderns viewed the religious situation in late Roman times, then, would be several mutually exclusive circles, totally separate enclaves in which religious adherents remain hermetically sealed from the doctrines of each other.

There are still many who take this view. And even those who do not may speak as if they do, by reifying gnosticism so that it appears as a "thing" with clearly delineated boundaries that cannot be stretched. On the other hand, there are those—myself included—who see gnosticism as not one but many things, shading off at some point into a recognizable form of Christianity or of Judaism. Similarly, the latter two religions no longer appear so fixed as never to permit the practice of something that surely appears "gnostical." Though we have no ready word for it—a consequence of carving up religious systems into competing alternatives and developing no vocabulary to describe what is common to all—it appears (in Morton Smith's words) that "Christian, magical, Gnostic, and Jewish material . . . must all derive from some common stock which existed, at the latest, in the first century C.E."[28]

Viewing the commonality of the whole, rather than the defensive posture of one of the parts, enables us to ask the usual questions in a different way. We will have to enquire not only as to how each religion protected itself from the others, but also how each one equipped itself to be readily recognizable as a valid alternative in the system in the first place. We will expect the normal reactive mechanism of polemic, many times in a liturgical context, such as the examples cited above. But we will also expect the liturgical inclusion of some common properties, such as metaphors or worship practices, which all parties agreed upon as necessary to religious life. Thus every group both includes itself in its society's generally accepted definition of licit religiosity and, at the same time, carves out its own niche within the system, defining what it is that differentiates "us" from "them." I call the former process "censoring in"; the latter, "censoring out."[29]

Religious identity is a composite of these two processes. Even as we censor others out by assuring our members that we are different, we censor ourselves into our society's definition of acceptable religiosity. We dare not be perceived as being precisely the same as others, but equally, we fear being labeled as so different that we do not count as a religion in the first place. Thus the first observation about what unites Otto's Europe with Palestine in Roman times is the realization that in both cases, however much competing religions differed, they shared their own distinctive version of a "common stock."

Another example of competing religions sharing a "common stock" can be postulated in the case of western European post-Enlightenment religion. Indeed, in our comparison of Rudolf Otto's Protestantism and Reform Judaism, we already demonstrated that. The precise nature of the common stock varied from that of late antiquity, of course, because the culture that spawned it underwent mutation. Neither Otto nor Reform Jews, for example, could see the world as the center of a seven-heavened universe, with God sitting on a chariot surrounded by angels; they had no desire to attain a mystical trance designed to gain access to the angelic band; they would never have fasted and put their heads between their knees during prayer; and they insisted on seeing semantic significance in each and every word, which they took apart philologically. But the *yordei merkavah* would have laughed at Reform Jews who stood quietly at attention while a four-part choir sang hymns. For them, God was not totally Other, but quite approachable, even desirous of being approached in His chariot. Thus the common stock differed, but there was one.

From this point on, we would do well to follow a semiological analysis. Semiology is the relatively new science of signs, what we signify by our choice of clothing, for example, or by the combination of food served at a formal dinner.[30] From a semiological perspective, the liturgy can be viewed as a series of signs. Our goal is to determine its system of signification. One such subsystem in the liturgical field, we posited, must be the numinous, though it now turns out that the specific signs favored at any given time to express the numinous are culturally determined. There is no inherent necessity for any of them. The signs are arbitrary. Numinous significance is assigned to them. Since the classical instance of an arbitrary semiology is language, we might consider liturgy as a language with its own rules of combination.[31]

Language is made of the combination of units into higher units, which are then combined into still higher units, and so on. The lowest determinative unit is the phoneme (a socially recognized sound); several phonemes combine to make morphemes (roughly equivalent to words); morphemes eventuate in sentences. At each step, the speaker chooses from among a relatively limitless set of alternatives, what Saussure called the "associatively" related units; the preferred term now is "paradigmatic."[32] The most elementary liturgical unit too must be a set of paradigmatic phonemes, so to speak, basic building blocks that exist on the same associative level, and from which we select one. We then select the next one, thus constructing a combination. The combinations all produce a syntax of prayer, A followed by B followed by C, and so on. The fact that we selected A, but not A', B, but not B', C, but not C', represents our paradigmatic selectivity. The fact that A is followed by B, but not by E, and that B is followed by C, but not by D, constitutes what is called the syntactical selectivity. Liturgy, then, is a sign system that defines itself according to the selection of some units from among others, and then combines them to form a syntax.

What shall we call our basic units? Phoneme is a term admirably fitted for speech, but our liturgical sign-system goes beyond speech to include gesture, dress, and special arrangement of objects—all the many things that good leaders of liturgy must keep in mind if their worship is to succeed. Since the analogy of a language is usefully retained, I suggest the word "vocabulary." Of course, worship must also obey the rules of its various subsystems, at their lower orders of determination: the rules of phonemes, for example (worshipers have to be able to sound the prayers), and of whatever is considered appropriate poetry (Frost's "I have been one acquainted with the night" or Blake's "It is an easy thing to triumph in the summer's sun" work well as worship today,[33] whereas *Ulysses* does not); or similar sets of rules for clothing and gesture that govern the pool of potential selectivity in the setting of prayer. But worship becomes worship, rather than speech or dress or gesture alone, because it combines all these other sign systems according to its own ends.[34] The units combined at that level we shall call "vocabulary."

But insofar as the numinous is concerned, liturgical vocabulary is unable to express fully the experienced reality that it seeks to represent. This is precisely the difficulty inherent in any ex post facto description of the mystical experience. Others who have had the same experience and who share the vocabulary will recognize the meaning, but the meaning is implied. We may, therefore, more precisely refer to numinous vocabulary as being synecdochal. It points to something beyond itself. It is but a part of the larger whole for which it must stand.

Theoretically, it should be possible to explicate the systematic combinatory

rules for each level, isolating the unit of selection (the paradigm) and the rules of
combination (the syntax). For our purposes, however, we do not require such an
exercise. Let us jump to the highest level, the final unit to which the entire sign-
system in all its permutations and combinations leads. I should like to call it the
"master image," by which I mean the whole of which the synecdochal vocabulary is the part. Our two earlier examples, Ottonian numinosity and Merkavah
mysticism, provide good illustrations.

Otto's vocabulary is in part explicit, in part not. The explicit part is the words
that he, himself, cites as indices of the numinous, and that are found throughout
the prayers that he presents as numinal material. "Awesome," "mysterious,"
"holy," "mighty"—these are some of the verbal vocabulary typical of Otto's
system, and, predictably, they are highly represented in Reform prayer books
too. But there were other vocabulary items that Otto's text-centered perspective
blinded him to: grand music, as opposed to simple melodies; the majestic organ
booming through cathedrals; Baroque churches with their palatial splendor and
elaborate architecture directing the gaze and the mind to a hidden deity far
beyond us miserable creatures down below;[35] the accentuation of social distance
between congregational laity and the clergy, achieved through differentiating
kinds of robing and diverse rules governing mobility during worship. No less
than the words, these are vocabulary items that point to that same transcendent
God whom Otto calls the *mysterium tremendum*.

The master image is a God of transcendence. God is beyond, totally Other,
outside the confines even of the church's high ceiling, brought to mind by the
mighty sweep of the music and the pageantry. God is an extension of the social
distance that differentiates worshiper from God's representatives on the pulpit.

Despite the surface similarity of some of the words ("holy," or "mighty," for
example) the Merkavah language of numinosity is quite different. To begin with,
even the words are not the same, since the Hebrew is equivalent to the German or
the English only in a loose way, and only on the plain of semantic convention. The
synecdochal vocabulary goes beyond that. True, it does contain words like
kadosh, *barukh*, and *kisei hakavod*, which we "translate" as "holy," "blessed,"
and "throne of glory," but note that in our worship, we have allotted semantic
significance only to the first two of these terms, whereas the third, which was
equally ripe with synecdochal meaning to the Merkavah worshipers, goes unrecognized as a significant expression in the Ottonian system of numinosity. And the
master image to which "blessed" or "holy" points should not be assumed to be
the same as that which *barukh* or *kadosh* suggests. At any rate, Merkavah
vocabulary has not only words, but gestures as well—dropping one's head
between one's knees, for example. There was also the deliberate choreographing
of prayer in antiphonal fashion, a habit that we retain in our responsive prayers, but

with this all-important difference: with us, it is merely an unimportant choreo-graphic style, a mannerism we have inherited and find pleasing; for the Merkavah worshipers, on the other hand, antiphony was selected with deliberate intent, because it represented the conscious patterning of human praise after Isaiah's description of the way the angels praise God. So here too, we find a metonymic association with the larger model of angelic worship, precisely the goal of the verbal vocabulary as well.[36] Here, the vocabulary points not to an unknowable God who is transcendent to the point of being totally Other, but to a very anthropomorphic deity who inhabits a chariot well within our grasp. The master image is the *merkavah* itself, God enthroned in heaven surrounded by angels singing praise.

In both cases we have three items that constitute our system of classifying numinous vocabulary in the liturgical sign-system: *synecdochal vocabulary,* a *master image,* and—finally—what we shall call *cultural backdrop.*

Cultural backdrop is that which is common to all competing religious claims to the numinous, the parameters according to which we censor ourselves in. With the Merkavah mystics, for example, God appears as a God of light in the mosaic floor of Beth Alpha;[37] and in the morning liturgy, God is described as renewing the work of creation every day, a reference to the sun rising and traveling, as if in a chariot, across the horizon, only to disappear mysteriously and ominously at night.[38] But similar iconography marks early Christian art, where, for example, we see Jesus in the form of the sun. For that matter, Clement of Alexandria (ca. 200) actually describes Jesus as driving his chariot across the sky, while fourth-century tomb mosaics in Rome repeat the imagery of Jesus as sun-god, entering the heavens in his chariot.[39] Helios, the sun-god, was a dominant divine motif in a world marked, as we said in chapter 2, by the ultimate categorization of reality according to the dichotomy of light and darkness. Religions generally of that age thus censored themselves into their own versions of this master image of light, filtering it through synecdochal vocabulary resonant with their own particu-larity.[40] One of the rules governing the selection of signs (paradigm) and their combination into meaningful units on a higher level (syntax) seems to be the dual need to censor in and yet to censor out.

The same is true, so much so that it hardly need be demonstrated, of post-Enlightenment Europe. Obviously Reform Jews and "Ottonian" Christians shared the same master image of transcendence, and expressed it with synec-dochal vocabulary that sometimes censored their communities into the dominant perception of licit religiosity and sometimes declared their independence from each other. Perhaps the best example is Reform Judaism's early preference for Christian hymns, rather than traditional Jewish chanting modes, which they perceived as cacophony. But they carefully denuded these hymns of any Christological vocabulary, thus implying that though they stood within the bounds of religious propriety, they did not inhabit the same place as their Christian neighbors.[41]

In each case the model holds. A chart will make the point clearly.

Yordei Merkavah

Cultural Backdrop	—Greco-Roman culture and cosmology —Gnostic cultural categories (such as light/darkness) and favored imagery (like the sun)
Master Image	—God enthroned in a chariot that rides through the sky, surrounded by angels who sing God's praise

Synecdochal Vocabulary	—Antiphonal worship pattern, modeled after angelic paradigm of Isaiah's *Kedushah* vision
	   1. in daily call to worship = to praise (N.B.) God, praise being that which humans do as emulation of angels
	   2. in *Hallel* = psalms of praise, again copying the angelic model
	   3. in *Kedushah* itself
	   4. in *amen* response to blessings (i.e., praises of God)
	—Favored words: *barukh, kadosh, kisei hakavod*
	—Favored imagery: chariot, angelic praise, sun, light vs. darkness (as in first blessing before *shema*)
	—Use of words for sound, not meaning, to achieve state of trance and join angels

Reform Judaism

Cultural Backdrop	—Post-Enlightenment Europe, post-Kantian philosophy emphasizing unknowable deity —German social system emphasizing social space between classes —Cultural heritage of classical music, particularly nineteenth-century discovery of romanticism and emotionality
Master Image	—Ottonian numinosity, transcendent deity, beyond being known, totally other *mysterium tremendum*

Synecdochal Vocabulary	—Cathedral architecture, art, and musical style; worship choreography: to emphasize social distance
	   1. robes marking status
	   2. rules reserving "manipulation of sancta" (e.g., carrying and reading Torah) to individuals charged with similar sacred status, generally only the rabbi
	—Favored words emphasizing majesty, grandeur, awe, reverence, "creatureliness" of worshiper standing reverently before God
	—Decorum limiting freedom of worshiper and accenting dependency on clergy as God's representatives

Many more details could be added, and, in fact, what is listed here is intended only as a sort of shorthand, a rough generalization abstracted from what we can call two separate worship systems. Any given instance within the set may vary slightly from that set's idealized pattern, so that, for example, a specific classical Reform congregation may or may not encode within its actual practice each and every one of the characterizing features typical of the worship system of which it is an instance. But despite this or that deviation, its membership in the set of classical Reform congregations will not be in doubt.

Thus, every liturgical field includes the apprehension of the numinous. But since the sign system that constitutes the liturgical language is arbitrary, no particular numinal vocabulary should be anticipated in advance of our observing any given case. Rather, the vocabulary will vary with the system. In all cases, however, the syntagmatic rules governing the combination of lower-order vocabulary units into ever higher orders will work eventually to suggest a particular master image, which, in turn, will be congruent with the cultural backdrop. The cultural backdrop contains the assumptions about reality that inform all religions within the religious system of society, so that they all will adopt its strictures and present to their adherents master images that are similar to one another (censored into society's definition of religion) yet different enough to be recognizable as religious options distinct from the claims of competitors (censoring out alternatives).

The cultural relativity of numinal vocabulary is crucial for us. Otherwise we should be obliged to search every liturgical language for identical evidence of the numinous, and, what is worse, to confuse the absence of specifically Ottonian language for the absence of the experience of the numinous itself. To underscore the vast range of alternative languages, we should consider the following two very diverse testimonies.

A. I felt a great inexplicable joy, a joy so powerful that I could not restrain it, but had to break into song, a mighty song, with room for only one word: joy! . . . I could see and hear in a totally different way. I had gained my enlightenment . . . and this in such a manner that it was not only I who could see through the darkness of life, but the same bright light also shone out from me, imperceptible to human beings, but visible to all spirits of earth and sky and sea, and these now came to me to be my helping spirits.

B. Then in a flash of illumination, I understood that this perfect genius of which I conceived was nothing more than a minute and miserable microcosm, containing but the barest hint of the infinitely more complex and enormously vast macrocosmic mind of God. . . . Somehow the attention of God was focused on me. . . . I was receiving enlightenment from Him. Tears came into my eyes, and I opened them upon a room in which it seemed to me that each object had been touched by God's sublime presence.[42]

These two examples are taken from I. M. Lewis's *Ecstatic Religion*. They contain enough Ottonian vocabulary for us to grant without further demonstration that they are numinal. That is because they are both ecstatic—that being the kind of report Lewis was searching for—and because the English vocabulary of ecstasy is similar to that of the majestic and awesome. But they do contain differences, not only from the Ottonian master image but also from each other.

The first is a report by an Eskimo shaman, whose enlightenment came when he was alone in the wilderness, while in the second account, enlightenment is a group experience. The shaman comes to see himself as essentially isolated from others, who do not even recognize the light emanating from him. But the individual in the second account is overcome by awe and humility and takes as his immediate reference point the very others among whom he is sitting. As he puts it, "God's sublime presence" rested everywhere. The second example, by the way, is a report by a subject in a psychological experiment, to whom LSD has been administered.

Each of our four examples—*yordei merkavah* mystics, Ottonian transcendence, the Eskimo shaman, and the LSD subject—presents us with a specific instance of a different vocabulary. Only a knowledge of the cultural backdrop behind them will elucidate their full meaning in the liturgical language of which they are a part. Speaking from our own theological perspective, we may well want to argue the question of the religious validity of some of them, but, empirically speaking, we can do nothing but accept the reports at their face value, thus learning to recognize diverse numinal vocabularies pointing toward alternative master images rooted in different cultural contexts.

But even Ottonian numinosity is not descriptive of religious trends today. Our present circumstance may be summarized by saying that the Ottonian language of transcendence is being replaced by yet a newer vocabulary, this one rooted in the American cultural backdrop. As we live through a changing expression of the numinous, we have the opportunity to see a language of liturgy in flux. As such, we have much to learn by consulting the history of numinal vocabulary during the course of this century.

Technically speaking, Reform Jews brought their Ottonian language of transcendence with them to this country. That European system was built into the great Reform temples that dotted the inner cities, when these Jews established their presence there. One can still observe the system in operation at such landmarks as Temple Emanu-El in New York or The Temple in Cleveland.

But there is good reason to doubt whether the cultural transplant ever took to the American soil. This tentative conclusion is derived from a study by Susan Abramson of Boston's old Temple Israel, a paragon of the classical Reform model under discussion here.[43] Preliminary reforms had been initiated there as early as 1873, in anticipation of the arrival of Rabbi Solomon Schindler, from Silesia. When Schindler arrived, however, he was struck by the fact that worship attendance was abysmally low. It might be imagined that it was only the conflict of a work schedule on Saturdays that militated against people's attendance, but that was not the whole story. People were apparently free enough to attend synagogue, but they chose not to, going instead to Jewish lodges for their "spiritual" nourishment. True, Schindler did in fact preach against men who worry more about business than about keeping the Sabbath, but in another sermon, he directed his remarks at those who attend the lodges, charging, "They consider their meetings and their prayers [at the lodges] to be a perfect divine service."[44] What congregation he had was made largely of women, to whom, of course, the all-male lodges were closed. So he took also to preaching to the women, urging them directly to use their influence at home so as not to let religious reform die because of lack of interest on the part of their husbands.[45] From 1884 to 1892, debate raged on the wisdom of holding services at all on Saturday morning, with some favoring an expanded Friday evening Sabbath service, and others supporting Sunday morning worship.[46] This entire debate, it should be noted, occurred in the context of a congregation that had just dedicated a new building (1880), replete with all the numinal vocabulary items typical of the classical Reform style, including a newly improved choir and an organ costing $2000.00.[47]

Yet despite the great care lavished on the creation of a magnificent service, both musically and intellectually, the problem of attendance did not go away. In June of 1898, the next rabbi, Charles Fleischer, reported to his board that "This Saturday morning, our congregation consisted of 1 man, 8 married women, 6 young women, 5 girls and 2 boys. Of these, only 10 were of the families of our own members."[48] How did the congregation respond to the obvious continual failure to attract worshipers? They resorted again to the usual means, a new and bigger building, and yet a more resonant organ, this one costing $9,000.[49] But it did not help. In 1910, only 26–31 people were attending Saturday morning services, all but one of them women. Sunday services were doing somewhat better, the average congregation numbering 215 persons, but only 20–25 of them were male.[50] Clearly, at least in Temple Israel, the enlightened western European model of worship, with its promise of experiencing transcendence, had failed to command the loyalty of most parishioners, who adopted the American freedom to seek ultimate meaning elsewhere in life's tasks.

Americans' lip service to the forms of traditional religion, combined with an operative disaffection in practice, has beset every religion here, not just Reform Judaism, and is by now the topic of a considerable body of literature. Perhaps the earliest recognition of the trend was the Lynds' perceptions when they returned to Middletown during the depression. People maintained their faith in an economic system that was in chaos, but found little consolation from their religious affiliation.[51]

Suburban living was the latest nail in the coffin. Study after study has demonstrated how suburbanization trivializes the religious enterprise.[52] As Herbert Gans summarizes, "The purpose of the synagogue was to keep the children in the fold . . . but to leave the adults uninvolved."[53] With the baby-boom children growing up in the newly developing suburbia in the fifties, Reform Jews discovered that they still belonged to temples, but that their temples had been made over into support systems for the two social classes "stuck" in the suburbs day in and day out: the children, on one hand, and on the other, their mothers, who struggled to keep house and home while their husbands went to work to earn enough money to pay the mortgage and car loans. Sunday-school centered synagogues serviced the former, and burgeoning temple sisterhoods supported the latter. The new architecture of places of worship told the tale. They were no longer places of worship, but places of meeting and education. Huge educational wings and enlarged social halls encroached on space once reserved for the sanctuary. In sum, even if the old numinous language had once worked, in some turn-of-the-century Reform temples, it surely was in a state of severe dysfunction by the fifties. And it has not gotten any better in the last thirty years.

Clearly, the cultural backdrop has undergone severe changes. We noted many of them in chapter 3. Here, we might recall just a few that are directly relevant to the numinous. Almost every item on the chart used earlier in this chapter has been altered. America is not Europe, and Americans neither know nor care about Kantian distinctions between noumenal and phenomenal, the basic dichotomy that underlay the concept of a God who fit into the former but not the latter. Class distinctions were consciously obliterated here; instead, the American corporation institutionalized a system of relationships in which people call one another by their first name, regardless of position of authority. High culture, so necessary for the production of grand music and magnificent art—artistic numinous vocabulary items typical of "cathedral-style" synagogues—was replaced by pop culture, which Gans describes as being user, not creator, oriented.[54] William James's hardheaded pragmatism, not Immanuel Kant's German idealism; Andy Warhol's Campbell soup cans, instead of Monet's water lilies; country music, Broadway, or (in the classics) "down-home" themes like Copland's *Rodeo*, in place of Handel's *Messiah* or Wagner's preoccupation with the mighty echoes of Germanic myth: these have been our cultural mentors and models.

So American pragmatists have not been taught to seek Otto's sense of the numinous in our churches and temples, with the exception, perhaps, of particularly holy days, which carry with them their own baggage of pomp and ceremony. But we have not on that account renounced the quest for God. We simply learned to search elsewhere, and, at the same time as traditional religions were slow to accommodate that search by a parallel openness to novel vocabular-ies of spirituality, new priests of new religions developed them. The best exam-ple, perhaps, is psychology, which invaded suburbia, particularly, filling the void left by shrinking religiosity.[55] Is there any way to differentiate empirically between Maslow's peak experiences, for example, and the reports of the re-ligiously enlightened that we looked at above? Maslow thinks not. Religious experiences, he writes, should be "a proper part of the jurisdiction of sci-ence. . . . Revelations or mystical illuminations, [that is,] core-religious experi-ences . . . can be subsumed under the head of peak-experiences.''[56] Jung's individuation process reads remarkably like initiation in the mystical secrets of the *yordei merkavah*, and Jung would be the first to grant the parallel between dreams and the symbolizing of religious realities.[57]

So both religion's supporters and its detractors have sought to express the experience of the numinous in this century. Religionists prefer traditional vocab-ulary, while psychologists do not. Growing numbers of secular Americans have learned to express their numinous experience in psychological rather than in traditional Jewish and Christian language. In a new cultural context, the old master image has grown pale, and its synecdochal vocabulary has lost its sym-bolic force.

But all evidence indicates not that experience of the numinous is impossible in our age, but the very reverse. People still experience the numinous, but interpret it according to whatever master image they have on hand. As we have seen, this has generally manifested itself in secular, usually psychological, imagery; or, when that fails, as it seems to have of late, in the vocabulary of the religious schemata of the East or of thoroughly westernized 'cults' that claim to have spiritual links to them.

Some observers, like Peter Berger, think we are only at the beginning of a grand confrontation between East and West.[58] Whether history shall prove him right or wrong, it is of the greatest importance that we understand why people find the need to express their numinous experience in synecdochal vocabulary and master imagery that are alien to their own religion. They do so only if their religion does not recognize that experience as valid, or, if, failing the necessary liturgical vocabulary, it denies them the possibility of expressing it and thereby bringing it to consciousness. Perhaps the most paradigmatic case in modern Jewish history is David Ben-Gurion, once the prime minister of Israel, who epitomized the modern self-conscious Jew controlling history, bent on maintain-ing the Jewish presence in history despite the Holocaust. Yet religiously, Ben-Gurion studied with Zen Buddhist masters, and took up yoga![59] Jewish religion in the modern state of Israel offered its prime minister no master image, and thus no synecdochal vocabulary, congruent with the cultural backdrop Israelis take for granted.

But a new numinous vocabulary is coming into being. Neither Merkavah mysticism nor Ottonian transcendence will do. We need only identify the new vocabulary, the new master image toward which it points, and the cultural backdrop that it presupposes.

The new master image is best summed up by the English word "community." Once, not long ago, the word was used to refer to the town in which one lived. Now it conjures up something like an extended family, bound together, however, not by blood but by mutuality of concern. This is Hunter and Suttles's "community of total liability," where we care for each other in every exigency.[60] Its opposite is the "community of limited liability," which we join with a predetermined arbitrary checklist of expectations in mind, according to which the efficiency of the community in question is judged. These limited-liability communities characterize institutional life, even institutional religious life. They are the very opposite of "community" as I use the term here.

By community as master image, I mean Victor Turner's liminal *communitas*, a cultural setting in which class structures are removed, social distance dispelled; where Buberian dialogue leads us to discover that, as Buber would have it, we discover the Eternal Thou in our relationships with every other Thou.[61] The new master image of community emphasizes the fellowship, the group, what in contemporary Hebrew parlance is known as the *chavurah*.[62] Its vocabulary includes words like "persons," "openness," "relationships," "sharing." It is joyful, celebrative, life-affirming. It glorifies what it calls honesty, openness, and sensitivity by members of a genuine religious community who meet each other, and in that meeting, meet God. Certainly this is no Merkavah journey through the heavens, nor the awesome encounter with the *mysterium tremendum* either. But it is the numinous clothed in different synecdoche, for our time.

The structural similarities between the new numinous vocabulary and the systems so far described are plain to see. We have explained the Merkavah system as being but a Jewish version of a general religious tendency toward a gnostic world view that characterized late antiquity; and we recognized a spectrum of adaptations within this tendency, by which all religions, in their own way, censored themselves into legitimacy. Otto's transcendence, similarly, was but a Protestant version of another pervasive sentiment, which had its own spectrum of adaptations running through Judaism as well. Today, we simply have another set of cultural assumptions, which glorify "persons," seek "honest, open communication," and convert "groups" into "communities."

As with the other cases, here as well, every religion is affected. We see the new numinous vocabulary in the present Roman Rite of Reconciliation, for example, where, in one instance, that of individual reconciliation, face-to-face dialogue between penitent and priest is called for. *A Manual for the Penitent*, published in 1976, depicts a simple table with an inviting chair on each side that beckons both participants to sit down and talk.[63] We see it in Judaism in the nostalgia for life in eastern Europe. Was it just accident that Zborowski and Herzog characterized their study of the life there, *Life Is with People*—a title resonant with the connotations of the old, now-vanished, somewhat romanticized, natural community of total liability that we imagine to have existed before the onset of modernity, and to which we aspire urgently to return?[64] The image is to be found in the fondness for simple Hasidic stories that more and more constitute the illustrative material in rabbis' sermons. It lies behind the Reform movement's recent deliberations on doing away with a hymnal, after almost a hundred years of using one.[65] People, it is said, want simple, singable music in their liturgy, often with the intimacy of a guitar or flute, not the grandeur of an organ. The new liturgies of Jew and Christian alike contain poems that may not say very much on the cognitive level but promote a sense of a community at prayer discovering God among themselves.[66]

The new numinous language has its own aesthetics. It is involving, demanding of participation.[67] New liturgies assert our responsibility to sing together, to act together, to discover one another in the liturgical field. We remove pews and sit in the round, suddenly aware that there are meaningful others in the room, not just ourselves alone before the majestic God and that God's clerics. With less transcendent awesomeness, we make fewer demands on the arts. Modern English style, says Daniel Stevick, is characterized by "an economy of means," by "understatements," by "sincerity."[68] Church architecture, asserts James White, is marked by flat roofs now, low profiles, instead of the sweeping Gothic spires. "Is the move away from high profile buildings simply a matter of economics and new construction methods?" he asks,

> Or is it a deeper move in worship away from a stress on God as transcendent to a recovery of the sense of His immanence? . . . Would we still want those tall structures even if we could afford them? The more restrained and modest buildings of our time show a move toward a *simplicity* that we previously failed to recognize as important. And it may reflect a deeper sense of the God who meets us in the midst of His people rather than up yonder in the distant haze.[69]

To be sure, there are people raised on Ottonian numinosity who distrust the whole contemporary enterprise and refuse to see the numinous in its new vocabulary. The names of Gary Wills and James Hitchcock come readily to mind.[70] These critics decry the death of true liturgy, the confusion of divine and human agencies, the transvaluation of transcendence into mere "groupiness." They abhor the willful abandonment of lofty language, awesome music, and grand ceremonialism. But "lofty," "awesome," and "grand" are Ottonian vocabulary, replaced in the new numinous language by "intimate," "touching," and "personal." Empirically judged, they amount to the same thing, a liturgical vocabulary of the numinous.

There are those who wonder aloud whether such "community" religion has the power to maintain itself, whether, that is, any new symbolic idiom can be created in today's world. Mary Douglas has argued, for example, that our age may not be open to symbolic language as such, and, insofar as symbolic language is the essence of describing and sharing—in fact, realizing—the numinous, religion may now be incapable of awakening genuine religious sentiment.[71] Douglas rests her case on Basil Bernstein's distinction between an elaborated and a restricted speech code, the former being the channel for "a relatively explicit meaning [in which] the condition of the listener is not taken for granted."[72] This elaborated code presupposes the ability to differentiate meaningfully among a wide variety of message units, at each stage of the utterance, and requires a lengthy period of formal and informal learning. The elaborated code lends specificity and precision to instructions, and the ability to "receive" in it is what generates higher levels of learning readiness.

The restricted code, on the other hand, is not intended to provide new information. The pure form of a restricted code would be

> one where the lexicon, and hence the organizing structure . . . are wholly predict-
> able. Examples of this pure form would be *ritualistic modes of communication*—
> relations regulated by protocol, religious services, etc. . . . The non-verbal compo-
> nent (expressive features) will be a major source for indicating changes in mean-
> ing. . . . How things are said, rather than what is said, becomes important. The
> intent of the listener may be taken for granted. Finally, the content of the speech is
> likely to be concrete, descriptive and narrative, rather than analytical and abstract.
> The major function of this code is to reinforce the *form* of the social relationship (a
> warm and inclusive relationship) by restricting the verbal signalling of individual
> responses.[73]

Douglas rightly understands Bernstein to be identifying this latter restricted code with ritual and religious symbol. But she sees society becoming less traditionally structured and more individually assertive. In such societies, she holds, the sum of shared symbolic language—the restricted code, that is, in which we should place synecdochal discourse—is reduced in favor of detailed explanatory language—the elaborated code—which prevents age-old "condensed symbols" from speaking to us as they once did.[74]

Possibly. Time will tell. But the societal macrocosm is not the religious microcosm of the *chavurah*, the fellowship, the community that meets regularly and becomes the positional or highly structured family that Bernstein posits as necessary for the restricted code to arise, and whose demise Douglas bemoans. It is precisely in these small groups that new vocabulary is developed and symbolic behavior shared.

Whether, in fact, religious institutions will continue in the direction of Turner's *communitas*, in the form of *chavurot* and fellowship groups that are by nature designed to facilitate communication in a restricted code, is an open question. But that is not our concern here. The purpose of this chapter was to take the bold step of looking at the liturgical field, committed in advance to admitting the validity of its claim to encounter the numinous. Unencumbered by theological presuppositions, we sought to develop a cross-cultural model by which the experience of the numinous in worship might be expressed systemically, the hope being that we might expand the model for worship to include even its most elusive element, what most religions would call the experience of God. Treating liturgy as a language, we found the numinous expressed by means of a form of communication that we labeled synecdochal vocabulary. We found that synecdochal vocabulary, in turn, pointed toward a master image that varied with time and place, but could always be said to be suggestive of and congruent with a specific cultural backdrop. The model held for the *yordei merkavah* of Roman Palestine, for Reform Judaism of nineteenth-century Europe, and for the experimentation with numinous expression in the Americanization of religion that characterizes our world today.

Expanding our agenda to include questions "beyond the text," then, yields what may be the most promising of all avenues of investigation: a means of studying, classifying, and appreciating, through textual remnants, that which makes prayer prayer: the human encounter with God.

EIGHT

Conclusion

A Holistic View of Liturgy

In chapter 1, I cited Clifford Geertz regarding the incredible wealth of alternative perspectives with which contemporary theorists describe society. "The woods are full of eager interpreters," he says, each with a different divining rod for uncovering the goings-on of human affairs.[1] The attempt of this book to take the liturgical text as a necessary starting point, but then to go beyond it, using a holistic view of the process by which that text is actually prayed to reconstruct the identity of the people who pray it, is but one of them. It deserves its own summary account here, lest the reader's perception of the various trees represented by the individual chapters obstruct the larger picture of the forest itself. At issue is not any particular claim, so much as the entire enterprise, a commitment to discover the identity of a praying community—its world view (the way things are), its ethos ("the tone, character and quality of its life, its moral and aesthetic style and mood"),[2] and the place it occupies in both—and to do so through an analysis of its praying, rather than going the other way around, that is, assuming that we know enough (relatively speaking) about the community's self-perception and need most now, on the basis of that knowledge, to reproduce the recension history of its prayers.

If our goal is the ultimate unveiling of communal identity, that is, knowledge of the community as the community knew itself, and as it played out its role in the world based on that knowledge, two independent starting points are required, and both of them come together, in a sort of pincers movement, in the liturgical study advocated here. First we have the purely textual disciplines—philology and form-criticism—by which reliable sets of prayers are attained; my indebtedness to the array of scholars, past and present, engaged in textual reconstruction should be patently evident at every turn of every argument here. We need also what has generally been the province of independent pursuits like history, which begin also with accurate facsimiles of texts, but which start from texts other than liturgical ones, and thus provide their own independent witness for a people's identity through time. Where these two directions converge is the act of prayer,

172

in which the people, as living reality, act out the world as it sees it, and from which its members return to their several homes to shape their lives about the contours of the world as presented in prayer. It is as if we had a liturgical Heisenberg principle, in which a particle's position and momentum are replaced by a people's history and its prayers. The liturgical principle of uncertainty would state that historical evidence of a people's identity and the prayer texts by which it ritualizes its role are two interdependent entities, both of which cannot be known fully, since each step in isolating a new truth about one brings about an improvement in our understanding of the other, which in turn reflects a novel recognition regarding the first, and so on, *ad infinitum*. Nevertheless, physicists study particles with some success, and we can do the same for a people's identity, as long as we remember—and this is my point—that discoveries in one direction, regardless of their scope and importance, cannot obviate the need to ask questions in the other direction too. We simply must go beyond an eternal re-creation of scientifically accurate texts; we need desperately to see how those texts, played out as lived liturgical practice, had consequences for the people who used them.

The focus of study should then not be the text at all, but what I have called the liturgical field, the holistic network of interrelationships that bind together discrete things, acts, people, and events into the activity we call worship—or better still, ritual. Within that field, one may single out any given relationship between or among any number of data for attention. I have here tried to isolate several such questions that seem to me crucial in the process by which ritualizing one's identity within religious communities fixes the sense of who one is.

Beginning with a look at *havdalah*, we saw the function ritual plays in establishing the categories with which we order experience. From the time of our birth, we human beings develop our capacity to encode events in meaningful patterns built on the simple recognition that to be one thing is not to be another. Whether it be the psychological development of the ego, as opposed to others; our group in contrast to theirs; the territorial imperative for our (but not their) space; or our equally serious claim that time is ours alone to name, to qualify, and even to quantify according to our own numbering system—things exist for us only if we master their patterns, and ritual seems to be above all the way we take possession of the patterns that others before us have handed down, a means of reminding ourselves that those patterns really count, and a ready-made theater for rehearsing them for our own benefit as well as for the next generation whom we socialize into them. Thus, Saturday night may be just the middle of a weekend for others, but for Jews enwrapt in (and enraptured by) *havdalah*, it is the guarantee that the very world is passing from a state of holy to one of profane.

Not that either one is necessarily evil—the English word "profane" deceptively misses the mark, insofar as it carries negative connotations, and the same is true of the word "holy" if it is taken necessarily to imply a higher order than its opposite—but simply that, for the Jew, there are two categories, holy and profane, and all that is must be either one or the other, but not both. Holy time is cosmically given—the seventh day (Shabbat), the tenth day of the seventh month (Yom Kippur)—and demands holy activity by holy people. But other days are by no means devoid of value; on the contrary, they have their own sets of responsibilities; it is just that they are nonholy, that is, profane, in the sense that they allow for ordinary labor, pedestrian activity, mundane thoughts and actions. ("Ordinary," "pedestrian," and "mundane" are as negatively charged as "profane" and fail to express the simple taxonomic discrimination without judgmental bias.) As for the holy people, Israel, it should be apparent that, like any religion or culture, Judaism has known its share of jingoes and xenophobes, but it has also its dominant acceptance of the nonholy other nations as equally deserving in the sight of God.

Much of Jewish life, however, revolves about acknowledging the distinction between the two realms: knowing where a blessing is in order, and where not; whether someone or something possesses sanctity, or its opposite. The very function of blessings over food, for example, is the releasing of holy produce from the earth (which belongs to God) so that it is no longer holy, but profane, and can thus be consumed by equally profane creatures (ourselves) living in a profane state.[3] (Apparently, the People Israel is holy, but the people who compose it are not.) Similarly, firstborn males are endowed with such heightened sanctity (by virtue of their birth order) that if they are neither priests nor Levites, a conflict arises. If the status with which they must act in the profane world is nonholy, then they must be redeemed by their fathers from the accident of their sanctified birth by yet another ritual (*pidyon haben*) that has as its focus this primal dichotomy of holy/profane.[4] The world is made of holy space, holy time, holy people, holy acts, and holy things—and their opposites: that much has been at the core of classical Jewish identity, insofar as *havdalah*, *pidyon haben*, and a variety of other rituals (like the *Kiddush* prayer inaugurating holy days)[5] inform us.

So the study of liturgy ought first to ask how liturgical rituals encode the world for those who ritualize. Like anthropologists at work among strangers, we ask for the "why" behind the phenomena, eliciting explanations beyond what the "text" of their testimony seemed immediately able to offer; but the strangers cease being strange only when we penetrate the surface of their language, only when the underlying categories with which they order things in the first place come to light.

But if, through their ritual and its implicit categories of meaning, Jews demarcate themselves from non-Jews, choosing, as it were, an alternative social universe to inhabit, so too do different groups of Jews develop in alternative ways from one another. For Orthodox/Conservative/Reform/(and others) today, read Pharisee/Sadducee/Essene/(and others) for the first century; Hasidim/Mitnagedim/(and, again, others) in eighteenth-century Poland, and the like. Moreover, sets of social divisions are hierarchical, so that within, say, the Reform, the Pharisaic, or the Hasidic camps themselves, there are any number of further subdivisions: classical Reform or its contemporary "revisionist" alternative (there is no ready name available yet), the followers of Hillel but not Shammai, and the court of the Satmar Rebbe rather than the Lubavicher Rebbe. And, to complicate matters, these exist on a spectrum, with identities shading off into one another at imprecise points.

How do simple human beings find their way through the maze of things they might be, if not, primarily, through ritual? Classical Reform Jews follow the dictates of Ottonian numinosity, see their history as Wise or Einhorn did, feature the prophets in their ritualized readings, favor the "old" *Union Prayer Book*, lean toward accenting social distance through a nonparticipational service in which high culture is present but traditionalist ritual objects and activities are not; the "revisionists" use a different book, and in a different way, featuring just those things that "classicists" omit. Equal ritual divisions, on the face of them picayune but really momentous for those who identify with one side or the other, mark the Hillelite/Shammaite debates from the first century, and the diatribes between rival Hasidic sects as well.

What we have is the process of censoring in and censoring out, another conceptual model we used here, an attempt to include oneself and one's group within the dominant definition of licit religiosity, yet to define oneself as holding a special place (in contrast to the "others") inside that generally recognized framework. If the focus of study is Roman religion in general, then it is late antiquity's dominant definition of religion that everyone emulates—Jews too sacrificed animals in their Temple, with all the drama and flourish that all cosmopolitans expected of religion then.[6] But they did so in their own way. And when the Temple ceased, they patterned their prayer after the cultic model, just as Christians too, without a Temple in which to sacrifice, emphasized the sacrificial aspect of their ritual observance.

Contrary to normal expectations, our rituals rarely censor out the obvious culprits in the vicinity—they are too evidently "not us" to warrant being singled out for negative mention. They exclude, instead, the close cousins, whose very similarity to us makes it imperative that we hedge our group's ego boundaries securely against their conceivable encroachment on our ideological turf. Thus, we looked at the growth of American Judaism and saw little ritualistic demarcation between Jews and non-Jews, but a great deal of censoring out of other Jewish possibilities: Reform (German immigrants) vs. "traditionalist" (eastern European immigrants); and Conservative movement vs. Reconstructionists. To the extent that a Reform ritual polemicizes against Christian influence, it is not, strictly speaking, Christians who are being censored out, but other Jews, who are charged—at least potentially—with borrowing too freely from Christians, crossing the divide between licit self-inclusion in society's norm and illicit living in someone else's camp. Similarly, in the past: the "so-called Gnostics," against whom Irenaeus railed, were not a foreign sect of some sort, but Christians who surely had an equally opprobrious epithet for Irenaeus in return; and the *minim* cursed in early Jewish liturgy were not Christians but other Jews, accused of going too far in the direction of Christianity.[7] The point is that group boundaries are fluid, always shifting, and observable only after the fact, where definers of group identity have successfully decided to erect them. Arbitrarily, people on the other side of the fence discover themselves marked off as strangers, even though they do not necessarily elect to be so. And after a period of years, subdivisions of people develop subdivisions of ritual, that is to say, rites.

So our study of rites documented no accident of geography, but a more basic underlying matter: the identity formation of subgroups within the larger social fabric. A second step in the holistic study of liturgy, then, is to identify changes in worship patterns not for their own sake but so as to recognize socially significant divisions in the religious identity of the worshipers; to trace prayer book revisions precisely because they entail *human* revisions of the worshipers' self-perception.

But identity in space through the knowledge that we keep the Sabbath precisely as it is kept by our cousins in Poland or in Jerusalem, say, is accompanied by identity through time, the myth of common origins that explains why we all do so in the first place. Hence, our next investigation dealt with what I called sacred myth, the history we tell one another in the course of our ritualizing together. Ritual is nothing if not time-bound, and specific occasions in the annual cycle take on their specificity because (among other things) they are anniversaries—either real or imagined—of occurrences in the past, occurrences that would have gone unnoticed but for the fact that the people celebrating their *re*currence have chosen to remember them as their own particular way of categorizing human history. Entire mythical tales are rarely included in these annual celebrations, but references to them are, and the religious community elsewhere socializes its members to recognize these allusions. As Lévi-Strauss remarks,

> Mythology exists in two clearly different modalities. Sometimes it is explicit and consists of stories which . . . rank as works in their own right. Sometimes . . . the mythic text is fragmentary. . . . Instead of the fragments being brought together in the light of some guiding principle, each remains linked to a particular phrase in the ritual, on which it serves as a gloss, and it is only recited in connection with the performance of ritual acts. [What we have is] implicit mythology in which fragments of discourse are bound up with non-linguistic actions.[8]

We thus see ritual serving as the locus for what we can call *normal exegetical mythologizing*. Each ritual action is pregnant with meaning and accompanied by exegetical interpretation, either in the form of obvious historical narrative, selectively perceived and honed in size to fit the ritual moment, or just in tacit acknowledgment of these larger truths, which are merely hinted at as the ritual proceeds. As textual instances of the first case, we have the Passover Haggadah and the *Avodah* rubric, both of which utilize moments of calendrical significance to recollect the past that made them so. In the latter category, we have selective prayers here and there in the prayer book (a citation we looked at from the *Musaf Tefillah*, for example), the prophetic lectionary cycle surrounding the Ninth of Av, or numerous other examples of prayers, old and new, that went unrecorded here.

Surely the liturgist's task is to unearth the system of significant history that religions present to their members at the moments most charged with religious import, the holy days and times that evoke the past.

Finally, I have made use of the common notion that religions postulate a certain "rightness" about who they are. In the course of human history, religious identity has sometimes been ascribed, sometimes chosen, but even when the latter, religious believers do more than join a group like all other groups. To switch the college one attends, or to take up golf but drop racquetball, is in the realm of taste; but to assume a new religious identity is, as we say, to convert, to be born again, to be made over. By definition, conversion—like naming ceremonies for all new things—is performative in nature, in that from the perspective of the person converting, it succeeds felicitously only if he or she professes commitment to the newfound faith. In the eyes of the convert, the medieval notion of "forced conversion" is an oxymoron, no less than forced free will or necessary choice. Religion is an identity, after all, not a pastime. It must, therefore, possess the means to impress its inherent "rightness" on those born to it, and those who choose it, both. In part, the sacred myth accomplishes this, but inevitably, recourse is had to ultimates, that is, at least in Western religions, to God. Hence the final chapter dealt with the apprehension of the divine in worship—an appropriate ending, since it is the divine-human encounter that makes worship what it is.

Here, my commitment to conceptualizing an underlying structure that unifies diverse cases of the same phenomenon should be evident, since the analysis revealed a threefold "generic" grid composed of *Cultural Backdrop, Master Image,* and *Synecdochal Vocabulary,* which should be applicable to all liturgical instances, independent of their specific cultural content; the examples given here being Judaism of late antiquity, nineteenth- to twentieth-century central Europe and America, and the contemporary strivings in which we find ourselves now. But other chapters are similar in approach. The study of prayer books was defined as a combined message of *manifest content, design or layout,* and *choreography,* for example.

What unifies this series of chapters is the common theme of religious community in search of self-definition through its life of prayer. At issue is an artistic impulse, however, so that if we are to ask the question, What is liturgy? without limiting our response in advance to the identification of some series of texts, we must eventually evoke the artistic potential in human behavior. There are, I think, at least three options open to us in this regard, and I should be explicit with regard to the one represented here.

There is first the nineteenth-century approach to phenomena in general, and religion in particular, which we can illustrate usefully for our purposes by a brief consideration of Freud. Freud is committed to a scientifically empirical observation of objective reality; he thus notes, for example, that religious ritual is empirically similar to what one observes in the study of neurotics, in that it is fraught with obsessive and compulsive behavior. But Freud is not interested in the sum total of empirical detail alone. Instead, he wants to understand diverse phenomena by revealing their underlying structure. He thus moves from the observed parallel between neuroses and ritual behavior to the unobserved, but underlying, connecting thread, and postulates a ritual-making mechanism in social behavior equivalent to a neurosis-producing tendency in individual life, both going back to the oedipal conflicts and the attendant fear of patricide. This summary of Freud's thinking, taken largely from his *Totem and Taboo*, is an oversimplification, to be sure, but a detailed description that would round out the account of Freud's theory would only deflect our attention from our primary topic, which is not the specific hypothesis erected by Freud, but the *type* of hypothesis that he sought, the particular model of explanation that Freud needed for his time.

Four features of Freud's treatment of ritual stand out here. To begin with, Freud believed that there is an independently existent real world of observable phenomena, and that the scientist's goal is to practice careful observation of the data "out there" until they are properly catalogued as to their connection with one another. That was what physical scientists thought they were doing, and Freud himself remained partial to their view, constructing his model of the psyche as if it were a homeostatic machine fueled by libidinal energy, and regularly likening it to other machines in the world of the "real" hard sciences.[9]

But Freud went further than the merely descriptive. Much as he supported his work by references to observable clinical data, the bulk of his writing is interpretive, and goes well beyond analyses of patients to include history and social theory as well, neither of which is empirically evident at all. Obviously, despite his claim to be merely an observer of phenomena, Freud had taken a necessary second step beyond the collection of clinical data, going past the observable realm of behavior to an unobservable domain of presumed infrastructure that supports the data. In a word, Freud was a structuralist. In the case before us, therefore, he did more than describe the wealth of diverse data regarding taboos of endogamy, and ritualistic totemic meals; he postulated nonobservable connections that lay behind them all, the theory of an original primal horde who killed and ate the father to obtain the mother, so that ever since, totemic systems (1) project the conflict over the father onto an animal, protecting the animal by prohibiting the tribe from hunting it; (2) yet also channel the urge to patricide into a ritual meal under the auspices of which the normally protected totemic animal—that is, the projection of the father—is again slaughtered by the group and consumed. Simultaneously, (3) totemism prohibits endogamous sexual relations as well. Freud was thus operating in a structural way, laying bare the grid of relationships beneath and behind appearances.

But as with any scientist of the period, Freud's dependence on nonobservable structural interpretations left him open to the charge that he had abandoned the empirical commitment with which he had begun. In this, he differed not at all from his contemporaries in the hard sciences, like Rutherford and Bohr, who were similarly postulating structural constructs underlying observable reality; with Freud, the issue was exacerbated, however, since he was studying human nature and laying bare hidden depths that his hearers denied, and about which they resisted even being told. Thus, Freud was careful, especially in his public lectures, to refer his theories back to observable phenomena, that is, the universal scientific test of hypotheses: does a theory predict events successfully or not?[10] Here we see the third characteristic of Freudian hypotheses: they are explanations of causes and effects, so that they can be tested for their predictive value in the laboratory or clinic. Cause-effect relationships are not the only conceivable bond between diverse phenomena—as Freud's disciple, Jung, was to hold with regard to what he called synchronicity;[11] but they are the only links that are structured to allow for the presence or absence of predictive testing, and so, Freud, like scientists of other sorts, admitted them alone as the litmus test of a successful theory of the underlying structure to phenomena.

Moreover, cause-and-effect connections are chronologically linear, the cause "happening" before its effect can occur. So scientific theories of the nineteenth century are diachronic. Also, ideally speaking, every cause is itself an effect of yet another cause prior to it, so that explanations like Freud's are not only diachronic but mythic, in the sense that they go back to supposed human origins, the very first cause of the whole causal sequence.

In sum, the first structural model that we might employ is illustrated by Freud, whose explanatory hermeneutic takes for granted four characteristics: (1) surface phenomena from which theories are extrapolated are objectively existent, and thus observable to an impartial outsider; (2) the theory explaining phenomena, however, must penetrate beneath observations to postulate a structural connective tissue that unifies discrete and variable data; (3) truth or falsity of theories is tested by their ability to predict other surface phenomena, that is, they are of a cause-and-effect nature; (4) interpretations are thus diachronic, often mythic, in terms of extending their causal chain back through time beyond the specific phenomena in question.

A second model is given to us by Lévi-Strauss, in many ways the paragon of structuralism. He was highly influenced by Freud, he says, since the Freudian system appealed to his preference for a geological model, whereby diachronic development is nevertheless present synchronically.[12] Nevertheless, Lévi-Strauss's criteria for acceptable hypotheses differ significantly from Freud's. Of the four assumptions that Freud held, Lévi-Strauss agrees with the first two, in that (1) phenomena are objectively present and empirically evident, and (2) explanations of them require the unearthing of structural grids supportive of the otherwise "seemingly incoherent mass" of "impenetrable" data.[13] Moreover, the underlying structures are mental constructs, for Lévi-Strauss, just as they are psychological ones for Freud.

But here, the similarity ceases. Lévi-Strauss's structures are not cause-and-effect relationships, but inbuilt constructs in the mind. Two events A and B are said to be explained not because A is the cause of B, but because A occurs with B as a related logical type, and so can be projected through cultural patterning upon the world we inhabit. With regard to totemism, then, Lévi-Strauss abandons cause-and-effect explanations and erects an internal logic of the system, what he calls the aesthetic component. It is "the arousal of aesthetic curiosity [that] leads directly to an acquisition of knowledge," a lesson he learned from Freud (!) he says. Thus, "ideas and beliefs of the totemic type . . . constitute codes, making it possible to ensure, in the form of conceptual systems, the convertibility of messages"; or, more specifically, in direct denial of the cause/effect hermeneutic, "How hopeless it is to attempt to establish a relation of priority between nutritional prohibitions and rules of exogamy. The relationship between them is not causal, but metaphorical."[14] Phenomena are explicable by the synchronic logical structure of the human mind itself, and we know an explanation to be true not because it predicts anything, but because it coheres aesthetically, providing "the important and valid category of the meaningful which is the highest mode of being of the rational."[15]

It is of the greatest importance to see that Lévi-Strauss has consciously crossed the boundary into the realm of art here, postulating an underlying mental structure according to which all phenomena are related not by cause and effect, nor in diachronic linear fashion, but with the same logic by which a painting or a symphony is "true," that is, by its presentation synchronically, all at one time, of internal harmony. Typically, Freud took a synchronic system, totemism, and reduced it to a diachronic myth of explanation; Lévi-Strauss takes a diachronic account, myth, and reduces it to a synchronic structure, mental logic.

It may be that Lévi-Strauss's postulate of the mind's internal structure that dominates cultural categorization is correct. But at the very least, it seems premature to make that judgment.[16] So we are left with a third possibility for our analysis here, one that retains Lévi-Strauss's emphasis on meaning, eschews the need for cause-and-effect demonstrations, and is content with seeing the presentations of ritual action as a structure enforced on phenomena, without that structure existing inherently in the human mind itself. For whether, in fact, it turns out that human beings are or are not genetically constructed to think in binary opposites (or any other logical paradigm) is, in a sense, a moot point, beyond what we need to make sense of culture. As long as the ritual patterning of the universe can be seen as a projection of the human need to order phenomena artistically, it matters little whether that need is biologically given via a particular type of necessary mental operation or not.

The third mode, and the one at use in these pages, then, is derived from a variety of theorists, but has been illustrated at such length here that multiple examples at this point would be superfluous. In general, it is a combination of the perspectives in the human sciences illustrated by Peter Berger, Mary Douglas, and Clifford Geertz. As in Freud and Lévi-Strauss, (1) phenomena are assumed to be real, though not necessarily completely objective, in that it is hard to see how we can penetrate the web of culturally enforced structure in order to see nature raw. (2) Interpretations of phenomena are structural too, though these structures are not necessarily given to reality by the workings of the psyche or the logic of the mind, as Freud or Lévi-Strauss would have it. Sometimes they can be traced in a functionalist sort of way to the social structure itself (as in the case of Ottonian transcendence), and they must be studied as synchronic presentations of meaning behind disparate data, apparent to human understanding because they are enforced upon the data by cultural patterns that are rehearsed in the ritual field. Therein lies the significance of ritual. And therein lies the extended study of liturgy for which I argue.

Liturgy should concern itself with the liturgical field as a whole because only there is the meaning behind the text made evident to worshipers. What we have is no linear presentation of verbal signs, but a symbol system that Susanne Langer has characterized as nondiscursive and presentational. Ritual, like art, is "judged on our experience of its revelations." Its assertions are neither true nor false but adequate or inadequate, expressive or not.[17] They are primarily solutions to "the problem of integration," whereby meaning, pattern, composition, and rhythm are bestowed on human existence in the world.[18] Or, to revert to Geertz's analogy with which chapter 1 concluded, "Analysis [I should say, *liturgical* analysis] is [or should be] the sorting out of the structures of signification. . . .

our constructions of other people's constructions of what they and their compatriots are up to."[19] Toward that end, the holistic study of liturgy may begin with the text but must eventually go beyond it—to the people, to their meanings, to their assumed constructs, and to their ritualized patterns that make their world uniquely their own.

Notes

CHAPTER 1: INTRODUCTION

1. Robert Taft, "Response to the Berakah Award: Anamnesis" *Worship* 59 (1985): 305.

2. Ibid., pp. 314–15.

3. Geoffrey Wainwright, "A Language in Which We Speak to God," *Worship* 57 (1983): 309.

4. Mark Searle, "New Tasks, New Methods: the Emergence of Pastoral Liturgical Studies," *Worship* 57 (1983): 306.

5. Stefan C. Reif, "Jewish Liturgical Research: Past, Present, and Future," *Journal of Jewish Studies* 35 (1984): 169.

6. See Clifford Geertz, "The Blurring of Genres," *American Scholar* 29 (1980).

7. See, for example, the report on "New Vogue: Company Culture" in the *New York Times*, January 5, 1983, which describes the "distinct identities and tones" for which corporations strive, and the way "companies instill their beliefs in their employees through rituals and heroes." Compare also a similar report in the *New York Times* (March 15, 1983) describing the replacement of church rituals with civic ones in the Soviet Union, including "a proposal to form an institute in Moscow where ethnographers, historians, folklorists, philosophers, writers and musicians would join to create modern rites 'uniting word and music true to national tradition.'"

8. For a history of modern scholarship, including the role of Zunz, see Richard Sarason, "On the Use of Method in the Modern Study of Jewish Liturgy," in *Approaches to Ancient Judaism: Theory and Practice*, ed. William Scott Green, Brown Judaic Studies I (Chico, Cal., 1978). The most current studies are discussed by Sarason in *The Study of Ancient Judaism*, vol. I, ed. Jacob Neusner (Chico, Cal., 1982); Cf. also Tzvee Zahavy, "A New Approach to Early Jewish Prayer," in *History of Judaism: The Next Ten Years*, ed. B. M. Bokser (Chico, Cal., 1980), pp. 49–65; and Stefan C. Reif, "Jewish Liturgical Research: Past Present and Future," *JJS* 34 (1983): 161–70.

9. See, particularly, recent works by E. Daniel Goldschmidt, who defended philology until his death in 1978. Cf. *Haggadah Shel Pesach Vetoldoteha* (Jerusalem, 1960); *Machzor Layamin Hanora'im*, 2 vols. (Jerusalem, 1970); and a posthumously published collection of articles that originally appeared individually in journals, *Mechkarei Tefillah Ufiyyut* (Jerusalem, 1979). See *Machzor*, vol. 1, p. 22, n. 23, for Goldschmidt's defense of philology against Heinemann's form-critical attack.

10. Joseph Heinemann, *Hatefillah Bitekufat Hatanna'im Veha'amora'im* (Jerusalem, 1966). Translated into English by Richard Sarason, entitled *Prayer in the Talmud: Forms and Patterns* (Berlin-New York, 1977).

11. See Sarason, "Method in Jewish Liturgy," pp. 131–47.

12. Ferdinand de Saussure, *Course in General Linguistics*, ed. Charles Bally, Albert Sechehaye, Albert Riedlingr (paperback ed., New York, 1966), pp. 1–2.

13. Arnold Goldberg, "Service of the Heart: Liturgical Aspects of Synagogue Worship," in *Standing Before God: Studies on Prayer in Scripture and Tradition in Honor of John M. Oesterreicher*, ed. Asher Finkel and Lawrence Frizzell (New York, 1981), pp. 195–211.

14. Leopold Zunz, *Die gottesdienstliche Vorträge der Juden, historisch entwickelt* (1832); Heb. ed., *Haderashot Beyisra'el*, ed. Ch. Albeck (Jerusalem, 1954), pp. 178–79.

15. On this benediction, see Reuven Kimelman, "*Birkat Haminim* and the Lack of Evidence for an Anti-Christian Prayer in Late Antiquity," in *Jewish and Christian Self-Definition, Volume Two, Aspects of Judaism in the Graeco-Roman World* ed. E. P.

Sanders, A. I. Baumgarten, and Alan Mendelson (Philadelphia, 1982), pp. 226–44, 392–403; and W. Horbury, "The Benediction of the Minim and Early Jewish Christian Controversy," *Journal of Theological Studies* 33 (1982): 19–61.

16. The best example of this approach is not Zunz, but Louis Finkelstein, "The Oldest Midrash: Pre-Rabbinic Ideals and Teachings in the Passover Haggadah," *HTR* 31 (1938): 291–317; idem, "Pre-Maccabean Documents in the Passover Haggadah," *HTR* 35 (1942): 291–332; 36 (1943): 1–38.

17. M. Taan. 2:1–4.

18. T. Taan. 1:10.

19. Taan. 16b.

20. J. Lévi, "Notices sur les jeûnes chez les Israelites," *REJ* 47 (1903).

21. V. Aptowitzer, *Die Parteipolitik* (Vienna, 1907), p. 51; Chanokh Albeck, *Shishah Sidrei Mishnah, Seder Mo'ed* (Israel, 1958), p. 493.

22. Cf. Joseph Heinemann, "The Meaning of Some Mishnayot in the Order Mo'ed" (Hebrew), *Tarbiz* 29 (1960): 25–29; idem, *Prayer in the Talmud*, pp. 106–111.

23. Ibid., pp. 110–11.

24. Philip Birnbaum, ed., *Hasiddur Hashalem: Daily Prayer Book* (New York, 1949), pp. 741–44. The essential blessings are tannaitic. See Tosefta & Shab. 137b.

25. Ibid., pp. 743–44. But the naming passage is medieval. Our version is cited in the thirteenth-century Italian work *Shibbolei Haleket*, Hilkhot Milah 4. Cf. Amram's Aramaic version, *Seder Rav Amram*, ed. D. Goldschmidt (Jerusalem, 1971), p. 179.

26. See Jacob Neusner, *A History of the Mishnaic Law of Women*, Part 5, *The Mishnaic System of Women* (Leiden, 1980), pp. 13–21, 267–72.

27. Michael Polanyi, *Knowing and Being* (Chicago, 1969); Gregory Bateson, *Steps to an Ecology of Mind* (New York, 1971).

28. Polanyi, *Knowing and Being*, p. 140.

29. See, for example, Paul H. Weiss, "The Living System: Determinism Stratified," in *The Alpbach Symposium: Beyond Reductionism, New Perspectives in the Life Sciences*, ed. Arthur Koestler and J. R. Smythies, esp. pp. 10–11; and Ludwig von Bertalanffy, *General System Theory* (New York, 1968). These authors use the term "holism" with different emphases, but generally they all approximate the view espoused here, in their opposition to what they call reductionism.

30. Clifford Geertz, *The Interpretation of Culture* (New York, 1970), p. 10.

31. Ibid., p. 9.

32. Daniel B. Stevick, "Responsibility for Liturgy," *Worship* 50 (1976): 301–302. Italics added.

33. Clifford Geertz, "Blurred Genres: The Refiguration of Social Thought," *The American Scholar* 29:2 (1980); reprinted in *Local Knowledge* (New York, 1983), pp. 20–21.

CHAPTER 2: *HAVDALAH*: A CASE OF CATEGORIES

1. Philip Birnbaum, ed., *Hasiddur Hashalem: Daily Prayer Book* (New York, 1949), p. 201. All translations of prayers are my own, unless otherwise indicated. To facilitate reference, however, I will regularly cite the places where liturgical passages may be found in published English sources, even though the translations there may vary from those used here. In this case I have borrowed Birnbaum's rendering of the last sentence.

2. Ibid., pp. 590–91.

3. Ibid., pp. 551–61. Birnbaum includes many songs but omits two folk elements that are standard in most households. The first is a welcome for Elijah, sung also at the Passover seder, *Eliyahu Hanavi* (Elijah the Prophet). The second is a refrain for the song *Hamavdil* (pp. 553–54), which reads, simply, *shavu'a tov* (A good week).

4. S. Baer, ed., *Seder Avodat Yisra'el* (Rödelheim, 1868).

5. The classic case, Elbogen, is discussed below, but see also Israel Abrahams, *Companion to the "Authorised Daily Prayer Book"* (1914; reprint ed., New York, 1966); or, on the High Holy Day *Machzor*, Max Arzt, *Justice and Mercy* (New York and Chicago, 1963). Abrahams even correlates his discussion with pagination of a specific prayer book, calling his commentary, "Companion . . . ," that is, a commentary that would otherwise appear below the line of the prayer text, were this to be the sort of edition that Baer issued.

6. Ismar Elbogen, *Der jüdische Gottesdienst in seiner geschichtlichen Entwicklung* (1913; German reprint ed., 1962); Hebrew ed., *Hatefillah Beyisra'el*, ed. Joseph Heinemann (Tel Aviv, 1972).

7. *Hatefillah Beyisra'el*, p. 93.

8. M. Pes. 8:1.

9. For my choice of dates for the geonic period, see justification advanced in Lawrence A. Hoffman, *The Canonization of the Synagogue Service* (Notre Dame, 1979).

10. See, for example, Naphtali Wieder, "The Old Palestinian Ritual—New Sources," *JJS* 4 (1953): 33–37.

11. Ber. 33a, cited twice, each time by a different tradent, both carrying the identical opinion, and identifying it as belonging to R. Jochanan. According to one version, Jochanan himself cited it; according to the other, someone else relayed it to him. In both cases, it appears as a given datum on which no disagreement is possible.

12. On Simon, see George Foot Moore, "Simon the Righteous," in *Jewish Studies in Memory of Israel Abrahams* (New York, 1927), pp. 351–59. On the Great Assembly, see discussion and literature cited in Salo Baron, *Social and Religious History of the Jews*, vol. 1, 2d ed. (New York, 1952), pp. 367–68, n. 35.

13. Solomon Zeitlin, "The Origin of the Synagogue," *PAAJR* 1 (1930): 79–80; reprinted in Zeitlin, *Studies in the Early History of Judaism*, vol. 1, pp. 11–12, and in *The Synagogue: Studies in Origins, Archaeology and Architecture*, ed. Joseph Gutmann (New York, 1975), pp. 14–26.

14. Kaufmann Kohler, "The Origin and Composition of the Eighteen Benedictions, with a Translation of the Corresponding Essene Prayers in the Apostolic Constitutions," *HUCA* 1 (1924): 388.

15. For the traditional list of enactments said to be by the Men of the Great Assembly, see the classic work by Z. H. Chajes, *The Student's Guide Through the Talmud*, trans. and ed. Jacob Schachter, 2d Eng. ed. (New York, 1960), pp. 83–87.

16. See below, chap. 7, for discussion.

17. Pes. 103a/b.

18. "Sea and dry land" and "seventh day and six days of work" actually have no scriptural basis, as the ensuing discussion makes plain. The scriptural citations on which the other oppositions are based are: (1) holy and profane, Lev. 10:10; (2) light and darkness, Gen. 1:4; (3) Israel and other peoples, Lev. 20:26; (4) unclean and clean, Lev. 10:10; (5) upper waters and lower waters, Gen. 1:7; (6) priests, Levites, and Israelites, 1 Chron. 23:13.

19. See R.H. 17b, for example. Later (ninth and tenth centuries, respectively) both Natronai and Saadiah know of the addition of terms beyond our usual formula, but in their case, we find not a continuation of an old custom but an instance of literary influence, as people had read the talmudic passage under discussion here and molded their custom to include what they read. It does not occur in the *Havdalah al hakos*, that is, the home ceremony, but in an extended poetic literary version, an elaboration of what I labeled A (p. 23, above). Cf. B. M. Lewin, *Otsar Hageonim*, vol. 3, p. 102; and *Siddur Saadiah*, p. 123, and n. 2. See also Naphtali Wieder, "The Old Palestine Ritual: New Sources," *JJS* 4 (1953), p. 36.

20. Claude Lévi-Strauss, *Structural Anthropology* (Eng. trans., New York, 1963), pp. 212, 216–17.

21. Claude Lévi-Strauss, *The Raw and the Cooked* (Eng. trans., Chicago, 1969), p. 8.

22. Claude Lévi-Strauss, *Myth and Meaning* (Toronto, 1978), p. 10.

23. Ibid., p. 8.

24. Ludwig Wittgenstein, *Lectures and Conversations on Aesthetics and Religious Belief*, ed. Cyril Barrett (Berkeley, n.d.), p. 55.

25. Claude Lévi-Strauss, *The Savage Mind* (Chicago, 1963), p. 75.

26. Mary Douglas, *Purity and Danger* (London, 1966), p. 39.

27. See, for example, Edward Sapir, *Selected Writings in Language, Culture and Personality*, p. 162; and idem, *Language* (New York, 1921), p. 17.

28. Douglas, *Purity*, p. 4. Italics added.

29. Ibid., pp. 34–35.

30. Ibid., p. 35.

31. Ibid., p. 38.

32. Margaret Mead, "Ritual and Social Crisis," in *The Roots of Ritual*, ed. James D. Shaughnessy (Grand Rapids, 1973), pp. 87–101.

33. On the relationship between worship and values, see Lawrence A. Hoffman, "Liturgical Basis for Social Policy: A Jewish View," in *Liturgical Foundations of Social Policy in the Catholic and Jewish Traditions*, ed. Daniel F. Polish and Eugene J. Fisher, pp. 151–68.

34. *Siddur Saadiah*, p. 123; and sources, n. 12.

35. *Hareshut beyado*, as Natronai puts it. See *Hamanhig, Hilkhot Shabbat*, no. 65.

36. Its normal appellation in the literature, "Creation," derives from a forced attempt to apply Rosenzweig's threefold theological scheme to the three blessings in the morning *Shema*. (On Rosenzweig, see his *Star of Redemption*, trans. William Hallo [New York, 1971]; for a summary of his scheme, see Eugene B. Borowitz, *A Layman's Introduction to Religious Existentialism* [New York, 1966].) But it is not creation per se so much as it is the distinction between light and darkness that counts here. The evening form of the same blessing in the standard Ashkenazic rite makes this point clearly: "He creates day and night; rolls away light from before darkness, and darkness from before light; and separates [N.B.] day from night." See Birnbaum, *Siddur*, p. 191.

37. Douglas, *Purity*, p. 6.

38. Birnbaum, *Siddur*, pp. 71–74, 191–92.

39. Arnold van Gennep, *The Rites of Passage*, Eng. ed. (Chicago, 1960); Victor Turner, *The Ritual Process* (Chicago, 1969).

40. Victor Turner, *A Forest of Symbols: Aspects of Ndembu Ritual* (Ithaca and London, 1967), p. 111.

41. See, for example, his treatment of *Tashlikh* or of covering the eyes during candle lighting, reprinted in his *Rabbinic Essays* (Cincinnati, 1951), pp. 299–433, 470; and idem, "The Origin and Development of Two Sabbath Ceremonies," *HUCA* 15 (1940): 367–424. Reprinted in *Beauty in Holiness: Studies in Jewish Customs and Ceremonial Art*, ed. J. Gutmann (New York, 1970), 203–61.

42. Douglas, *Purity*, p. 97.

43. Ibid., p. 113.

44. *Seder Rav Amram*, p. 93.

45. See *Tur* OH, no. 299; *Machzor Vitry*, p. 116; *Hamanhig*, no. 65; *Sha'arei Simchah* (Fürth ed.), vol. 1, p. 15.

46. See, for example, confusion over the angel's name, discussed in *Machzor Vitry*, p. 116, n. 30.

47. Ber. 5:2.

48. *Machzor Vitry*, p. 116.

49. For a representative text, see *Sefer Harazim*, ed. Mordecai Margoliouth (Jerusalem, 1967). On Antioch, see Robert Wilken, "The Jews of Antioch," *Society of Biblical Literature 1976 Seminar Papers*, p. 73, and Wayne A. Meeks and Robert L. Wilken,

Jews and Christians in Antioch in the First Four Centuries of the Common Era (Chico, Cal., 1978), p. 51, n. 172. The classic work on central Europe is Joshua Trachtenberg, *Jewish Magic and Superstition: A Study in Folk Religion* (Cleveland, 1961).

50. Douglas, *Purity*. The parallel avoidance of danger from demons, recited daily at nightfall, is *Hashkivenu* (see Birnbaum, *Siddur*, p. 197). There, God is asked to protect us from Satan. Thus the daily evening liturgy parallels the Saturday night *havdalah* insofar as (1) both are said when light becomes darkness; (2) both underscore the basic light/darkness categorization by a *havdalah*, the former in the first blessing before the *Shema*, the latter in the *havdalah* itself; and (3) both call on outside forces for protection in the liminal state of being.

51. Jacob Mann illustrates Jewish messianism then in "Messianic Movements During the First Crusades" (Hebrew), in *Hatekufah* 23 (1925): 243–61, and 24 (1926): 335–58; reprinted in *The Collected Articles of Jacob Mann*, vol. 1 (Israel, 1971), pp. 182–225. For Christian parallels, see Norman Cohn, *The Pursuit of the Millennium*, 1957 (rev. ed., Oxford, 1970).

52. On the original meaning of *leil shimurim*, see J. Derenbourg, "Haggadah et Legende," *REJ* 9 (1884): 303–304. The seder eve *piyyut*, *Vayehi bechatzi halayelah*, compresses all redemptive history into that one night. See Birnbaum, *Haggadah*, pp. 136–39.

53. Ber. 54a.

54. See Joseph Gutmann, "The Messiah at the Seder," in *Raphael Mahler Jubilee Volume* (Israel, 1974), pp. 29–38. The illustrations themselves are carried in Mendel Metzger, *La Haggadah enluminée* (Leiden, 1973), plates LV–LVII.

55. Turner, *Ritual Process*, p. 110.

56. See Bonnie Ann Steinberg, "Elijah's Cup: A Search for the Origins of a Custom" (Master's thesis, Hebrew Union College, 1979), where relevant postbiblical lore is collected.

57. Turner, *Ritual Process*, pp. 109–110.

58. Ibid., p. 106. On *communitas*, see discussion below, pp. 168–71.

CHAPTER 3: RITES: A CASE OF SOCIAL SPACE

1. L. Zunz, *Ritus der synagogalen Gottesdienst* (Berlin, 1859), p. 2.

2. L. Zunz, *Die Gottesdienstliche Vorträge der Juden, historisch entwickelt* (1832), chap. 21; trans. into Hebrew by Chanokh Albeck, *Haderashot Beyisra'el* (Jerusalem, 1954).

3. See, for example, the collection of studies on rites by Goldschmidt, assembled in his *Mechkarei Tefillah Ufiyyut*.

4. Joseph Heinemann, *Tefillot Yisra'el Vetoldotehen* (Jerusalem, 1966), p. 2, and cited in Eng. trans. (as here) in Jakob J. Petuchowski, "Guide to the Prayer Book" (ms., Cincinnati, 1968), p. 10.

5. Solomon Schechter, "Genizah Specimens," *JQR*, o.s., 10 (1898): 654–59; reprinted in Jakob J. Petuchowski, *Contributions to the Scientific Study of Jewish Liturgy* (New York, 1970), pp. 373–79.

6. Jacob Mann, "Genizah Fragments of the Palestinian Order of Service," *HUCA* 2 (1925), reprinted in Petuchowski, *Contributions*, pp. 379–449. Cf. Israel Abrahams, "Some Egyptian Fragments of the Passover Haggadah," *JQR* o.s., 10 (1898): 41–51; Israel Levi, "Fragments de Rituel de Prières, *REJ* 53 (1907): 231–43; Ismar Elbogen, "Die Tefillah für die Festtage," *MGWJ* 55 (1911): 586–99. See also the later publication that complements these works, Simchah Assaf, "Miseder Hatefillah Be'erets Yisra'el," in *Sefer Dinabourg*, ed. Isaac Baer (Jerusalem, 1949).

7. Compare his works on the Passover Haggadah, cited above, chap. 1, n. 16, and

"The Birkat Hamazon," *JQR*, n.s., 19 (1928–29): 211–62; and "The Development of the Amidah," reprinted in Petuchowski, *Contributions*, pp. 379–449.

8. See Heinemann's critique in *Prayer in the Talmud*, chap. 2, esp. pp. 43–45.

9. Mann, "Genizah Fragments," p. 380.

10. A. I. Schechter, *Studies in Jewish Liturgy* (Philadelphia, 1930). For Italian liturgy, see the classic introduction to *Machzor Minhag Italiani* by SHaDaL (Samuel David Luzzatto), vol. 1 (Livorno, 1846), and subsequent studies by Goldschmidt, reprinted in his *Mechkarei Tefillah*, pp. 80–122, 153–87, 220–22.

11. Discussed in detail in Hoffman, *Canonization*. For secondary works on *Siddur Saadiah*, see bibliography there.

12. Gregory Bateson, *Steps to an Ecology of Mind*, Introduction, p. xx.

13. See William Popper, *The Censorship of Hebrew Books* (1899; reprint ed., New York, 1969).

14. This reverence is best seen in the *minhag* literature, with its penchant for reporting the customs of individual worthies, and in the earlier works of the disciples of Meir of Rothenberg (d. 1293). See the many times that Meir's personal examples became normative for them (Isaac Ze'ev Kahana, *Maharam Merotenberg: Teshuvot, Pesakim, Uminhagim*).

15. See evidence assembled by B. M. Lewin, *Iggeret Rav Sherira Gaon* (Haifa, 1921; reprinted Jerusalem, 1972), Introduction, pp. 49–50.

16. Jacob R. Marcus (*Israel Jacobson* [Cincinnati, 1972], pp. 86–94) notes that Jacobson turned to worship reform as his most immediate task.

17. *Gates of Prayer* and *Gates of Repentance*, the American Reform movement's basic liturgical texts for weekdays, Sabbaths, and festivals, are directly dependent on *Service of the Heart* and *Gate of Repentance*, the liturgy of Great Britain's Union of Liberal and Progressive Synagogues. Chaim Stern, general editor of the American works, served previously as coeditor of the British volumes. The Central Conference of American Rabbis recognized this dependence legally by paying a royalty to their British colleagues for liturgical material borrowed and used in the United States.

18. *A Hagada de Pessach*, ed. Herbert Bronstein, trans. Kathe Windmüller (Sao Paulo, 1977).

19. See Anan's *Sefer Hamitsvot*, published by Harkavy, *Studien und Mittheilungen*, vol. 4 (Berlin, 1887), and vol. 8 (St. Petersburg, 1903). Cf. also description by Jacob Mann, "Anan's Liturgy," *Journal of Jewish Lore and Philosophy* 1 (1919): 329–53, reprinted in Philip Birnbaum, *Karaite Studies* (New York, 1971), pp. 283–308. This is true of the tenth and eleventh centuries as well. See Leon Nemoy, "The Liturgy of al-Qirqisani," in *Studies in Jewish Bibliography, History and Literature in Honor of I. Edward Kiev*, ed. Charles Berlin (New York, 1971); and, in general, Judah Hadassi's *Eshkol Hakofer*, which still follows Karaite liturgical sensitivities obediently.

20. Zevi Ankori (*Karaites in Byzantium: The Formative Years; 970–1100* [New York, 1959]) surveys the situation generally. For the Bashyazi family, see Ankori's "Beit Bashyazi Vetakanotav," in *Aderet Eliyahu* (Jerusalem, 1967). Ankori emphasizes the shrinking social distance between Karaites and Rabbinites as a factor causing ritual borrowing, in "Eliyahu Bashyazi, Hakara'i," *Tarbiz* 25 (1956): 183. Jacob Mann (*Texts and Studies*, vol. 2 [Philadelphia, 1935], pp. 654–55) documents the issue of Sabbath lights and notes that in seventeenth-century Poland, where Jews and Karaites barely maintained any social distance from each other at all, Karaites even sang Sabbath songs "in imitation of *Lekha Dodi* and in honor of the Sabbath bride!" It is difficult to say when, precisely, Anan's insistence on limiting his liturgical sources to the Bible was no longer honored, and at what point each successive genre of prayer was added to the biblical material, but Nemoy (*Karaite Anthology* [New Haven and London, 1952], p. 273) suggests it was the thirteenth-century Aaron ben Joseph who first made the breakthrough.

21. The adoption of *Nusach Sefarad* became the most visible symbol of that distance. See Goldschmidt, "Al Nusach Hatefillah shel Kehillot Hachasidim," in his *Mechkarei Tefillah*, esp. pp. 314–316. A sense of the crisis entailed in this choice can be gleaned from *Siddur Hageonim Vehamekubalim Vehachasidim*, vol. 1 (Jerusalem, 1970), *ma'amar sheni.*

22. See Jakob J. Petuchowski, *Prayerbook Reform in Europe* (New York, 1968), chap. 3, "Reform From Within."

CHAPTER 4: AMERICAN JEWISH LITURGIES

1. David Philipson, ed., *Reminiscences by Isaac Mayer Wise* (Cincinnati, 1901), pp. 23, 24, 37. Wise's opponents, on the other hand, railed against what they adjudged to be deficiencies in Wise's own Judaic knowledge! See Joseph Gutmann, "Watchman on the Rhine," *American Jewish Archives* 10 (1958): 135 ff.

2. For details, as well as publication history of *Minhag America*, see Lawrence A. Hoffman, "The Language of Survival in American Reform Liturgy," *CCAR Journal* 24 (1977): 90–93.

3. See below, on Gotthard Deutsch, p. 126.

4. See above, n. 2.

5. Hoffman, "Language of Survival," pp. 93–95; and Eric L. Friedland, "Olath Tamid by David Einhorn," *HUCA* 45 (1974): 307–32.

6. Wise, who died in 1900, was followed for three years by Moses Mielziner, as president pro tem, and then, for a day (February 18, 1903) by Gotthard Deutsch. But Kohler was technically the second permanent appointment. See Michael Meyer, *Hebrew Union College–Jewish Institute of Religion at One Hundred Years* (Cincinnati, 1976), p. 52.

7. Quoted from an article by Einhorn in Isaac Leeser's *Occident*, by W. Gunther Plaut, *The Growth of Reform Judaism* (New York, 1965), p. 24. The actual text that was signed by Wise, and against which Einhorn railed, is reproduced in part in Herbert Parzen, *Architects of Conservative Judaism* (New York, 1964), p. 10; and is quoted by Jakob J. Petuchowski, "Abraham Geiger and Samuel Holdheim," *Leo Baeck Yearbook* 22 (1977): 156, which cites also Einhorn's attack on Wise from *Sinai* (1856).

8. An 1892 prayer book edited by Isaac Moses and dependent almost entirely on Einhorn's perspective was the first step in the process. But it was quickly withdrawn, probably at the insistence of Jews in New York, and replaced by the *Union Prayer Book* (1894/1895), which censored many of Einhorn's strongly held views on Jewish particularism. Cf. Hoffman, "Language of Survival," pp. 87–107; and Lou H. Silberman, "*The Union Prayer Book*: A Study in Liturgical Development," in *Retrospect and Prospect*, ed. Bertram Wallace Korn (New York, 1965), pp. 46–81.

9. Immigration figures are cited differently by different authors. Lloyd P. Gartner notes that there were about 280,000 Jews here in 1880, but a million by 1900 ("Jewish Education in the United States," in *The Jewish Community in America*, ed. Marshall Sklare [New York, 1974], p. 232). For our purposes, we note that the numbers do not increase dramatically until close to 1900, the very time that the Reform movement identified itself through its liturgy in such a radical way. Parallel figures are derived from Samuel Joseph, *Immigration to the United States from 1881 to 1910* (New York, 1914), pp. 95–96. Russian immigration from 1880 to 1890 totaled only 135,003 persons, and from 1890 to 1900, still only 279,811. But the next decade it jumped to 704,245. The figures from Rumania, though smaller, are even more striking when compared according to decades. They go from 6967 (1880s) to 12,789 (1890s) to 47,301 (1900s). But even by 1900, immigrants clustered in recognizable ghettos, particularly in New York and Chicago, where, in fact, the radical reformers were strong, led by Kohler and Hirsch,

Einhorn's sons-in-law. See 1900 census figures and comment in *Report of the Commission of Immigration of the State of New York*, April 5, 1909, p. 12, n. 3.

10. Herbert Parzen, "The Early Development of Conservative Judaism," *Conservative Judaism* 3:4 (1947): 17; and, in general, idem, *Architects of Conservative Judaism* (New York, 1964).

11. Parzen, "Early Development of Conservative Judaism," 4:4 (1948): 12.

12. Solomon Schechter, "Dedication Address," *Jewish Theological Seminary Biennial Report*, 1902–1904, p. 102.

13. Mordecai Kaplan, "Unity and Diversity in the Conservative Movement," *Conservative Judaism* 4:1 (1947): 1; and Robert Gordis, "The Tasks Before Us," *Judaism* 1:1 (1945): 3.

14. Mordecai Kaplan, "The Rabbinical Assembly at the Crossroads," *Conservative Judaism* 2:3 (1946): 1–2.

15. It contains "prayers, readings and hymns which can be used by public assemblies, patriotic societies, schools, civic centers, churches and synagogues, to celebrate these holidays in a religious spirit." (*Faith of America*, ed. Mordecai Kaplan, J. Paul Williams, Eugene Kohn [New York, 1951], Introduction, p. xxiv.) It is "a sort of liturgy" (p. xxx) for holidays, ranging from Independence Day and Memorial Day to Flag Day and Arbor Day.

16. *The Reconstructionist* 1 (1935): 2.

17. *Siddur Tefillot Yisra'el Lashabbat Uleshelosh Regalim: Sabbath and Festival Prayer Book* (New York, 1946).

18. *Tefillot Lashabbat Uleshelosh Regalim: Sabbath and Festival Services*, ed. Morris Silverman (Hartford, 1937).

19. Morris Silverman, "A Prayer Book Which Meets Present Needs," *The Reconstructionist* 4 (1938): 14–16.

20. Robert Gordis, "The Tasks Before Us," p. 4.

21. It is actually far less liberal than Silverman's original (1937) work. It omits transliterations, for example. Given the thesis proposed here, this conservative tendency would be expected, since the book is seen as an expression of movement identity, defined not so much against the foil of religious Orthodoxy (as was the case with Reform) as against the religious liberalism of Reform and Reconstructionism.

22. Robert Gordis, "A Jewish Prayer Book for the Modern Age," *Conservative Judaism* 2 (1945): 1–20.

23. Ibid., p. 4.

24. Ibid., p. 8.

25. See Gordis's scathing critique of this practice of alternating services in order to avoid "monotony" (ibid., p. 4). He dates it to Samuel Holdheim's *Gebetbuch* of 1856. Jonah B. Wise stated the problem well in 1930: "The reading preacher faces the serious implications of a shortened manual of translated prayers read weekly to the same group." (Jonah B. Wise, "The Devotional Value of the *Union Prayer Book*," *CCAR Yearbook* 40 [1930]: 295.) On this congregational passivity—people are read "to," note—see discussion below regarding the tendency to involve worshipers, typical of liturgical trends today, pp. 168–70.

26. See collected comments through the ages, assembled by A[braham] A[lexander] Wolff, *Ateret Shalom Ve'emet: Die Stimmen der ältesten glaubwerdigsten Rabbinen über die Pijutim* (Leipzig, 1857).

27. See above, chap. 3.

28. Personal communication from publisher, Jacob Behrman, among others.

29. For more extended treatment, see Lawrence A. Hoffman, *Gates of Understanding* (New York, 1977), pp. 135–50.

30. Back cover, *Conservative Judaism* 1 (1945).

31. Personal communication from Rabbi Cohen of Lincoln Square Synagogue, New

York, who recalls the adoption of the book in 1970 after the synagogue's rabbis received the personal approval (*haskamah*) of Rabbi Soloveitchik.

32. By contrast, wealthy upper- and middle-class worshipers in large European cities sought a Hazzanic style that bespoke grandeur and musical sophistication, a tendency personified best by the illustrious Salomon Sulzer (1804–90), the chief cantor of the Jewish community in fin-de-siècle Vienna. Sulzer described his own goal as the recasting of "the old national melodies and modes . . . according to the rules of art," and apparently succeeded so well at his task that even non-Jewish music connoisseurs came to hear him. In a passage resonant with the romantic temperament of the age, Franz Liszt testified of one such occasion, "Only once we witnessed what true Jewish art could be. . . . For moments we could penetrate into his real soul and recognize the secret doctrine of the fathers. . . . Seldom were we so deeply moved by emotion as on that evening, so shaken that our soul was entirely seized by meditation and given to participation in the service" (cited in Eric Werner, *A Voice Still Heard* [University Park and London, 1976], pp. 212, 215).

33. For a study of the Conservative movement's choreography, see Marshall Sklare, *Conservative Judaism* (Glencoe, 1955), pp. 83–128; reprinted with some alterations in idem, *The Jews: Social Patterns of an American Group* (Glencoe, 1958), pp. 357–77. For a more recent study of the choreography of modern Orthodoxy, see Samuel Heilman, *Synagogue Life* (Chicago, 1976), chaps. 3 and 4.

34. For the significance of these events in terms of their appearance in liturgical recollections of Jewish history, see discussion below, chapter 6.

35. Cf. Lawrence A. Hoffman, "Creative Liturgy," in *Jewish Spectator* (Winter 1975): 42–50; and, for an account of how Jewish acculturation in America has altered "traditional" rituals generally, Abraham G. Duker, "Emerging Culture Patterns in American Jewish Life," *Publications of the American Jewish Historical Society* 39 (1950): 351–89.

36. Jakob J. Petuchowski, "Conservative Liturgy Comes of Age," *Conservative Judaism* 27 (1972): 3.

CHAPTER 5: SACRED MYTHS: I. PREMODERN JEWISH PERSPECTIVES

1. Peter L. Berger and Thomas Luckmann, *The Social Construction of Reality* (1966; Anchor ed., New York, 1967), pp. 25–27.

2. George Charbonnier, *Entretiens avec Claude Lévi-Strauss* (1961; Eng. trans., *Conversations With* . . . , London, 1969), p. 49.

3. Cf. for example, Ernst Cassirer, *Language and Myth* (1945, trans. Susanne K. Langer); Claude Lévi-Strauss, "The Structural Study of Myth," in *Structural Anthropology*; Edmund Leach's popular but valuable introduction and critique of Lévi-Strauss in *Claude Lévi-Strauss* (New York, 1970), pp. 57–91. Mircea Eliade, *Myths, Dreams and Mysteries*, pp. 23–38; Carl G. Jung, et al., *Man and His Symbols* (London, 1964), Index, s.v. "Myth"; Heinrich Zimmer, "Myths and Symbols," in *Indian Arts and Civilization* (New York, 1946).

4. For examples of the former, see Jacob Mann, "Changes in the Divine Service Due to Religious Persecution," *HUCA* 4 (1927): 241–311. For the question of whether the *piyyut* itself arose as a response to persecution, see short summary discussion by Petuchowski, in Joseph Heinemann with Jakob J. Petuchowski, *Literature of the Synagogue* (New York, 1975), pp. 206–207, and sources listed there. For the latter, see Heinemann, *Prayer in the Talmud*, pp. 193–207, and for elaboration of the theme, see Anson Hugh Laytner, "*Hutzpa K'lapei Shamaya*: The Tradition of Arguing with God" (Ordination Thesis, Hebrew Union College, 1979).

5. For Polanyi, see above, chap. 1, n. 27.

6. The *Hasidei Ashkenaz*, on whom, generally, see Yosef Dan, *Torat Hasod Shel Hasidut Ashkenaz* (Israel, 1968); Ivan Marcus, *Piety and Society* (Leiden, 1981). For an example of their liturgical commentary, see *Siddur of R. Solomon ben Samson of Germaise*, ed. Moshe Herdler (Jerusalem, 1971).

7. See Peter Berger, *The Sacred Canopy* (New York, 1969), pp. 45–51.

8. M. Bik., chap. 3.

9. Deut. 26:5–10.

10. Deut. 26:14–15.

11. Ber. Rabbah 1:1, and elsewhere.

12. "In time to come, when Jews will enter the Land [of Israel] for the third time, they will begin [again] to calculate *shemitah* and *yovel*" (*Hilkhot Shemitah Veyovel* 12:16); hence, it is characteristic of the age of history, from the Temple's destruction until the advent of the messiah, that the *yovel* is not kept.

13. Opinions differ, however, on whether, in fact, it was offered anyway. See sources cited by Alexander Guttmann, *Rabbinic Judaism in the Making* (Detroit, 1970), p. 282, n. 62.

For the view—unconvincing, in my opinion—that the Temple cult, in general, continued to operate even after 70, see K. W. Clark, "Worship in the Jerusalem Temple after A.D. 70." *New Testament Studies* 6 (1959–60): 269–80; reprinted in *The Gentile Bias and Other Essays* (Leiden, 1980), pp. 9–20. Cf. short rebuttal by Shaye J. D. Cohen, "The Significance of Yavneh: Pharisees, Rabbis and the End of Jewish Sectarianism," *HUCA* 55 (1964): 27, n. 1: "The present tense used by Josephus and some of the apostolic fathers when describing the sacrifical cult proves nothing, since the same phenomenon can be observed even after 135, by which time even Clark admits that the sacrificial cult must have ceased."

14. For a short collection of sources analyzed as to the philosophical conception of time in Jewish tradition, see Menachem M. Kasher, "Musag Hazeman Batorah Besifrei Chazal Veharishonim," *Talpiyot* 3–4 (1942): 799–829. The problem of reconstructing history from rabbinic sources is dealt with in Michael Meyer, *The Idea of History* (N.Y., 1974); Ellis Rivkin, "The Saadiah–David ben Zakkai Controversy," in *Essays in Honor of Abraham A. Newman*, ed. Meir ben Horin, Bernard D. Weinryb, Solomon Zeitlin (Philadelphia, 1962); Jacob Neusner, "The Babylonian Talmud as a Historical Document," *Conservative Judaism* 24 (1970): 48–57; idem, *Beyond Historicism, After Structuralism: Henry Spindell Memorial Lecture* (Bowdoin College, 1980). See also classic essay by Salo Baron, "Emphases in Jewish History," *Jewish Social Studies* 1 (1939), reprinted in Baron, *History and Jewish Historians* (Philadelphia, 1964), pp. 64–89.

15. This principle is stated early, and then repetitively through the ages. The *tannaim* know of it (see, for example, *Sifre* to Nu. 9:1, Horowitz ed., p. 61; *Mekhilta* to Ex. 15:9, Horowitz-Rabin ed., p. 139, Lauterbach ed., vol. 2, p. 54). Both the Babli (Pes. 6b) and the Yerushalmi (Shek. 6:1, Sotah 5:3) assume it. It is the basis for exegesis by later medieval midrashim as well (Koh. Rab. 1:31, e.g.), and is repeated from earlier sources by commentators whose interpretations became standard (Rashi to Nu. 9:1, e.g.).

16. Even in the so-called triennial cycle, wherein the necessary cycle occupied some three to four years, a private annual reading of the entire Pentateuch was the norm, so that individuals would be able to read every word, each year. On this cycle, see Adolph Buechler, "The Reading of the Law and Prophets in the Triennial Cycle," *JQR*, o.s. 5 (1893) and 6 (1894); reprinted in Petuchowski, *Contributions*, pp. 181–302; Ben Zion Wacholder, "Prolegomenon" to *Jacob Mann's The Bible as Read and Preached in the Old Synagogue*, vol. 1, Ktav ed. (New York, 1971), pp. xi–xliii; Joseph Heinemann, "Machzor Hatelat Shanati Velu'ach Hashanah," *Tarbiz* 33 (1964): 362–68; Michael J. Klein, "Four Notes on the Triennial Lectionary Cycle," *JJS* 32 (1981): 65–73; and Marc Bregman, "The Triennial Haftarot and the Perorations of the Midrashic Homilies," *JJS* 32 (1981): 74–85.

17. For an interesting introduction to the way in which different cultures structure time, and the arbitrary nature of Western linear time, see Edward T. Hall, *The Silent Language*, Doubleday Anchor ed. (New York, 1973), pp. 1–19, 140–61. On Western time, see Benjamin J. Whorf, *Collected Papers on Metalinguistics* (Washington, 1952).

18. M.R.H. 2:1.

19. Exactly when this consecutive message came about is debatable. It is known to Abudarham (fourteenth-century Spain), who says he got it from the writings of Rabbenu Hananel (tenth-century North Africa). See *Abudarham Hashalem*, p. 303. Tos. Meg. 31b, however, attributes it to *Pesikta Rabbati*, even though (in our printed version, at least) the message there is hardly as patterned as it is in Abudarham's account. Yet Abudarham cites the *Pesikta*, or, possibly, he cites Hananel, who quoted the *Pesikta* (*ve'amrinan bapesikta*), so the origin of the idea that we have a consecutive serialized message conveyed by Haftarah readings probably goes back to the sixth century or before, when different lectionaries were being combined and the *Pesikta* collection was taking shape. The vision of a connected message in the combined lectionaries was arrived at some time later and was known to Hananel, who read it into the *Pesikta*. Cf. Lewis M. Barth, "The Three of Rebuke and the Seven of Consolation: Sermons in the Pesikta de Rav Kahana," *JJS* 33 (1982): 503–15.

20. See, e.g., *Kinot for the Ninth of Av According to the Ashkenazic Rite*, ed. Abraham Rosenfeld (London, 1965), which prescribes elegies on Tish'a B'av not only for the destroyed Temple but also for the martyrs of the Hadrianic persecution, those of the 1173 York massacre, and even "our 6,000,000 martyrs who perished during 1939–1945" (pp. 168–75). Here, through the liturgy, historical time is collapsed and various tragedies are recalled ritualistically, as if they were one.

21. For a discussion of the pre-rabbinic description of the Passover seder, as well as for an analysis of the rabbinic era that followed, see Baruch M. Bokser, *The Origins of the Seder* (Berkeley and Los Angeles, 1984). Joseph Tabory's "The Passover Eve Ceremony, an Historical Outline," in *Immanuel* 12 (1981): 32–41, is a brief synopsis of that author's 1977 doctoral dissertation and must be considered point by point in the light of evidence that only the dissertation, but not the article, provides.

22. M. Pes. 10:4. The theme is explicit in the new Reform liturgy. See *A Passover Haggadah*, ed. Herbert Bronstein (New York, 1974), p. 34.

23. For a collection of opinions, see M. Kasher, *Haggadah Shelemah* (Jerusalem, 1967), pp. 90–95. The telescoping of history is particularly evident in Rabbi Levi's insistence that the cups stand for "the four kingdoms" that have oppressed Israel, these being spelled out in a later version of the same idea by Rabbenu Joel. See citations, pp. 91, 95. The Fifth Cup of Rabbi Tarfon may already in his time (second century) have reflected the idea that the final redemption, though still unrealized, is expected to occur imminently on Passover Eve. See Lawrence A. Hoffman, "A Symbol of Salvation in the Passover Haggadah," *Worship* 53:6 (1979): 527, n. 32.

24. See S. Stein, "Influence of the Symposia Literature on the Literary Form of the Pesah Haggadah," *JJS* 8 (1957): 32.

25. Scholars are not unanimous in identifying such an early stratum. See, e.g., Solomon Zeitlin (*Rise and Fall of the Judaean State*, vol. 3 [Philadelphia, 1978], p. 441), who dates *Midrash Tannaim* in the Middle Ages.

26. Louis Finkelstein, "The Oldest Midrash: Pre-rabbinic Ideals and Teachings in the Passover Haggadah," *HTR* 31 (1938).

27. Nahum Glatzer, *The Passover Haggada* (New York, 1953), pp. 30–31.

28. Ruth Stragow Newhouse, "The Music of the Passover Seder from Notated Sources, 1644–1945" (Ph.D. diss., University of Maryland, 1980), vol. 1, p. 16.

29. E. D. Goldschmidt, *Haggadah Shel Pesach Vetoldoteha* (Jerusalem, 1960), pp. 30–47.

30. Though it is outdated, see G. Alon, *Toldot Hayehudim Be'eretz Yisra'el Bitekufat*

Hamishnah Vehatalmud, vol. I (Israel, 1962), pp. 164–66; and translation thereof, *The Jews in their Land in the Talmudic Age*, trans. Gershon Levi (Jerusalem, 1980), pp. 261–72.

31. Reuven Kimelman, "Rabbi Yohanan and Origen on the Song of Songs: A Third-Century Jewish-Christian Disputation," *HTR* 73 (1980): 575 and n.51.

32. This is the same text adduced by Goldschmidt as the necessary precursor of our Haggadah narrative. The tale continues with his being charged as being worse than Pharaoh, etc. Goldschmidt's argument is cited, and my objection to it noted, above, p. 90.

33. For the entire midrash as recited today, see Birnbaum, *Haggadah*, pp. 76–85.

34. Land was probably also lost, insofar as it was allotted as war payment to Roman troops. In this particular case, Josephus's discussion is ambiguous, but such awarding of territory was the general rule in Roman military policy. Certainly, even in Palestine, that rule was followed to some extent. See discussion by E. Mary Smallwood, *The Jews under Roman Rule* (Leiden, 1976), pp. 340–41. Smallwood interprets Josephus to mean that "the territory of Jews who had fought to the point of capture (*captivi*) or surrender (*dediti*) was appropriated as punishment" (p. 341). Later too, after the uprising of 115–17, we find that land belonging to Jewish rebels in North Africa and Cyprus was expropriated (p. 405). On the situation in Judaea, see Benjamin Isaac, "Judaea after AD 70," *JJS* 35 (1984): 44–50; who emphasizes the fact that Jewish land holding did not altogether cease after 70. Still, the Roman custom of confiscating rebels' land, in general, is reaffirmed "undoubtedly" (p. 48).

35. Built by Onias III or IV, but in either case, during the reign of Ptolemy VI (181–45). See Victor Tcherikover, *Hellenistic Civilization and the Jews* (Philadelphia, 1961), pp. 275–81. Tcherikover sees it as a private shrine for troops regularly stationed at Leontopolis, however, not as a rival to the Jerusalem Temple. See also Smallwood, *The Jews under Roman Rule*, pp. 367–68, and Robert Hayward, "The Jewish Temple at Leontopolis," *JJS* 33 (1982): 429–43.

36. Tcherikover, *Hellenistic Civilization and the Jews*, pp. 284, 286.

37. This and other rabbinic legends regarding the grandeur of Alexandrian Jewry and its synagogue are assembled in Samuel Krauss, *Synagogale Altertümer* (Berlin, 1922), p. 262. Cf. H. L. Gordon, "The Basilica and the Stoa in Early Rabbinic Literature," *Art Bulletin* 13 (1931): 361; Joseph Gutmann ("Origin of the Synagogue" in idem, *The Synagogue: Studies in Origins* [New York, 1975], p. 76, n. 16) doubts the veracity of the report on the grounds that the synagogue type presupposed by it is "the basilica with double aisles and galleries [which are really] contemporary Galilean in nature." He is undoubtedly correct to see the text as highly stylized by Palestinian authors, but it is the fact that Palestinian writers and readers would have taken the report as credible that matters here.

For brief summaries of scholarly attempts to reconstitute the history of early synagogue architecture, see the series of essays published in J. Gutmann, ed., *Ancient Synagogues: The State of Research* (Chico, Cal., 1981), esp. Andrew R. Seager, "Ancient Synagogue Architecture: An Overview," pp. 39–43; and Marilyn J. Chiat, "First-Century Synagogue Architecture: Methodological Problems"; see also Chiat's *Handbook of Synagogue Architecture*, Brown Judaic Studies, no. 29 (Chico, Cal., 1982), and "Ancient Synagogues in Erez Yisrael," *Conservative Judaism* 35 (1981): 4–17; and E. M. Meyers, "Ancient Synagogues in Galilee: Their Religious and Cultural Setting," *Biblical Archeologist* 43 (1980): 97–108.

38. For data and summary of information regarding migration to Alexandria, see Smallwood, *Jews under Roman Rule*, p. 222. Smallwood indicates the difficulty in estimating these figures before the year 72, since only then did a newly legislated Jewish tax result in distinctive census returns for the Jewish community. Philo's figure of a million settlers there by the first century, though "conjectured and too high," nonetheless "can be taken as evidence that the number of Jews there was impressively large."

39. During the period in question here, "when Palestinian circumstances favored large-scale emigration from the country, there was almost certainly a constant trickle of Jews into Egypt" (Smallwood, p. 222). Even the Sicarii fled there (p. 364)!

40. For other instances of identical use of *'Arami* as Rome, see Finkelstein, "Oldest Midrash," pp. 300–301, n. 20.

41. See Jacob Neusner, *Between Time and Eternity* (Belmont, Cal., 1975).

42. See Birnbaum, *Haggadah*, pp. 65–75. Primary sources are collected in Kasher, *Haggadah Shelemah*, pp. 19–33, and discussed in brief by Eugene Mihaly, "The Passover Haggadah as PaRaDiSe," *CCAR Journal* 13 (1966): 3–27.

43. Birnbaum, *Haggadah*, pp. 83, 85. I have slightly altered Birnbaum's translation here and added the Hebrew in transliteration.

44. Ibid. The redundant ending to the introductory sentence is clear. Literally, it reads, (A) "These (*elu*) are the ten plagues of Egypt which the Holy One brought upon the Egyptians in Egypt," (B) "and these are they (*ve'elu hen*)." (A) was originally the subscription to the exegetical interpretation of Deut. 26:8, which elicited the numbering of ten plagues, but not their specification. (B) is the superscription that introduces their specification. Birnbaum gets around the difficulty by translating, "These make up the ten plagues . . . namely . . ." (*Haggadah*, p. 85). But the fact remains that the second "These are they" looks more like an independent introduction of its own, not a conclusion for the sentence, as it now stands. Birnbaum, however, is unable to see the composite nature of the piece, since he follows the traditional understanding that assumes that the listing of the plagues by name is an early liturgical unit that concluded the midrash from the very beginning. It could not, therefore (from this perspective), have been added later; and our sentence must be the bridge between the midrash and the plagues, introducing the fact that the plagues are about to be enumerated. It seems more logical to me, however, to divide the sentence at Point B, that is, before "And these are they," and to assume that only to that point do we have the original midrash. (Even then, we ought not to speak of an original midrash, in the sense of there being only one. But we do have, at least, the earliest liturgical stratum, probably borrowed from a midrashic exegesis.) What follows in the Haggadah, i.e., the further midrashic expansion of ten plagues until they number 50, 200, or 250, would probably, but not necessarily, have been added to the Haggadah later still. The material is itself tannaitic and constitutes a later ritualized use of earlier literary sources.

45. Birnbaum, *Haggadah*, p. 87; see Goldschmidt, *Haggadah*, p. 47.

46. Scholars are unanimous in dating this piece early, before the Temple's destruction, though they differ widely on when and why it was composed. See Eric Werner, "Melito of Sardis: the First Poet of Deicide," *HUCA* 37 (1966): 193, n. 1; Werner relies on Finkelstein, "Pre-Maccabean Documents," and Goldschmidt, *Haggadah*. See the latter, pp. 48–51, for summary of opinion. Despite what Finkelstein takes to be an allusion to *Dayyenu* in the tannaitic work, *Sifre*, Goldschmidt concludes (p. 50) that the only real reason for such an early dating, i.e., "in the Second Temple period" is that "after the Temple's destruction, they (the rabbis) no longer concentrated on the building of the Temple as one of the great acts of God's mercy." In other words, the end of the song postulates the Temple's erection as the pinnacle of Jewish history, so it must have been composed before 70, when Jews stopped believing that. But how does Goldschmidt know that Jews no longer adored the Temple, even after its demise? On the contrary, they studied about it, lionized it even, and prayed for its reconstitution. See, e.g., the stirring accounts in M. Tamid 3:8 and 7:1–3. The first is an obvious *post facto* glorification of the once-magnificent cult, and the second concludes, "This was the rite of the daily whole offering in the service of the house of our God. May it be His will that it be built up speedily and in our days, amen." Thus, the *Dayyenu* may really be late indeed, any time in the Middle Ages, as long as the conceptualization of history argued here remained in effect. Saadiah (tenth century) knew of the *Dayyenu*, so it was common by then, but he still considered it optional, unlike the midrash to Deut. 26, which he prescribes. Antiquity

of a piece was one of Saadiah's criteria for inclusion (see Joseph Heinemann, "Yachaso shel Rav Saadiah Gaon Leshinu'i Matbe'a Tefillah," *Bar Ilan Yearbook* 6 [1963]: 220–33, and remarks in *Siddur Saadiah*, itself, p. 11), so Saadiah may himself have recognized the relatively recent vintage of the *Dayyenu* composition; on the other hand, he surely knew that the material expanding the number of plagues to 50, 200, and so on, was also ancient, since he would have recognized it as a citation from the tannaitic midrash. But he lumps the *Dayyenu* together with this material, as one large chunk of optional text (p. 143). So it might be argued that Saadiah believed the *Dayyenu* to be equally early, but still not mandated, since the Mishnah omits it. To this objection, however, there are two answers. First, Saadiah by no means omits all non-Mishnaic material, and there is no reason why he should have done so here—unless, of course, he knew it to be a late addition to the liturgy. Second, while it is clear that the midrash, also a late addition to the liturgy, could have originated in its own midrashic form at an early date and then been transformed into liturgy later, it is not clear that *Dayyenu* could have been composed as anything but liturgy to begin with, since it is written in the familiar litany style of ritual. So in sum, (a) Saadiah generally included all authentically old liturgical Haggadah practices that reached him, both those of the Mishnah and those outside it; (b) he made an exception to the tannaitic midrash on the plagues, and to the *Dayyenu*, because both were recent, in terms of their being an accepted part of the Haggadah corpus; (c) the midrash was old, in its original midrashic form, but still young insofar as it was used liturgically; (d) the *Dayyenu*, though conceivably also old (but just never accepted into any forms of the Haggadah before Saadiah's time, insofar as we know them from the fragments uncovered to date), should more probably be dated late in the first place. We thus avoid the necessity of postulating the existence of earlier fragments that were subsequently lost.

47. There are manuscript differences, of course. See Goldschmidt, *Haggadah*, pp. 48–49, n. 4.

48. See Birnbaum, *Siddur*, pp. 81, 196.

49. See, e.g., list of authorities in *Shulchan Arukh* O.H. 473:6. Oral translations became less common after printing made available facing translations in the prayer books themselves. See *Arukh Hashulchan* O.H. 473:20.

50. See Birnbaum, *Siddur*, p. 398.

51. See Birnbaum, *Haggadah*, p. 132.

52. Birnbaum, *Siddur*, p. 89.

53. M. Tamid 5:1.

54. Zunz, *Haderashot*, pp. 178–79.

55. Elbogen, *Der jüdische Gottesdienst*, p. 55.

56. On the relationship between Temple cult and nascent synagogue service, see Richard Sarason, "Religion and Worship: The Case of Judaism" in *Take Judaism for Example: Studies toward the Comparison of Religion*, ed. Jacob Neusner (Chicago, 1983), pp. 49–65; and Jakob J. Petuchowski, "Jüdische Liturgie," *Judaica* 41:2 (1985): 99–107.

57. Birnbaum, *Siddur*, p. 54.

58. See biblical basis, Deut. 26:13–15, esp. vv. 14b–15; M. M.S. 5:10–13.

59. See interpretation of Deut. 26:15 in M. M.S. 5:13: " 'Bless Thy People Israel': with sons and daughters; 'and the ground which You have given us': with dew, wine, and young cattle; 'as You swore to our ancestors, a land flowing with milk and honey': that You may give flavor to the fruit."

60. See esp. Richard S. Sarason, "Religion and Worship," pp. 49–65.

61. Isa. 1:18.

62. Details drawn from M. Yoma; citation of "a protracted absence" is 5:1. The use of the altar, not the ark, as liturgical focus is due to the fact that the ark was no longer in existence; even though the now empty Holy of Holies (which the priest alone entered) constituted the pinnacle of the day's cultic events, it was the visible sacrificial altar that

had become the center of attention. I suspect this was true also of the preexilic cult after Josiah's centralizing reforms. On Josiah's cultic reform, see esp. W. E. Claburn, "The Fiscal Basis of Josiah's Reforms," *JBL* 92 (1973); on the artistic consequences of that reform, see introductory essay to Joseph Gutmann, ed., *The Image and the Word: Confrontations in Judaism, Christianity and Islam* (Missoula, Mont., 1977), pp. 5–25. For a history of the ark itself, see Gutmann, "History of the Ark," *Zeitschrift für die Alttestamentliche Wissenschaft* 83 (1971): 29; and for a later treatment of ark accoutrements in the Middle Ages and modern times, see his essay "Return to Zion in Mercy," in Lawrence A. Hoffman, *Land of Israel: Jewish Perspectives* (Notre Dame, Ind., 1986).

63. Ezra Fleischer, *Shirat Hakodesh Ha'ivrit Bimei Habeinayim* (Jerusalem, 1975), pp. 93–95. For short introduction to *piyyut* as a liturgical poetic form in Jewish liturgy, see Joseph Heinemann with Jakob J. Petuchowski, *Literature of the Synagogue* (New York, 1975), pp. 205–13.

64. Jakob J. Petuchowski, *Prayerbook Reform in Europe* (New York, 1968).

65. Ibid.

66. See Shalom Lilker, *Kibbutz Judaism: A New Tradition in the Making* (New York, 1982); Charles S. Liebman and Eliezer Don-Yehiya, *Civil Religion in Israel: Traditional Judaism and Political Culture in the Jewish State* (Berkeley, Los Angeles, and London, 1983), pp. listed in index s.v. "Haggada/haggadot—kibbutz"; and Yehuda Sharett, "Foreword to the *Haggada*," *Shdemot* 20 (1983): 49–56.

CHAPTER 6: SACRED MYTHS: II. AFTER THE ENLIGHTENMENT

1. See Petuchowski, *Prayerbook Reform in Europe*, esp. chap. 3, for examples of novel liturgical creations.

2. Petuchowski goes so far as to identify the attitude toward the Temple cult as the single most unifying doctrinal point among the otherwise diverse representative thinkers responsible for the creation of Reform prayer books. See *Prayerbook Reform*, p. 293.

3. See above, chap. 4, for details of Wise's and Einhorn's roles.

4. *Minhag America: The Divine Service of American Israelites for the New Year*, 1866 ed., pp. 127–37. Further references are cited as MA/NY 1866.

5. Ibid., p. 131.

6. On Wise's particularism, see Lawrence A. Hoffman, "The Language of Survival in American Reform Liturgy," *CCAR Journal* 24 (1977): 90–93.

7. See Eric L. Friedland, "*Olath Tamid* by David Einhorn," *HUCA* 45 (1974); and Hoffman, "The Language of Survival," pp. 93–95. Citation is from *Olath Tamid: Gebetbuch für Israelitische Reform-Gemeinden*, 1858 (italics added). I cite from his "Fest [!] der Zerstörung Jerusalems," pp. 394–400. All translations are my own or (when indicated) drawn from the translation of *Olath Tamid* by Emil G. Hirsch, *Dr. David Einhorn's Olath Tamid*, 1896. On the latter, see Hoffman, "The Language of Survival," pp. 95–102. Further references to the former are cited as OT; to the latter, OT Hirsch. Despite their aversion to the theology of the traditional Tish'a B'Av service, a reaction they shared with one another and with Einhorn, most European prayer book authors had chosen to retain its original nature. In general, they included a traditional Torah and Haftarah reading, continued the recitation of the biblical book of Lamentations, and incorporated selective elegies (*kinot*), that particular form of *piyyut* reserved for this single great day of mourning. On the other hand, their ambivalence shone through in the extra prayers that they composed for the occasion. Geiger, for example, "translates" the traditional *Rachem* addition as: "Enough of mourning for Zion and Jerusalem! God buildeth the indestructible walls of the eternal Jerusalem." Stein, even while mourning the destruction, adds, "The bright morning of a better time dawned." Only the 1848 Berlin *Gebetbuch*, belonging to what Petuchowski characterizes as "the most radical

congregation on the European continent,'' went as far as Einhorn in doing away with *all* traditional mourning, and replacing it with a statement of celebration. Its prayer for the occasion glorifies the fact that ''Here on the soil of a new homeland, Thou has restored to us the fatherland which we have lost forever in the land of our fathers.'' (See Petuchowski, *Prayerbook Reform in Europe*, pp. 292–96.) Geiger's theoretical extremism but practical traditionalism, explored by Petuchowski elsewhere (*New Perspectives on Abraham Geiger* [Cincinnati, 1974], pp. 42–54) is evident in this instance as well. Einhorn broke no new ground, but went farther than his predecessors, and seems to be the first reformer to apply the prophetic message to his own time, as justification for his reforms.

8. P.T. Taan. 4:6.

9. See Gershom Scholem, *Sabbatai Zevi: The Mystical Messiah*, Eng. ed. (Princeton, 1973), pp. listed in index s.v. ''Fasts, abolition of,'' esp. proclamation translated on pp. 616–17. A prayer ms. published by Scholem (''Seder Tefillot shel Hadonmeh Me'izmir,'' *Kiryat Sefer* 18 [1942] may be the sectarian liturgy of celebration for that day, thus following the proclamation's edict and paralleling the celebrative tone of Einhorn's liturgy! See Michael D. Mayersohn, ''The Sabbatian Siddur: The Liturgy of a Messianic Movement'' (Ordination Thesis, Hebrew Union College, 1979). The relationship between Kabbalistic and Reform messianism is explored further in Lawrence A. Hoffman, ''Liturgical Bases for Social Policy,'' in *Liturgical Foundations of Social Policy in the Catholic and Jewish Traditions*, ed. Daniel F. Polish and Eugene J. Fisher (Notre Dame, Ind., 1983), pp. 151–68; and, from a historical perspective, by Scholem, who traces Reform families back to Sabbatian sectarians (Gershom Scholem, ''A Sabbatian Will from New York,'' in Scholem, *The Messianic Idea in Judaism* [New York, 1971], pp. 167–75).

10. Cf. Petuchowski, ''Geiger and Holdheim,'' p. 155.

11. OT Hirsch, pp. 181–82.

12. MA for the Day of Atonement, 1866, p. 245. Hereafter referred to as MA/YK (=Y[om] K[ippur]) 1866.

13. MA/NY 1866, p. 129.

14. Detailed in Friedland, ''*Olath Tamid* of David Einhorn,'' *HUCA* 45 (1974).

15. OT Hirsch, p. 188.

16. Ibid.

17. Reform Jews saw themselves as continuers of Temple times, in that they had their own temples, where their own *avodah* (worship as prayer, not as sacrifice) was the norm. They denied the old myth's fervent hope for a restoration of the cult and hoped instead to present themselves as that cult in its proper modern form. For example, ''In order to deny the traditional Jewish messianic expectations of a future Temple . . . [Reform temples even] introduced the seven-branched Temple lampstand into their sanctuaries'' (Joseph Gutmann, ''A Note on the Temple Menorah,'' in idem, *No Graven Images: Studies in Art and the Hebrew Bible* [New York, 1971], p. 38). They thus outfitted themselves as continuers of the Temple of old. On the other hand, they were not the first to call their synagogues ''temples''; on which, see Michael A. Meyer, ''Hakamato shel Haheikhal Behamburg,'' in *Perakim Betoldot Hachevrah Hayehudit* (Jerusalem, 1980).

18. *The Union Haggadah: Home Service for Passover* (1923), pp. 30–31.

19. See Bertram W. Korn, *American Jewry and the Civil War* (Philadelphia, 1951), pp. 20–23.

20. See Simeon H. Maslin, ''Language of Survival: Social Action,'' *CCAR Journal* 24 (1977): 24–25.

21. On the social gospel, and what the author calls ''moral reconstruction,'' see, for example, Herbert Wallace Schneider, *Religion in Twentieth-Century America* (New York, 1964), pp. 78–118.

22. *Union Prayer Book*, vol. 1, 1894, p. 236; further references given as UPB 1.

23. Ibid., p. 236.
24. Quoted by Plaut, *Growth of Reform Judaism*, p. 34. Italics added.
25. *Union Haggadah*, p. 33.
26. Michael A. Meyer, "A Centennial History," in *Hebrew Union College–Jewish Institute of Religion: One Hundred Years*, ed. Samuel Karff (Cincinnati, 1976), p. 79.
27. *Future of an Illusion* (1927; Norton ed., trans. James Strachey, New York, 1961), p. 9.
28. Meyer, "Centennial History," p. 119.
29. See above, chap. 4, n. 9.
30. Landon Y. Jones, *Great Expectations: America and the Baby-Boom Generation* (New York, 1980), pp. 20–27.
31. On Masada, see Charles S. Liebman and Eliezer Don-Yehiya, *Civil Religion in Israel*, pp. 41–44, 148–51. The authors identify two stages in the myth, which can be traced to Yitzchak Lamdan's 1927 poem *Masada*. The first stage recognizes the suicide of Masada's defenders as an ultimate act of will in the face of impervious opposition. It served the early pioneers as a reflection of the fact that Zionist ideology taught them to succeed through resolute will, yet real-life circumstances—like malaria, economic failure, and their neighbors' hostility—seemed at times to prevent success no matter how hard one willed it otherwise. By the 1960s, however, the suicide motif was troubling and had to be denied by explicit statements such as that made by Yigael Yadin as late as 1980: "The true lesson we learn from Masada is not blind worship of the acts of courage of Ben Yair and his comrades [who committed suicide in the end]. The lesson is in the words of Yitzchak Lamdan, 'Masada will not fall again.' " But "The Masada myth does not begin in the twentieth century," says Shaye J. D. Cohen ("Masada: Literary Tradition, Archeological Remains and the Credibility of Josephus," *JJS* 32 [1981]: 405). See his excellent analysis of the historical reliability of Josephus's Masada account there.
32. See Irving Greenberg's series of three essays published by the National Jewish Resource Center, New York, under the general title of "The Third Era," in *Perspectives*, Oct. 1980, Sept. 1981, and Oct. 1982.
33. See his *American Judaism: Adventure in Modernity* (Englewood Cliffs, 1972), and his collection of essays from the sixties and seventies published together in his *Stranger at Home: The Holocaust, Zionism and American Judaism* (Chicago and London, 1981).
34. Charles Liebman, "Myth, Tradition and Values in Israeli Society," *Midstream* (Jan. 1978), pp. 44–53; idem, "Religion and Political Integration in Israel," *Judaism*, pp. 17–27.
35. Jonathan Woocher, "Civil Judaism: The Religion of Jewish *Communitas*," National Jewish Conference Center *Policy Study* (May 1979), and "Sacred Survival: American Jewry's Civil Religion," *Judaism* 34 (1985): 151–63.
36. Leon Festinger, Henry W. Riecken, Stanley Schachter, *When Prophecy Fails* (New York, 1956), p. 26.
37. M. Pes. 10:4.
38. J. L. Austin, *How to Do Things with Words* (Cambridge, Mass., 1962), p. 6.
39. Ibid., p. 8.
40. Arak. 16a.
41. See Kasher, *Haggadah Shelemah*, pp. 21–33.
42. See Birnbaum, *Haggadah*, pp. 64–65.
43. M. Pes. 10:5–6; cf. Birnbaum, *Haggadah*, pp. 96–97.
44. S. Stein, "Influence of the Symposia Literature on the Literary Form of the Pesah Haggadah," *JJS* 8 (1957).
45. M. Pes. 10:5–6.
46. Harold Bloom, *A Map of Misreading* (New York, 1975; paperback ed., 1980), p. 3.
47. *A Passover Haggadah*, ed. Herbert Bronstein (New York, 1974), p. 34.

48. Ibid., pp. 41, 46.
49. Ibid., p. 46.
50. Ibid., pp. 44–45.
51. Ibid., p. 77.
52. Cf. *Sabbath and Festival Prayer Book* (New York: Rabbinical Assembly of America and United Synagogue of America, 1946), p. 150; and citation of traditional *Musaf Tefillah* prayer, above, p. 108.
53. *Passover Haggadah: The Feast of Freedom*, ed. Rachel Anne Rabinowicz (New York: Rabbinical Assembly, 1982), p. 9. Italics added.
54. Ibid., p. 47.
55. Ibid., p. 66.
56. Ibid., p. 68.
57. Ibid., p. 69.
58. Ibid.
59. Ibid., p. 111.
60. Ibid., p. 97. The mythic role of the Maccabees as a historical precursor of modern-day Israel is evident in popular works. See, e.g., Moshe Pearlman, *The Maccabees* (New York, 1973), whose author explained to me that he was moved to write the book by his experience in the Israeli army, as he crossed back and forth over terrain that had been the scene of battles fought "by another small citizen army" centuries before.
61. *A Passover Haggadah*, p. 78.
62. *Feast of Freedom*, p. 103.
63. Ibid., p. 85.
64. Cf. Reform movement's use of poem by Shlonsky, *Passover Haggadah*, p. 46; The Warsaw ghetto recollection by Bunim Heller, *Feast of Freedom*, p. 95; and the Partisan Song, reproduced in *Gates of Repentance*, the High Holy Day volume of the Reform movement, p. 441. Hereafter referred to as GOR.

APPENDIX: THE CASE OF WOMEN

1. See above, p. 13.
2. See address by David Einhorn, reproduced, in part, in Lawrence A. Hoffman, *Gates of Understanding, vol. 1, Companion Volume to the New Reform Liturgy, Gates of Prayer* (New York: Central Conference of American Rabbis, 1977), pp. 25–26.
3. *A Passover Haggadah*, p. 43.
4. See, e.g., GOR, p. 61.
5. *A Passover Haggadah*, p. 30.
6. GOR, p. 414.
7. GOR, p. 421.
8. GOR, p. 437.
9. GOR, p. 249.
10. See *Gate of Repentance* [of the Union of Liberal and Progressive Synagogues, London] (1973), p. 131. The author is John Rainer (see p. 464, n. 20).
11. GOR, pp. 418, 427.
12. See, e.g., *Gates of Prayer*, pp. 97, 134.
13. *A Passover Haggadah*, pp. 45–46.
14. *Out of the House of Bondage*, ed. Annette Daum and Edith J. Miller (New York: New York Federation of Reform Synagogues, 838 Fifth Ave., 1981).
15. See, for example, Gail Ramshaw Schmidt, "De Divinus Nominibus: The Gender of God," *Worship* 56 (1982): 117–32.
16. *Gates of Forgiveness*, ed. Chaim Stern (New York, 1980), pp. 31–33.

CHAPTER 7: THE NUMINOUS

1. See above, p. 77.

2. Kurt Lewin, *Field Theory in Social Science: Selected Theoretical Papers* (New York, 1951), p. 140.

3. Victor Turner, *Dramas, Fields, Metaphors* (Ithaca, 1974), p. 127.

4. Rudolf Otto, *The Idea of the Holy*, trans. John W. Harvey (Oxford, 1958), p. 6.

5. Ibid., p. 8.

6. Ibid., p. 10.

7. Ibid., pp. 186–90.

8. Cited by Jakob J. Petuchowski, *Prayerbook Reform in Europe* (New York, 1968), pp. 106–107.

9. Nathan Perilman, "The Union Prayer Book," *CCAR Journal* 14 (1967): 43, 46, 45.

10. *Union Hymnal Compiled and Published by the Central Conference of American Rabbis*, 3d ed. (New York, 1957), p. 4. Author unknown; composed by H. W. Hawkes. Italics added.

11. As opposed to *Kedushat hayom*, "Sanctification of the Day," which is recited on Sabbaths and Festivals.

12. T. Ber. 1:9.

13. See Theodor Klauser, *A Short History of the Western Liturgy*, 2d Eng. ed. (Oxford, 1979), pp. 16–17, 133–34.

14. For sources of various opinions, see Heinemann, *Prayer in the Talmud*, p. 230, n. 32.

15. Ibid., p. 233.

16. Ibid., p. 241. He acknowledges his debt to Otto (n. 56) and to Kaufmann Kohler too, who had already adopted Otto's perspective; see Kaufmann Kohler, *MGWJ* 37 (1893).

17. Ibid., p. 244, n. 61.

18. See Lawrence A. Hoffman, "Censoring In and Censoring Out: A Function of Liturgical Language," in *Ancient Synagogues*, ed. Joseph Gutmann (Chico, Cal., 1981), and sources cited there; also, Itamar Grünwald, *Apocalyptic and Merkavah Mysticism* (Leiden, 1980).

19. Philipp Bloch, "Die Yordei Merkavah, die Mystiker der Gaonenzeit und ihr Einfluss auf die Liturgie," *MGWJ* 37 (1893): 18–25, 69–74, 257–66, 305–11.

20. On Moore's "Normative Judaism," see Jacob Neusner, "Judaism After Moore: A Programmatic Statement," *JJS* 31 (1980): 141–56; and idem, *Judaism: The Evidence of the Mishnah* (Chicago, 1981). A contrary view is provided by Jakob J. Petuchowski, in his review of Neusner's work, in *Religious Studies Review* 9 (1983): 111–12.

21. Cf. Gershom Scholem, *Major Trends in Jewish Mysticism* (1941; reprint ed., New York, 1961), pp. 49–54; and idem, *Jewish Gnosticism, Merkabah Mysticism, and Talmudic Tradition* (New York, 1960).

22. Alexander Altmann, "Shirei Kedushah Besifrut Hahekhalot Hakadumah," *Melila* 2 (1951): 1–25.

23. Cf. Itamar Grünwald, "Piyyutei Yannai Vesifrut Yordei Merkavah," *Tarbiz* 36 (1967): 257–58; Chaim Schirmann, "Yannai Hapayyetan Shirato Vehashkafat Olamo," *Keshet* 6 (1964): 45–66.

24. Jacob Neusner, "Jewish Use of Pagan Symbols after 70 C.E.," *Journal of Religion* 43 (1963): 290.

25. David J. Halperin (*The Merkabah in Rabbinic Literature*, American Oriental Series, vol. 62 [New Haven, 1980]) has recently argued that the Merkavah mystical texts demonstrate merely an exegesis of Ezekiel's visions, rather than an ecstatic mystical praxis (see, e.g., p. 182). But even if he is right, that is to say, even if for some rabbis

Merkavah lore functioned merely exegetically, it does not follow that it was so limited in the purview of them all. I think it more likely, in any event, that exegesis, though always present, only *eventually* replaces texts intended for actual practice, but this should not be taken to imply that there was originally no practice at all. Mircea Eliade (*Myths, Dreams and Mysteries: The Encounter Between Contemporary Faiths and Archaic Realities* [1957; Eng. trans., London and New York, 1960; paperback ed., 1975], pp. 32, 36) describes this phenomenon of a praxis being transmuted into ritualized instruction when he says, "It is not difficult to recognize, in all that modern people call instruction, education and didactic culture, the function that is fulfilled by myth in archaic societies. . . . Reading replaces not only the oral folk tradition, such as still survives in rural communities of Europe, but also the recital of the myths in the archaic societies." Similarly, we find elsewhere in Jewish worship that (1) actual sacrifices cease in 70, but the Mishnah continues teaching about them, at least, and (2) those teachings enter the daily prayer texts recited by Jews to this day, as if their contents could actually be realized cultically; (3) *piyyutim* too maintain Merkavah lore by preserving its terminology—see above, n. 23—but in the process, convert it into a literary phenomenon dependent on the ability of prayer "readers" to recognize the metonymic trope involved in citing technical terms that belong to a certain larger body of lore (see my discussion in Lawrence A. Hoffman, "Censoring In and Censoring Out," p. 25). Consider also (4) the contemporary practice of most modern westernized religions to limit ritual action to congregational reading, this being yet a further transformation, not, in this case, from sacrifice to prayer, or even from mysticism to literature, but from high ritual emphasizing affect to rote recitation of text emphasizing didactic transmission of data, and absence of affective nonverbal communication. Cf. Mary Douglas's polemic against just this sort of blindness to expressive symbolic communication that goes beyond cognition, so evident (for her) in the restructuring of Catholic ritual among the Bog Irish, which she attributes to "those ecclesiastics acting as if the liturgical signal boxes are manned by colour-blind signal-men." She concludes, regarding these very Bog Irish in their new condition, "Echoes of Reformed [*sic*] Judaism!" (*Natural Symbols* [Great Britain, 1970; paperback ed., N.Y., 1973], pp. 64, 66). Thus exegetical literary form is not always symptomatic of absence of praxis at the outset. Recall our Haggadah midrash that was only eventually relegated to literary, even didactic, form, but that originated as actual ritual. See also review of Halperin's otherwise generally excellent account by David Sperling (*Journal of Near Eastern Studies* 44 (1985): 153–55), who points out other difficulties with the thesis.

26. M. Ber. 5:3.

27. See Birnbaum, *Siddur*, p. 71.

28. Morton Smith, "Observations on Hekhalot Rabbati," in *Biblical and Other Studies*, ed. Alexander Altmann (Cambridge, 1960), p. 152. The debate as to the essence of gnosticism is vast. Most recently, see P. S. Alexander, "Comparing Merkavah Mysticism and Gnosticism: An Essay in Method," *JJS* 35 (1984): 1–18. I agree with R. McL. Wilson ("Jewish Gnosis and Gnostic Origins: A Survey," *HUCA* 45 [1974]: 177–89), who proposes separate terms for the "common stock" on one hand (gnosis) and the specific Christian heresies such as we find in Nag Hammadi, on the other (Gnosticism). Our interest here is the fact that although the latter clearly exists, so too does the former, which corresponds to no distinct sects but was a common element throughout Hellenistic religion, Judaism included. Indeed, Gerard Valée argues that distinct sectarianism did not even exist until Irenaeus polarized "the true gnosis . . . the doctrine of the Apostles," from "gnosis falsely so-called." (Gerard Valée, "Theological and Non-theological Motives in Irenaeus's Refutation of the Gnostics," in *Jewish and Christian Self-Definition*, ed. E. P. Sanders [Philadelphia, 1980], pp. 174–75.) It was then that gnosticism slowly emerged from gnosis (Wilson's terms) as a result of a slow reification process brought about by certain "Orthodox" speakers trying to "identify themselves clearly and unambiguously, to describe their own social outline," and, thus, to define boundaries between

themselves and gnostic expressions that they considered beyond the pale. (See Raoul Mortley, "The Past in Clement of Alexandria," in Sanders, *Jewish and Christian Self-Definition*, p. 186.)

29. See Lawrence A. Hoffman, "Censoring In and Censoring Out," and idem, "Assembling at Worship," *Worship* 55 (1981).

30. See Roland Barthes, *Elements of Semiology* (1964; English trans., N.Y., 1967), pp. 23–30, 63, for summary of these systems.

31. The arbitrary nature of signs is critical to all semiological analysis, following the lead of Saussure (*Course*, pp. 67–70). An excellent introduction to Saussure and semiology is Jonathan Culler, *Ferdinand de Saussure* (Penguin pb., 1977). It is Saussure himself who first suggested that rituals would appear in a new light if studied as systems of signs (*Course*, p. 17).

32. See Culler, pp. 44–48. Barthes calls the paradigmatic "systematic" (*Elements*, pp. 60, 63). Paradigmatic/syntagmatic is paralleled by Jakobson's metaphor/metonymy dichotomy (R. Jakobson, "Deux Aspects du langage et deux types d'aphasie," *Les Temps Modernes* 188 [1962]).

33. These actually appear in *Gates of Prayer*, pp. 670, 686–87. Cf. notes thereto in *Gates of Understanding*, vol. 1, ed. Lawrence A. Hoffman (New York: Central Conference of American Rabbis, 1977), pp. 258, 260.

34. Following Barthes's suggestion regarding other systems, *Elements*, p. 41.

35. See Klausner, *A Short History of the Western Liturgy*, pp. 138–50.

36. See n. 54 in Hoffman, "Censoring In and Censoring Out," pp. 36–37.

37. The *payyetanim*—already identified as being sensitive to Merkavah imagery (see n. 23, above)—were also aware of these inscriptions: for example, Kalir's poetic references to the Zodiac tally with actual iconographic displays in the synagogues with which he was familiar: see Joseph Yahalom, "Synagogue Inscriptions in Palestine—a Stylistic Qualification," *Immanuel* 10 (1980): 54–55. Beth Alpha and the Helios motif are discussed by: E. R. Goodenough, *Jewish Symbols in the Greco-Roman World*, vol. 8 (New York, 1958), pp. 2, 214; E. L. Sukenik, *The Ancient Synagogue of Beth Alpha* (London, 1932), p. 36; Rachel Wischnitzer, "The Beth Alpha Mosaic: a New Interpretation," *Journal of Jewish Social Studies* (1955): 133–44; and Chiat, *Handbook of Synagogue Architecture*, p. 125.

38. Birnbaum, *Siddur*, pp. 71–72.

39. Henry Chadwick, *The Early Church* (London, 1967), p. 126. See Jesus as Helios in mid-third-century burial chamber mosaic under the Church of St. Peter, reproduced in André Grabar, *Early Christian Art* (N.Y., 1968), fig. 74.

40. See for example, Robert Hayward, "The Jewish Temple at Leontopolis," *JJS* 33 (1982): 434–37, whose analysis of the Temple's candlestick traces the motif of God as light back through a variety of sectarian systems all the way to Ps. 84:12.

41. See summary by Lawrence A. Hoffman, "The Debate on Music," in Hoffman, *Gates of Understanding*, pp. 27–30. Esp. interesting is A. Z. Idelsohn's diatribe against this preference for Christian hymnody ("Synagogue Music Past and Present," *CCAR Yearbook* 33 [1923]: 344–55). Not wanting to be censored in so completely to western religiosity, Idelsohn emphasized censoring out the alternative of Christianity.

42. Ioan Lewis, *Ecstatic Religion* (Great Britain, 1971), pp. 37–38.

43. Susan Abramson, "History of Temple Adath Israel, Boston, as Seen Through the Evolution of the Worship Service" (Honors Thesis, Brandeis University, 1966).

44. Ibid., p. 120.

45. Ibid., p. 118.

46. Ibid., pp. 129–33.

47. Ibid., pp. 127–28.

48. Ibid., p. 176.

49. Ibid., p. 179.

50. Ibid., p. 191.

51. Robert and Helen Lynd, *Middletown in Transition* (N.Y., 1937); discussed in context of other urban studies by Maurice R. Stein, *The Eclipse of Community* (Princeton, 1960). See esp. p. 226.

52. Stein, *Eclipse of Community*, p. 226.

53. Herbert J. Gans, *The Levittowners* (Vintage ed., New York, 1967), p. 77. Cf. P. London, *The Modes and Morals of Psychotherapy* (New York, 1967), who explains the rise of psychotherapy as a response to religion's failure to address American adults. Psychotherapists are a sort of secular priesthood.

54. Herbert J. Gans, *Popular Culture and High Culture* (New York, 1974), p. 25. Creator-oriented culture, which corresponds here to the musical heritage of enlightened Europe, "is viewed with the belief that the creator's intentions are crucial and the values of the audience almost irrelevant" (p. 62); it sees itself "as setting aesthetic standards and providing the proper culture for the entire society" (p. 78); in the eyes of its devotees, it has a life of its own, which they, the aesthetically enlightened public, have learned to appreciate, so that they must now protect the cultural product from the masses of users. User-culture is that which the public chooses for its own purposes. It is treated by culture consumers as a means to the satisfying of a further goal or need, and has, therefore, no life of its own beyond its function for those who use it. The conflict between these two perspectives is the most important element exacerbating the alienation of the artist from the audience (p. 25). When the artists have sufficient power to enforce creator-culture, they have no need to criticize "lower-class" aesthetics. But "when intellectuals lose power and the status that goes with power," they launch just such a critique (p. 7). The American clergy may thus be likened to artists who have recently lost power and status in their own churches and synagogues. Hence, they criticize popular (user-culture) music, charging it with being false to some objective aesthetic standard. The charge on aesthetics is couched in appropriate religious rhetoric, to the effect that proper religiosity in worship demands only the highest cultural accompaniment; it must not pander to popular taste.

55. This constitutes much of the theme of John R. Seeley, Alexander R. Sim, and Elizabeth W. Loosly, *Crestwood Heights* (New York, 1956). See also P. London, *The Modes and Morals of Psychotherapy*, n. 53 above.

56. Abraham H. Maslow, *Religions, Values and Peak Experiences* (Viking Compass ed., New York, 1970), pp. 11–12, 19–20.

57. See Mitchell Chefitz, "A Study of the Merkavah Mystics" (Ordination Thesis, Hebrew Union College, 1975). Chefitz compares reports of dreams by people undergoing Jungian analysis with visions of the *yordei merkavah* mystics.

58. Peter Berger, *The Heretical Imperative* (New York, 1980).

59. Reported in Moshe Pearlman, *Ben Gurion Looks Back* (N.Y., 1965), pp. 184–94. I am grateful to Professor Stephen J. Whitfield for directing me to this source.

60. Albert J. Hunter and Gerald D. Suttles, "The Expanding Community of Limited Liability," in Gerald D. Suttles, *The Social Construction of Communities* (Chicago, 1972), pp. 44–82.

61. Victor Turner, *The Ritual Process* (Chicago, 1969), pp. 131–65.

62. See Lawrence A. Hoffman, "The Synagogue, The Havurah, and Liable Communities," *Response* 38 (1979–80): 37–41.

63. *A Manual for the Penitent* (New York, 1976), beginning of Rite for Reconciliation of Individual Penitents.

64. Mark Zborowski and Elizabeth Herzog, *Life Is with People: The Culture of the Shtetl* (New York, 1952).

65. For a history of the hymnal, see Jeffrey Stiffman, "The Hymnal as a Reflection of Change" (diss., St. Mary's Seminary and University Ecumenical Institute of Theology, 1974). On the history of singing in the Reform movement, see above, n. 41. The decision referred to was made at a Publications Committee of the Central Conference of American

Rabbis meeting in New York in February 1981, but has since been rescinded after a stormy reaction was encountered. The book is scheduled for publication in 1987.

66. For diverse attitudes toward this liturgy, see Robert N. Bellah, *Beyond Belief: Essays on Religion in a Post-Traditional World* (New York, 1970), pp. 209–15; and Lawrence A. Hoffman, "Creative Liturgy," pp. 42–50.

67. I take this also to be both modern and American, following the thinking of Dewey in the latter regard. See John J. McDermott, *The Culture of Experience* (New York, 1976), pp. 21–63.

68. Daniel Stevick, *Language in Worship* (New York, 1970), pp. 141–42.

69. James H. White, *Christian Worship in Transition* (Nashville, 1976), p. 151.

70. Gary Wills, *Bare Ruined Choirs*; James Hitchcock, *The Decline and Fall of Radical Catholicism* (New York, 1972); see also James Buckley's debate with Father Leo Malania and Professor Harold Weatherby, aired in 1975 by the Southern Educational Communications Association and available in transcript form from them; a deliberately anonymous review of *Gates of Prayer*, in *Brief*, the quarterly newsletter of the American Council for Judaism, Summer–Fall, 1976; Cleanth Brooks, "God, Gallup, and the Episcopalians," *American Scholar* (1980): 313–25; Margaret A. Doody, "'How Shall We Sing the Lord's Song upon an Alien Soil': The New Episcopalian Liturgy," in *The State of the Language*, ed. Leonard Michaels and Christopher Ricks; and Edward Graham, "Liturgical Reform," *Judaism* 23 (1974): 52–60.

71. Mary Douglas, *Natural Symbols* (New York, 1970), p. 27. " . . . I argue [that] people at different historical periods are more or less sensitive to signs as such."

72. Basil Bernstein, "Linguistic Codes, Hesitation Phenomena, and Intelligence," *Language and Speech* 5 (1962): 31–46; reprinted in Bernstein, *Class Codes and Control* (New York, 1975), pp. 76–94. Quotation is from p. 78.

73. Ibid., pp. 77–78.

74. Turner's term, following Sapir. See Victor Turner, *A Forest of Symbols: Aspects of Ndembu Ritual* (Ithaca and London, 1967), pp. 28–30.

CHAPTER 8: CONCLUSION

1. See above, chap. 1, n. 6.

2. Following the dichotomy of Geertz; see his *Interpretation of Cultures*, pp. 126–27.

3. T. Ber. 4:1; cf. Baruch Bokser, "*Ma'al* and Blessings over Food: Rabbinic Transformations of Cultic Terminology and Alternative Forms of Piety," *JBL* 100 (1981): 557–74; and Lawrence A. Hoffman, *Land of Israel: Jewish Perspectives* (Notre Dame, Ind., 1986), Introduction.

4. Birnbaum, *Siddur*, pp. 749–51.

5. Ibid., pp. 290, 598.

6. Compare, for example, Ramsay MacMullen's survey, *Paganism in the Roman Empire* (New Haven, 1981), with descriptions of the cult in Jewish tradition.

7. See above, chap. 1, n. 15.

8. Claude Lévi-Strauss, *The Naked Man* (Harper and Row paperback ed., New York, 1981), p. 669, 671.

9. This is generally recognized by now, but see his preference, especially when he lectured, for analogies with machines, e.g., *Five Lectures on Psychoanalysis* (Norton ed., trans. James Strachey, New York, 1977), pp. 18, 54; and his fetish for reading himself into the normal science of his day by prefacing his studies with a review of the literature and by emphasizing the role of others, like Breuer, from whom he claims to have borrowed (see *Lectures*, p. 21).

10. In general, the acid test for him is his patients' progress, but see, as indicative of his constant concern for scientific rectitude, *Lectures* (pp. 32–33), where he cites Jung's

associative tests that are "indispensable for . . . *objective* demonstration . . . in the examination of the psychoses."

11. "Jung himself did not use the term transcausal, but the deeper we move into his thinking on Synchronicity, the clearer it becomes that this is the core of his concept. The operation of the Synchronicity principle depends on a factor that moves *across and beyond causality.*" Ira Progoff, *Jung, Synchronicity, and Human Destiny* (New York, 1973; Delta ed., 1975), p. 163.

12. Claude Lévi-Strauss, *Tristes Tropiques* (1955; Washington Square Press ed., New York, 1977), pp. 47, 49.

13. Ibid., p. 49.

14. Ibid., p. 49. *Savage Mind*, pp. 31, 105.

15. *Tristes Tropiques*, p. 47.

16. See, however, essays in *Zygon* 18 (1983): 221–326, which investigate the possibility that cultural patterning is rooted in the brain's structure.

17. Susanne K. Langer, *Philosophy in a New Key* (Mentor ed., New York, 1941), pp. 222–23.

18. See Gregory Bateson on art, *Steps to an Ecology of Mind*, pp. 128–52.

19. Geertz, *Interpretation of Cultures*, p. 9.

Index

Abaye, 34
Abrahams, Israel, 49, 185 n.5
Abramson, Susan, 164–65
Abudarham, 193 n.19
Adam, 25
Aesthetics, 169, 204
Alexandria: Jews in, 99–100, 194 n.38
Altar, 196–97 n.62
Altmann, Alexander, 156
American Council for Judaism, 129
Amram, 43
Anan ben David, 56
Anthropology, 13, 16, 21–22, 41–42, 46
Antiphony, 160–61, 162
Aramean, 79–80, 96–97, 100
Aram Tsova (Yemenite rite), 56
Architecture, church, 169
Ark, 196–97 n.62
Art: use in holistic study of liturgy, 17
Artist: alienation from audience, 204 n.54
Ashkenazic Jews, 61
Ashkenazic rite, 48–49, 54–55, 57–58, 69, 70, 72
Atonement, 84–86, 110, 112–13
Austin, J. L.: on performative language, 133, 134, 137
Avodah, 108–13, 116, 132, 198 n.17; emendation of sexist language in, 147–48; in Reform prayer books, 121–23, 125

Baby boom, 128, 166
Babylonia, 39, 99
Babylonian rite, 48–51, 55
Babylonian Talmud, 32–35, 70, 91. *See also* Talmuds
Baer, Isaac Seligman, 24–26
Bar Mitzvah: celebrated at Masada, 130
Barukh (blessed): use of, in Merkavah liturgy, 155, 160, 162
Bateson, Gregory, 15, 52
Benedictions. *See* Blessings
Ben-Gurion, David, 167
Berakhot. *See* Blessings
Berger, Peter, 77, 167
Bernstein, Basil, 170
Betrothal: role of women in, 14
Bialik, Chaim Nachman, 140, 147
Bible, 20–21, 40–41, 87. *See also* Scripture; Torah
Birnbaum: on the ten plagues, 195 n.44
Birth: and *brit milah*, 13–14, 15
Blessed (*barukh*): use of, in Merkavah liturgy, 155, 160, 162

Blessings (benedictions; berakhot), 7–12, 28, 31, 136–37, 174; *Avodah* as, 108–13; in *havdalah* ritual, 23–25, 27–28, 35, 40
Bloch, Philipp, 155
Bloom, Harold, 137
Brit milah (covenant of circumcision), 13–14, 44
Buber, 168

Categorization, 28–31, 149, 154, 173; of culture, 37–39, 42; *havdalah* as ritual of, 22, 31, 39–42; of rites, 47–59
Censoring in and censoring out, 158, 161, 175, 203 n.41
Censorship: role in liturgical differences, 53
Central Conference of American Rabbis, 60, 62
Chariot: as symbol, 155, 161, 162
Chavurah, 27, 168, 170–71. *See also* Community
Chefitz, Mitchell, 204 n.57
Chmielnicki, Bogdan, 129
Christianity, 122, 155, 161–62, 176, 203 n.41; and gnosticism, 157; social activism in, 124–25
Christian liturgy, 1, 56, 57, 151; inclusion of women in, 145–46; renewal in, 74, 169; use of the *Kedushah*, 153
Church architecture, 169
Church fathers, 57, 157
Circumcision, covenant of (*brit milah*), 13–14, 44
Citizenship, rights of: as goal for Jewish people, 114
Commentaries, 20, 25–26, 185 n.5
Common stock: competing religions from, 157–58, 202 n.28
Communism, 127, 129
Community (*communitas*), 45, 168–71
Community, worshiping, 8, 11–12, 75, 150, 172; and development of rites, 55–59, 69, 71–72; relationship with God, 150–51
Community of limited liability, 168
Community of total liability, 168
Confessions: as category of liturgy, 30
Conjuration, 41, 42–43
Conservative Judaism, 64–70, 72–74, 128, 175–76; Passover texts for, 141–43; and sacred myth, 130, 132, 141–43
Conservative Judaism, 66
Conversion, 177
Corporations: use of rituals, 3, 183 n.7
Court jester: role of, 44

Covenant, 13–14, 82, 92, 117, 118; and *avodah* as cult, 110–11; First Fruit ritual as loyalty to, 79, 80
Creation, 40, 186 n.36
Creator-oriented culture, 204 n.54
Creature-consciousness, 151
Crusades: and liturgical differences, 53
Cultural backdrop, 161–64, 166, 167, 177
Cultural categorization, 37–39, 42
Cultural diffusion, 53

Darkness. *See* Light and darkness
Davening, 71
Day of Atonement. *See* Yom Kippur
Dayyenu, 105–108, 113, 123, 126
Dead Sea sects, 40
Degradation (*genut*): use of, in Haggadah, 132–33, 134, 135–38
Degradation to dignity (*migenut leshevach*), 139, 143. *See also* From Degradation to Dignity
Deliverance, 139, 140
Depression, economic, 127–128
Deutsch, Gotthard, 126
Diaspora, 99, 114, 116, 121
Differentiation, 37–38, 47–48, 53–54
Dignity (*shevach*): use of, in Haggadah, 132–33, 134, 135–38
Divorce: role of women in, 14
Doctors' Plot of 1953, 129
Doresh, 91
Dormitive hypothesis, 52
Douglas, Mary, 170, 201–202 n.25; on culture, 38, 42, 43
Dreams: and mysticism, 167, 204 n.57
Dress: role in liturgy, 159

East, religious schemata of, 167
Eastern Europe: Jews from, 48, 127–29
Ecstasy, 164
Ecstatic Religion (Lewis), 163–64
Egypt, 50, 98–100; exodus from, 79–81, 86–88, 105–108, 135
Egyptian rite (Genizah), 48–50, 51
Einhorn, David, 62, 63, 117, 118–24, 129, 138, 189 n.8
Elazar, Rabbi, 33
Elbogen, Ismar, 26–27, 49, 109
Eleazar ben Yair, 142
Eliade, Mircea: on myth, 201–202 n.25
Elijah, 24, 25–26, 41, 43–45, 105
Elijah Bashyazi, 57
Enlightenment, 163–64
Enlightenment, the, 21, 58, 121
Eskimo shaman: ecstatic experience of, 163–64
Eulogies: in fast-day ritual, 9–12; in *havdalah*, 33–34, 35, 40
Exile, 114, 116, 138

Exodus from Egypt, 79–81, 86–88, 105–108, 135
Ezra, 28, 118

Fast day, 8–12, 14–15, 119–20
Fasting: role in Merkavah mysticism, 155
Federation of Jewish Philanthropy, 130
Festinger, Leon, 131
Fichte, 46
Field, 149–51
Field of meaning, 76–78, 149–50, 151
Finkelstein, Louis, 50, 90, 92, 195–96 n.46
First Fruit myth, 79–81, 89, 91, 98, 107–108
Form-criticism, 5–6, 8, 11–13, 36, 77–78, 172; on categorization of rites, 48, 50; field of meaning in, 149; on the *Kedusha*, 153–54
Four cups of wine: as symbol, 88, 193 n.23
France: history of rites in, 48, 54, 55
Frank, Anne, 139, 148
Freud, 127, 178–81
From Degradation to Dignity, 88, 89, 102–103, 107, 132–38. *See also* Degradation to dignity

Gans, Herbert J., 166, 204 n.54
Gate of Repentance, 188 n.17
Gates of Forgiveness, 146, 148
Gates of Prayer, 72, 146, 188 n.17
Gates of Repentance, 146, 188 n.17
Geertz, Clifford, 15–16, 18, 172, 181
Geiger, Abraham, 197–98 n.7
Genizah (Egyptian rite), 48–50, 51
Genizah fragments, 26, 49–50, 55, 90, 91
"Genizah Fragments of the Palestinian Order of Service" (Mann), 49–50
Genut (degradation): use of, in Haggadah, 132–33, 134, 135–38
Geography: and classification of rites, 47–52, 53–56, 58–59, 69
Geonim, 23
German language: use by American Jews, 61, 126
Germany, 4, 48, 53–56, 58, 126–28, 162
Gestalt, 15, 31, 71–72, 149
Gesture: in liturgy, 159
Ge'ullah (Redemption): as blessing in Haggadah, 136, 137
Ghettos: social class in, 71
Gluckman, Max, 44
Gnosis, 202–203 n.28
Gnosticism, 156–57, 162, 176, 202–203 n.28
God-language: in Reform liturgy, 146–47, 148
Goldschmidt, E. D., 90–91, 194 n.32, 195–96 n.46
Gordis, Robert, 64, 66, 190 n.25
Great Assembly, 28–29, 30, 31–32
Great Britain: Reform liturgy in, 54, 58, 188 n.17

Greco-Roman society, 39, 40, 157, 162; symposium tradition, 88, 137
Greenberg, Irving, 130

Haftarah readings, 83, 193 n.19
Haggadah, 17, 74, 82, 89–102, 116, 132–38; contemporary sacred myth in, 132, 133–43; emendation of sexist language in, 146–48; medieval additions to, 103–108
Hallel, 136, 137, 162
Halperin, David J., 201–202 n.25
Hamanhig: havdalah ritual in, 43
Hashkivenu, 187 n.50
Hasidei Ashkenaz, 77, 129
Hasidism, 54–55, 57, 68, 69
Havdalah, 20, 22–36, 37, 39–45, 173–74; as home ritual, 23–24, 185 n.19; as part of synagogue ritual, 22–23, 28
Havdalah al hakos, 23–24, 185 n.19
Havdalot. See Separations
Hazzanic style of worship, 191 n.32
Hebrew, 56, 61
Hebrew Union College, 60
Heinemann, Joseph, 4–5, 7–8, 11–12, 78; on categorization of rites, 48–50, 51, 52, 55; on the *Kedusha*, 153–54
Heroes: and sexism in sacred myth, 145, 147
Herzl, Theodor, 143
Herzog, Elizabeth: *Life Is with People*, 169
High Priest: and *avodah* as cult, 111–12
Hirsch, Emil G., 62, 124
History, 5, 7–8, 29, 53. *See also* Myths, sacred
Hitchcock, James, 169
Hitler: Pharaoh identified as, 139
Hoffman, David, 89–90
Holism, 15–16, 18, 184 n.29
Holland: Jews in, 56
Holocaust, 73, 126, 129–32, 139–43
Holy (*kadosh*), 151, 155, 160, 162
Holy, Holy, Holy: See *Kedushah*
Holy and profane, 37, 40–41, 173–74; in *havdalah* ritual, 22–24, 32–35, 40, 42, 185 n.18
Holy days, 23, 166
Holy of Holies, 111–12, 196–97 n.62
Homosexuality: culture's attitude toward, 39
Hope, message of, 138
How to Do Things with Words (Austin), 133
Hunter, Albert J., 168
Hymns, 161–62, 169, 203 n.41

Ibn Giyyat, Isaac, 24, 43
Iconography, 161–62
Idea of the Holy, The (Otto), 151
Idelsohn, A. Z., 203 n.41
Identity, 61, 63, 176
Identity, communal, 68, 76, 172–73
Identity, Jewish, 69, 71–73, 118–19

Identity, religious, 59, 158, 177
Idolatry: *genut* as, 136
Immigrants, 58, 61, 62–63, 126–28, 189–90 n.9
Individuation process, 167
Initiation liturgy: into convenantal status, 13–14
Irenaeus, 176
Israel (people), 132, 136; differentiated in *havdalah*, 23–24, 32–35, 40, 185 n.18; as suffering servant, 119, 121, 123
Israel, State of, 73, 129, 130, 132, 139–43
Isserles, Moses, 24, 43
Italy: history of rites in, 48, 51, 53, 55

Jacob bar Abba, Rabbi, 33
Jacobson, Israel, 152
Jesus: and Jewish liturgical system, 57
Jewish studies, 20–22
Jewish Theological Seminary, 64–65
Jochanan, Rabbi, 28, 29–32, 185 n.11
Jonah, story of, 84–85
Joshua ben Levi, Rabbi, 33–34
Jubilee Year. *See* Time-Past
Judah, Rabbi, 34, 40
Judah HaNasi, 33, 35, 120, 156
Judeo-German, 56. *See also* Yiddish
Jung, 167, 179, 204 n.57, 205–206 n.10, 206 n.11

Kabbalah, 54–55
Kaddish, 75
Kadosh. See Holy
Kaplan, Mordecai, 64–66, 67, 69
Karaites: liturgy of, 56–57, 188 n.20
Kedushah (Holy, Holy, Holy; *Kedushat Hashem*; sanctification of the name of god), 28–31, 153–55, 162
Kimelman, Reuven, 92
Koestler, Arthur, 127
Kohler, Karumann, 62, 189 n.6
Korbanot: as category of liturgy, 30
Korei, 91

Ladino, 56
Lake City sect, 131
Lamdan, Yitzhak: *Masada*, 199 n.31
Langer, Susanne, 181
Language, 38, 55–56, 159–64
Langue, 36
Leil shimurim, 44
Lévi, Israel, 11
Lévi, Jacob, 49
Lévi-Strauss, Claude, 36–38, 76, 176, 180–81
Lewin, Kurt, 75, 149–50
Lewis, I. M.: *Ecstatic Religion*, 163–64
Liebman, Charles, 130
Life Is with People (Herzog and Zborowski), 169

Light and darkness, 37, 40–41, 186 n.36, 187
    n.50; in *havdalah* ritual, 23–24, 32–35, 40,
    42, 185 n.18
Liminality, 42, 44–45
Linguistics: use in study of myth, 36
Liszt, Franz, 191 n.32
Literature, 3–6, 78; liturgy as, 26–27, 47–48,
    51–52; use in defining academic areas, 20–
    21
Liturgical field, 150–51, 163
Liturgical renewal, 74, 146, 169
Lodges: used in place of synagogue, 165
London, P., 204 n.53
LSD experience, 163–64

Maccabees, 143, 200 n.60
Maccabees, The (Pearlman), 200 n.60
Machzors, 23, 43, 74
Machzor Vitry, 23, 43
Magical, the: in *havdalah*, 43
Maimonides, 52, 148
Mann, Jacob, 49–50, 188 n.20
Mantra, 155
Manual for the Penitent, A, 168
Manuscript errors: as cause of liturgical dif-
    ferences, 53, 55
Marriage (wedding), 1, 14
Masada: as symbol, 130, 142, 199 n.31
Masada (Lamdan), 199 n.31
Masculine language: use in liturgy, 145–48
Maslow, Abraham H., 167
Master image, 160–64, 167–68, 177
Matchil bigenut umesayem beshevach. See
    From Degradation to Dignity
Mead, Margaret, 39
Meaning, field of, 76–78, 149–50, 151
Medieval era (Middle Ages), 23–24, 70, 77,
    117–18, 122–23; additions to Midrash,
    102–13
Men: role in Jewish ritual, 13–14
Menachem ben Solomon, 51
Merkavah mysticism (*yordei merkavah*), 154–
    56, 158, 160–62, 164, 167–68, 201–202
    n.25, 203 n.37, 204 n.57
Messianism, 44, 118, 121, 126, 131
Metaphors, 86, 158
Methodology: and fields of meaning, 76–78,
    149
Meyer, Michael, 126, 127
Middle Ages. *See* Medieval era
Midrash, 20–21, 89, 93, 98; medieval addi-
    tions to, 102–13; on Passover, 89–102
Midrash Hagadol, 89–90
Midrash Tannaim, 90
Mielziner, Moses, 189 n.6
Migenut leshevach. See Degradation to dignity
Millenarianism (millennialism), 44, 105, 131
Minhag America, 61–63, 117–18, 122
Minhag Polin, 48

Minhag Rinus (Rhineland rite), 48
Miracles: recounted in *Dayyenu*, 105–13
Mishnah, 14, 18, 79, 87, 91, 195–96 n.46;
    Avodah ritual in, 111–12; as source of From
    Degradation to Dignity, 132–33, 135, 136–
    37
Mishnah Taanit, 8–12
Moore, George Foot, 156
Moral of history: found in Passover seder,
    102, 138
Morphemes, 159
Moses, Isaac, 189 n.8
Musaf Tefillah, 108, 113, 141
Mysterium tremendum, 151, 154, 160, 162
Mysticism, 154–56, 158, 159–62, 164, 167,
    201–202 n.25
Myths, 16, 22, 35–36, 201–202 n.25; of com-
    mon origin, 176; Lévi-Strauss on, 176
Myths, sacred, 75–115, 116–44, 176; of clas-
    sical Reform Judaism, 116–26; and contem-
    porary Reform Judaism, 126–33, 138–41;
    definition of, 76; inclusion of women, 145–
    48

Nation-folk, 4–5
Natronai, 185 n.19
Neusner, Jacob, 130, 156
Ninevites, 84–85
Ninth of Av (Tish'a B'av), 81, 82, 85, 116,
    193 n.20; ritual for, 119–20, 197–98 n.7
Normative Judaism, 156
North American Academy of Liturgy, 1
Numeration: as critical method, 77
Numinous, the, 151–70
Nusach seferad, 49, 54–55, 57, 68

Objects, arrangement of: role in liturgy, 159
Olam Haba. See Time-to-Come
Olath Tamid, 62, 119, 121–23
Oppositions, 32–35, 37, 40–41; in Haggadah
    benediction, 136; in *havdalah*, 22, 32–35,
    39–40, 42
Oral tradition, 5, 36, 90–91
Orthodox Judaism, 62, 65, 68–69, 70–71, 72,
    129, 131
Oshaiah, Rabbi, 33, 35
Other, the, 151, 158, 160
Otto, Rudolf, 151–54, 155, 158, 160, 163–
    64, 166, 168

Pale of Settlement, 71, 127
Palestine, 56, 99–100
Palestinian rite, 48–51, 55
Palestinian Talmud, 43, 120. *See also* Tal-
    muds
Paradigmatic, 159–60, 203 n.32
Parole (linguistic term), 36
Parzen, Herbert, 64
Passover Haggadah, A, 138, 139–41, 146

Passover Haggadah: The Feast of Freedom,
142–43
Passover seder, 44, 82, 86–102, 103–108,
132, 141–43. *See also* Haggadahs
Patristic literature, 57, 157
Payyetanim, 203 n.37. See also *Piyyutim*
Pearlman, Moshe: *The Maccabees,* 200 n.60
Pentateuch: reading of, 83, 192 n.16
Performative framing, 133–36, 137–38
Performatives, 133–36, 137–38, 177
Perilman, Nathan, 152
Persians: cultural effect on Judaism, 39, 40
Personal example: role in liturgical differences,
53–54, 188 n.14
Pesikta, 193 n.19
Petuchowski, Jakob, 114, 197 n.2, 197–98
n.7
Pharaoh, 80, 88, 100; identified as Hitler, 139
Phenomenology of religion, 151–52
Philology, 4–6, 8, 11–13, 77–78, 172; field
of meaning in, 149; on the *Kedushah,* 153;
on Midrash texts, 90–91; use in analysis of
myth, 35–36; use in study of *havdalah* rit-
ual, 24–27
Philosophy: role in Judaism, 99
Phoneme, 36, 159
Pidyon haben, 174
Pietism, 129
Pittsburgh Platform (1885), 124, 125
Piyyutim (synagogue poetry), 112, 156, 201–
202 n.25
Plagues: Haggadah text on, 103–104, 195
n.44
Plausibility structure, 77
Poetry, 7, 46–48, 111, 159; synagogue poetry,
112, 156, 201–202 n.25; use in *havdalah*
ritual, 24, 41
Poland, 48, 54, 55–56; decade of disaster in,
129; Jews from, 127–28
Polanyi, Michael, 15, 77
Pool, David de Sola, 68, 70–71
Postbiblical literature (Rabbinics), 20–21, 151
Postwar baby boom, 128, 166
Prayer, act of, 6–7, 172–73
Prayer books, 6, 16, 47, 70, 116; written in
America, 60–63, 65–74, 189 n.8, 190 n.15
Prayer leader (precentor), 11–12, 13
Prayers (*tefillot*), 1–2, 5, 36–37, 69–70; as
category of Jewish liturgy, 28–31; relation-
ship to worshipers, 75; role in *avodah* cult,
109–10; used by merkavah mystics, 155;
use of second or first person in, 111–12
Prayer text, 4–8, 11–12, 77, 172–73; field of
meaning around, 149; mystical nature of,
156
Precentor (prayer leader), 11–12, 13
Priests, 12, 34, 79–81, 111–12, 185 n.18
Profane. *See* Holy and profane
Prophets, 121–23, 125–26

Protestantism: and the numinous in worship,
151–52, 153, 158
Psalms: as category of liturgy, 30
Psychology, 167
Psychotherapy, 204 n.53
Pumbeditans, 33–34
Punishment, 84–86, 129

Questions: use of, in Passover seder, 88–89

Rabban Gamaliel II, 92
Rabbinical Assembly, 66
Rabbinic Judaism, 32–35, 40–41, 81, 121–
22, 156; conception of time, 82–86, 117–
18; and the Passover seder, 88–102, 103–
104
Rabbinics (postbiblical literature), 20–21, 151
Rabbinites: liturgy of, 56–57, 188 n.20
Rashi of Troyes, 48, 55
Rav, 33, 34
Rava, 33, 35, 39–40
Rav Judah, 33, 34
Reality, 15–16, 41, 37–38, 49, 40–41; repre-
sented by the numinous, 159; and sacred
myths, 75
Recitation: compared to prayer, 6–7
Reconciliation, Rite of, 168–69
Reconstructionist, 66
Reconstructionist Foundation, 65
Reconstructionist movement, 65–66, 69, 72,
175–76
Redemption (*Ge'ullah*): as blessing in Hag-
gadah, 136, 137
Reductionism, 18, 36, 52, 184 n.29
Reform Judaism, 54, 57–59, 60–74, 164–66,
175–76; on exile and the diaspora, 114; in-
clusion of women in liturgy, 145–48; and
the numinous in worship, 152–53, 158,
160, 161–63, 164–66; Passover ritual in,
89, 139–41; prayer book revisions for, 117–
26; and sacred myths, 116–33, 138–41
Religions: as minority cultures in America, 39
Revisionism, 2, 175
Rhineland massacres of 1096, 129
Rhineland rite (*Minhag Rinus*), 48
Riecken, Henry W., 131
Rites, 46–59, 176; as different from rituals,
46; U.S. development of, 60–74; Zunz's
categorization of, 47–50, 53–54
Rites of passage, 14, 39, 130
Ritual, 1, 3, 13–17, 172–82; as different from
rite, 46; Freud on, 178–80; as performative,
132–35; role in cultural categorization, 38–
39; use of, by corporations, 3, 183 n.7
Roman Catholicism, 146, 168–69, 201–202
n.25
Roman rite, 51
Romans, 81, 98–99, 194 n.34
Romantic era: philology in, 4

Rosh Hashanah, 83, 117
Rubrics, 47, 91
Rules: and cultural categories, 38–39
Russia: Jews from, 63, 127–28

Saadiah, 48–49, 51, 55, 175 n.19, 195–96 n.46
Sabbatai Zevi, 120, 129, 131
Sabbath, 22–23, 106, 107; differentiation from weekdays, 23–24, 32–35, 37, 40, 185 n.18
Sabbath and Festival Prayer Book, 141
Sabbath of Repentance (*Shabbat Shuvah*), 85
Sabbatical Year. *See* Time-Past
Sacred myths. *See* Myths, sacred
Sacrifice, 87, 110
Samaritans: liturgy of, 56
Samuel (of 3rd-century Babylonia), 34
Sanctification of the name of god. See *Kedushah*
Saussure, Ferdinand de, 6, 159, 203 n.31
Schachter, Stanley, 131
Schechter, Abraham I., 51
Schechter, Solomon, 49, 50–51, 64
Schindler, Solomon, 165
Scholem, Gershom, 156
Science: and contemporary sacred myth, 130–31; Freud's use of, 178–80
Scripture, 24–25, 28, 93–97. *See also* Bible; Torah
Sea and dry land: as opposition in *havdalah*, 34, 185 n.18
Second person: use in fast-day liturgy, 11–12
Sect: mystics as, 156
Sectarianism, 63, 67
Secularism, 57
Secularity, 130–31
Seder. *See* Passover seder
Seder Chibbur Berakhot, 48–49, 50–51, 55
Seder Rav Amram, 43, 70, 91, 101
Seminarians: performative frame for instructions for, 134–35
Semiology, 158–64. *See also* Signification
Separations (*havdalot*), 20, 28–31, 32–35, 38
Sephardic Jews: as immigrants to U.S., 61
Sephardic rite, 48–49, 54–55, 56, 57, 72
Service of the Heart, 188 n.17
Shabbat Shuvah (Sabbath of Repentance), 85
Shaman, 16, 164
Shavuot, 79, 81, 87, 112
Shema, 40–41, 187 n.50
Shemitah. See Time-Past
Shemoneh Esrei. See Tefillah
Shevach (dignity): use of, in Haggadah, 132–33, 134, 135–38
Shimurim, 44
Shlonsky, Abraham: "A Vow," 139–40
Shofarot, 9
Siddur, 61
Siddur Lashabbat Veyom Tov; The Traditional

Prayer Book for Sabbath and Festivals, 68, 70–71
Sifre (Midrash): on Passover, 89–90, 101
Signification, 14, 15–17, 93–95, 158–64
Silverman, Morris, 66; prayer book, 66–67, 70, 73
Simon the Hasmonean, 28
Simon the Just, 28
Sin, 84–86, 110, 113
Sinai, Mount, 81, 92, 113
Sisyphus, myth of, 138
Slavery: *genut* as description of, 136
Smallwood, E. Mary, 194 n.38
Social activism, 124–26
Social class: and style of worship, 71, 162, 191 n.32
Social distance, 55–59, 68, 69, 72, 162; between congregation and clergy, 160; and Jewish mystics, 156
Social gospel, 124
Socialism, 124–25, 127, 129
Social justice, 120
Social sciences, 21, 37, 46
Soloveitchik, Rabbi, 68, 190–91 n.31
Songs: use in *havdalah* ritual, 24, 25, 28, 41
Soviet Union: use of civic rituals, 183 n.7
Spain: history of rites in, 48, 50, 54, 56, 57
Spanier, Arthur, 5
Speech codes, 170–71
Stalin, 127, 129
Stein, S., 137
Stevick, Daniel, 17, 169
Structuralism, 36–37, 179–81
Suburbanization: effect on religious enterprise, 166–67
Suffering servant: Israel as, 119, 121, 123, 138
Sukkot, festival of, 84, 85
Sulzer, Salomon, 191 n.32
Sun: as symbol, 161
Suttles, Gerald D., 168
Symbolism, 38, 88, 170, 181
Synagogue, 1–2, 11–12, 26, 71, 109, 165–66
Synagogue poetry (*Piyyutim*), 112, 156, 201–202 n.25
Synchronicity, 25–26, 179, 180, 206 n.11
Synecdochal vocabulary, 159–64, 177
Syntax, 159–60, 163

Tableship rites, 137
Taft, Father Robert, 1–2
Talmuds, 10–11, 17–18, 20–21, 70, 90–91, 120; on *havdalah*, 25, 32–35, 43
Tamid, 108–109
Tammuz, 84
Tannaim, 33–34, 89–90, 190
Tefillah (*Shemoneh Esrei*), 7–8, 9–10, 28, 108–13, 147
Tefillot. See Prayers

Temple, 12, 71, 108–109, 110–13, 175
Temple, destruction of, 84–86, 98, 100–102, 108, 116–21
Temple Israel (Boston), 164–65
Text, 1–7, 16–17, 20–21, 172–73; use in study of *havdalah* ritual, 24–41; use in study of myth, 35–36. *See also* Prayer text
Time: rabbinic conception of, 82–86, 89
Time-Now (*Zeman Hazeh*), 82–83, 84–86, 114–18, 138, 143; and Passover seder, 100–101, 102, 105, 107–108
Time-Past (Jubilee Year; Sabbatical Year; *shemitah*; *yovel*), 82, 85, 138
Time-to-Come (*Olam Haba*; *Yemot Hamashiach*), 82–83, 86–87, 110, 116, 139, 140; and contemporary myth, 126; for Einhorn, 120–21; and the Passover seder, 100–101, 107–108
Tish'a B'av. *See* Ninth of Av
Tithes, presentation of, 80–81, 110
Torah, 34, 81, 83, 117–18, 185 n.18. *See also* Bible; Scripture
Totemism, 179, 180
Tradition, 1, 4, 5, 36, 76, 90–91; and *havdalah* ritual, 25, 27, 41, 43–45
Trance: role in merkavah mysticism, 155, 162
Transcendence, 160, 161, 164, 168, 169
Tur, 43
Turner, Victor, 42, 44–45, 149–50, 168

Unclean and clean: as opposition in *havdalah*, 34, 185 n.18
Union Haggadah, 89, 123–24, 126
Union of American Hebrew Congregations, The, 60
Union Prayer Book, 63, 67, 70, 72–73, 117, 123–24, 125
Upper waters and lower waters: as opposition in *havdalah*, 34, 185 n.18
User-culture, 204 n.54

Valée, Gerard, 202 n.28
Van Gennep, Arnold, 42, 44
Vatican II, 146

Vocabulary: as basic unit of liturgy, 159–64, 167–68
"Vow, A" (Shlonsky), 139–40

Wedding (marriage), 1, 14
Westphalian preamble of 1810, 152
Wills, Gary, 169
Wilson, R. McL., 202–203 n.28
Wise, Isaac Mayer, 60–63, 117–19, 121–24, 128, 138, 189 n.6
Wise, Stephen S., 124
Wittgenstein, 37–38
Wolff, Friedrich August, 4
Women, 13–14; inclusion in liturgy, 145–48
Woocher, Jonathan, 130
World War I, 126
World War II, 126
Worship, 1, 2, 152, 155, 177; act of, 15, 69, 71–72, 191 n.32; and categories of liturgy, 30–31; and the numinous, 150–71; semiological analysis of, 159–64
Worshiping community. *See* Community, worshiping

Yemen: history of rites in, 52
Yemenite rite (*Aram Tsova*), 56
Yemot Hamashiach. See Time-to-Come
Yeshivah, 21
Yiddish, 143. *See also* Judeo-German
Yom Kippur (Day of Atonement), 83, 84–85, 111–13, 121–22, 132
Yordei merkavah. See Merkavah mysticism
Yose ben Yose, 112
Yovel. See Time-Past

Zaken: as prayer leader, 13
Zborowski, Mark: *Life Is with People*, 169
Zechariah, 120
Zeman Hazeh. See Time-Now
Zerubabel, 118
Zikhronot, 9
Zionism, 66, 114–15, 125, 199 n.31
Zoroastrianism, 40
Zunz, Leopold, 3–4, 5, 7–8, 20–21, 69, 72; on categorization of liturgical rites, 46–50, 51, 53–55